The new great tra

The post-communist societies of Eastern Europe are examples of a social formation of great theoretical interest with distinctive features of its own. They reveal that Soviet imposed 'real socialism' has produced more fundamental and enduring changes in the region than had generally been believed. That this is so is most evident in the societies which have historically been the most Western-oriented and in which political and economic reforms are now most advanced: Poland, the Czech Republic, Slovakia and Hungary. Their governments are trying to effect a transition to democracy and the free market in conditions which are not necessarily propitious. It is already clear that many of the immediate benefits which neo-liberals expected to flow from dismantling the old system have not materialized; what the eventual outcome of the changes will be is open to question. For this reason it is better to speak of a transformation from a known past to an unknown future than a transition to a guaranteed end-state.

Among the central issues discussed are the legacy of real socialism, the efficacy of neo-liberal economic reforms and the demand for social protection, the status of *homo economicus*, the social conditions of economic reconstruction and the social dimensions of privatization and marketization, the regeneration of civil society, and interest representation and the prospects for democracy. Some of the issues recall elements of Polyani's analysis of the original great transformation to a market economy in nineteenth-century Western Europe and North America.

The editors have long-standing interests in developments in post-war Eastern Europe and have collaborated over twenty years. Contributors to the volume come from East-Central Europe, the UK and the USA. They include scholars in sociology, politics and economics.

The new great transformation?

Change and continuity in
East-Central Europe

Edited by Christopher G.A. Bryant
and Edmund Mokrzycki

London and New York

First published 1994
by Routledge
11 New Fetter Lane, London EC4P 4EE

Simultaneously published in the USA and Canada
by Routledge
29 West 35th Street, New York, NY 10001

Typeset in Times by J&L Composition Ltd, Filey, North
Yorkshire
Printed and bound in Great Britain by
TJ Press (Padstow) Ltd, Padstow, Cornwall

British Library Cataloguing in Publication Data
A catalogue record for this book is available from the British
Library

Library of Congress Cataloging in Publication Data

The New great transformation?: change and continuity in
   East-Central Europe / edited by Christopher G.A. Bryant
and Edmund Mokrzycki.
      p. cm.
   Includes bibliographical references (p.   ) and
index.
      ISBN 0–415–09249–3: $55.00. — ISBN 0–415–09250–7:
$17.95
      1. Europe, Eastern—Social conditions.   2. Post-
communism—Europe, Eastern.   3. Europe, Eastern—
Economic conditions—1989–   .   4. Europe, Eastern—
Politics and government—1989–   .   I. Bryant,
Christopher G.A. II. Mokrzycki, Edmund.
HN380.7.A8N49 1994
306′.0947—dc20   93–20938

ISBN 0–415–09249–3 (hbk)   0–415–09250–7 (pbk)

To Elizabeth and Hanna

Contents

Contributors

Andrew Arato is a professor at the New School for Social Research. His latest books are *From Marxism to Democratic Theory* (1992) and *Civil Society and Political Theory* (with Jean Cohen, 1992). Address: New School for Social Research, 66 West 12th Street, New York, NY 10011, USA.

Zygmunt Bauman is Emeritus Professor of Sociology in the University of Leeds. He won the Amalfi European Prize in 1989. His most recent books are *Modernity and Ambivalence* (1991), *Intimations of Postmodernity* (1992) and *Postmodern Ethics* (1994). Address: Department of Social Policy and Sociology, University of Leeds, Leeds LS2 9JT, UK.

Christopher G.A. Bryant is Professor of Sociology and Director of the Institute for Social Research at the University of Salford. His recent publications include *What Has Sociology Achieved?* (edited with Henk Becker, 1990) and *Giddens' Theory of Structuration* (edited with David Jary, 1991). Address: Department of Sociology, University of Salford, Salford M5 4WT, UK.

Arista Maria Cirtautas is an assistant professor in the Department of Government at Claremont McKenna College. She held an Alexander von Humboldt Fellowship for research in Germany during 1990–91 and an IREX fellowship for research in Poland, 1991–92. Address: Department of Government, Claremont McKenna College, Claremont, CA 91711, USA.

Vic Duke is Senior Lecturer in Sociology in the University of Salford. He has published *A Measure of Thatcherism* (with Steven Edgell, 1991). Address: Department of Sociology, University of Salford, Salford M5 4WT, UK.

Maurice Glasman is a Research Fellow at the European University Institute. Address: European University Institute, Badia Fiesolana, Via dei Roccettini 9, San Domenico di Fiesole, 50016 Florence, Italy.

Keith Grime is Lecturer in Geography in the University of Salford. He is the Eastern and Central Europe editor of *Regions*, the bi-monthly newsletter of the Regional Studies Association. Address: Department of Geography, University of Salford, Salford M5 4WT, UK.

Tadeusz Kowalik is Professor of Economics and Humanities in the Polish Academy of Sciences. During 1991–92 he was a fellow at the Stockholm Institute of Eastern European Economics. Address: Institute of Economics, Polish Academy of Sciences, Pałac Staszica, ul. Nowy Świat 72, 00–330 Warsaw, Poland.

Steven Lukes is Professor of Political and Social Theory at the European University Institute. He is a fellow of the British Academy. His latest book is *Moral Conflicts and Politics* (1991). Address: European University Institute, Badia Fiesolana, Via dei Roccettini 9, San Domenico di Fiesole, 50016 Florence, Italy.

Petr Mareš is Assistant Professor of Sociology in the Masaryk University of Brno. In 1992 he was a postdoctoral fellow at the Institute for Social Research of the University of Amsterdam. He is a joint author of *Searching for Flexible Organisation* (in Czech, 1993). Address: Department of Sociology, Social Policy and Social Work, Masaryk University, Arne Nováka 1, 660 88 Brno, Czech Republic.

Edmund Mokrzycki is Professor of Sociology and Chair of the Theoretical Sociology Unit at the Polish Academy of Sciences. During 1992–93 he was a Jean Monnet Fellow at the European University Institute in Florence. His latest books in Polish are: *Sociology in Philosophical Context* (1990), *Theory and Practice of Empirical Sociology* (edited with Anna Giza, 1990) and *Modes of Thought and Rationality* (co-edited, 1992). Address: Institute of Philosophy and Sociology, Polish Academy of Sciences, Pałac Staszica, ul. Nowy Świat 72, 00–330 Warsaw, Poland.

Libor Musil is Assistant Professor of Sociology in the Masaryk University, Brno. He is joint author of *Searching for Flexible Organisation* (in Czech, 1993). Address: Department of Sociology,

Social Policy and Social Work, Masaryk University, Arne Nováka 1, 660 88 Brno, Czech Republic.

Ladislav Rabušic is Assistant Professor in Sociology in the Masaryk University, Brno. During 1992–93 he was a fellow at the Woodrow Wilson School of Public and International Affairs at Princeton University. Address: Department of Sociology, Social Policy and Social Work, Masaryk University, Arne Nováka 1, 660 88 Brno, Czech Republic.

Erzsébet Szalai is a Research Fellow in Economics at the Hungarian Academy of Sciences. In 1991 she was a fellow at the New School for Social Research in New York, and during 1992–93 she held a fellowship at the Budapest Collegium. Her latest book is *Economy and Power* (in Hungarian, 1990). Address: Institute of Economics, Hungarian Academy of Sciences, Budaörsi út 45, 1112 Budapest, Hungary.

Acknowledgements

Chris Bryant thanks the Economic and Social Research Council, and Dr George Kolankiewicz, the Co-ordinator of the East–West II Initiative, for a grant which, *inter alia*, funded his participation in the 'Democracy in Context' research seminars from December 1991 to April 1993 – a programme in which Edmund Mokrzycki also took part. Seminars in Warsaw, Rotterdam, Salford and Prague enabled the editors to meet and spared them the travails of having to confer entirely by post and fax. In addition, papers presented at, and work done for, each of the four seminars have indirectly informed the content of this volume.

Edmund Mokrzycki thanks the British Academy for funding a visit to England in September 1991 which included an editorial meeting in Salford; and the European University Institute, Florence, for the 1992–93 Jean Monnet Fellowship which enabled him to benefit from its support and its facilities during the most intensive period of editing.

Both editors thank Paul Piccone for permission to publish a revised and extended version of an article by Zygmunt Bauman which first appeared in *Telos*, no. 92, summer 1992.

Chris Bryant, Salford
Edmund Mokrzycki, Florence   April 1993

Chapter 1

Introduction
Theorizing the changes in East-Central Europe

Christopher G.A. Bryant and Edmund Mokrzycki

REVOLUTION, CONVERGENCE, TRANSITION OR TRANSFORMATION?

The collapse of state socialism in Eastern Europe in 1989 seemed like a revolution at the time to many participants in the East and observers in the West. Garton Ash (1990), for example, referred to the revolutions in Prague, Berlin and Bucharest – although he attributed to Warsaw and Budapest 'refolutions' which effected reform from above in response to pressure for revolution from below. But, as Dahrendorf (1990), following the French historian, Furet, quickly pointed out, the revolution in Eastern Europe was always an odd one in so far as there was no new revolutionary idea whose time had come. Indeed insistent demands for liberal democracy, and rather less insistent demands for a capitalist economy, might have been thought more a counter-revolutionary demand for the restoration of pre-communist traditions – except that, Czechoslovakia apart, there was no tradition of democracy and little tradition of bourgeois capitalism to restore. Revolutions, according to Skocpol, are also 'accompanied by and in part carried through by classed-based revolts from below' (Skocpol, 1979: 4). In Eastern Europe, however, one could speak variously of civil society against the party-state, popular demonstrations, even national liberation, but not properly of class-based revolts. The collapse of communism in Eastern Europe in 1989 was so quick, so dramatic and so complete, that references to revolution will no doubt continue, but for many the term has the wrong associations to capture the character of the who, the what and the why of the changes in 1989 and after. Perhaps the best one can hope to do is find some qualification which at least captures the character of events in 1989 itself. Bruszt (1990) refers to the 'negotiated revolution' in Hungary, a more euphonious term than Garton Ash's 'refolution'. Many Hungarians speak even less dramatically of *rendszerváltás*, an exchange of systems (cf. Arato in Chapter 6, this volume). Similarly, the common description of a 'velvet revolution' in Czechoslovakia recalls a tradition of non-violence in that country.

Some social scientists, such as those who organized the ISA Sociological Research Committee meeting in Uppsala, Sweden, in June 1992, have asked whether 1989 and after represent less a new departure than a convergence of East with West (*Theory*, 1991). Certainly the peoples of East-Central Europe do aspire to convergence in so far as they would like to establish liberal democracy and a capitalist market economy quickly. The character of the latter demand, however, is open to question; very many would like the prosperity of the West and the job security of the East. Be that as it may, the convergence theory of Kerr, Aron and others in the 1960s was not about aspirations but rather a common logic of development in industrial societies which gave rise to social structures much more comparable than the ideological apologists for capitalism and socialism would lead one to expect (Kerr *et al.*, 1960; Aron, 1967). There are two obvious reasons why returning to this idea now is inappropriate. First, what we have witnessed in the societies of East-Central Europe before and after 1989 is not some internal developmental dynamic which slowly compelled their convergence with capitalist societies in Western Europe or North America to a point at which continued protestations of a different ideology became insupportable. Rather, what we have seen is the exhaustion of the developmental potential of the state socialist mode of production, and the inability of communist party-states to resist demands for transformative change. In terms of technology, economic development and occupational structure, the societies of East-Central Europe had been diverging from the range of capitalist formations in the West at least since the mid-1970s. For all the talk of a return to Europe (and all the attachments of youth to American cultural icons), the onerous legacy of real socialism may well preclude convergence on some dimensions for the foreseeable future. Second, convergence theory is inattentive to differences, many of them immense, within capitalism. (The same might be said of much of the discourse of capitalism versus socialism which succeeded it in the late 1960s and 1970s.) If one considers equity structures, the role of stock exchanges, the role of banks and relations between finance and industrial capital, the role of the state, industrial relations and the segmentation of labour markets, state and private welfare provision, non-tariff barriers to trade, corruption and connections with organized crime, and the social relations and cultural forms which accompany them, then American, British, German, Italian, Swiss, Swedish and Japanese – and Taiwanese, Brazilian and Kenyan – capitalisms are each very different. With which of these is it supposed East-Central Europe is converging or could converge?

If 'revolution' and 'convergence' fail to provide the motif for post-communist changes, what about 'transition'? Political scientists have done important work on the 'transition to democracy' in three groups of countries: the post-war democracies of Germany, Italy and Japan; the new southern European democracies of the 1970s in Portugal, Spain and Greece; and the democratic super-session of South American authoritarian regimes in the 1980s in Argentina, Brazil, Uruguay, Chile and Paraguay (O'Donnell *et al.*, 1986). It is tempting to make Eastern Europe a fourth, as Przeworski (1992) has done, but it is also misleading. The collapse of communism is different from the defeat or the collapse of fascism and authoritarianism in so far as it involves not just political transition, but also economic. As Offe argues, the societies of Eastern Europe face a problem not faced before:

> the transfer of the hitherto state-owned productive assets to other forms of property, and, to this end, the creation of an entirely new class of entrepreneurs and owners in a way that has to be decided and justified in a political way and through political actors.
>
> (Offe, 1991: 4).

Whilst great efforts have long been made to analyse the transition from capitalism to socialism, the seeming irremovability of the state socialism imposed by the Soviet Union in East-Central Europe used to discourage systematic consideration of movement the other way. In short, there is neither model nor precedent for the transition from real socialism to democracy and capitalism. The very language of transition assumes an outcome which in reality is far from guaranteed. As Stark says, seemingly descriptive notions like 'transition to capitalism' and 'transition to a market economy' hide 'teleological constructs in which concepts are driven by hypothesized end-states. Presentist history finds its counterpart here in futurist transitology' (Stark, 1992: 22).

Like Stark we prefer to speak not of transitions, with the emphasis on destinations, but rather of transformations, with the emphasis on actual processes 'in which the introduction of new elements takes place most typically in combination with adaptations, rearrangements, permutations, and reconfigurations of already existing institutional forms' (ibid.). The legacy of real socialism cannot simply be discounted. Quite what the longer-term outcomes of the 'transformative politics' of which Bruszt (1992) writes, or of the transformative economics which accompanies them, turn out to be remains uncertain. We may well, on occasions, have to find new terms for new phenomena rather than try to fit everything into familiar Western moulds.

At the same time we think it instructive to ask whether one might reasonably expect a new 'great transformation'. Others, such as Ramet (1991), have alluded to such a transformation – and arguably the scale and the speed of the attempted change to capitalism and democracy alone justifies the epithet 'great' – but we wish to go further by making explicit what features of Polanyi's celebrated work, *The Great Transformation: The Political and Economic Origins of our Time* (1944), we mean to recall.

Polanyi's book deals with the establishment and consolidation in the nineteenth century of a civilization which was fundamentally different from anything that had gone before. Its central feature was the self-regulating market (in contrast to the absorption of the economic within the social in all previous societies). And central to the self-regulating market was Economic Man. Adam Smith had famously invoked man's natural 'propensity to barter, truck and exchange', but, contrary to Smith, Economic Man was not, according to Polanyi, a universal feature of human life but rather a cultural development which was to come to prevail in much of the world in the next century. Polanyi's thesis is that:

the idea of a self-adjusting market implied a stark utopia. Such an institution could not exist for any length of time without annihilating the human and natural substance of society; it would have physically destroyed man and transformed his surroundings into a wilderness. Inevitably society took measures to protect itself, but whatever measures it took impaired the self-regulation of the market, disorganized industrial life, and thus endangered society in yet another way.

(Polanyi, 1944: 3)

Economic liberalism had to be counter-balanced by social protection, and indeed everywhere it was – with measures enacted by politicians of every ideological persuasion. The consequence was a civilization organized around two contrary principles. For long periods the tension between them was creative but the balance had been lost by the 1930s with fateful consequences, and 'the origins of the cataclysm lay in the utopian endeavor of economic liberalism to set up a self-regulating market system' (Polanyi, 1944: 29). Writing in 1944, Polanyi was in no doubt that the balance between economic liberalism and social protection would have to be re-established.

Polanyi says surprisingly little about democracy. His general line is that 'the liberal state', one of the four institutions of nineteenth-century civilization (along with the balance-of-power system, the international gold standard and the self-regulating market), 'was itself a creation of the self-regulating market' (ibid.: 3). The 1832 Reform Bill in Britain, for example, and the Poor Law Amendment that followed it in 1834, 'put an end to the rule of the benevolent landlord and his allowance system' (ibid.: 80). But social protection, too, is presented as consistent with democracy. Thus 'Socialism is, essentially, the tendency inherent in an industrial civilization to transcend the self-regulating market by consciously subordinating it to a democratic society' (ibid.: 234).

We do not ourselves wish to push the reference to Polanyi as far as Glasman does in his highly original analysis in Chapter 10. Clearly, the circumstances of East-Central Europe today are very different from those of emergent industrial societies in the nineteenth century. In particular, their politicians and people look to make changes in a few years which took many decades in the West. Also, Polanyi emphasizes how the beginning of the economic transformation in the West preceded democratic reform and establishment of the liberal state. In East-Central Europe political change has, by contrast, and with the limited exception of Hungary, come first (on Hungary cf. Böröcz, 1993). Most fundamental of all, the legacies of the pre-capitalist and pre-democratic West were very different from the legacy of real socialism in East-Central Europe today.

Having said that, there are some parallels. In both cases we have
to consider change on the grand scale and with similar putative
end-states. In the first case liberal thinking (more precisely the
laissez-faire of the 1820s onwards), in the second neo-liberal
economic thinking – with its assumptions about the natural (as
distinct from cultivated or socially constructed) economic propen-
sities of men and women, and its inattention to the fabric of social
life and moral order – was of immense influence. Then and now
we have to consider what happens when economic utopia (in the
technical, not normative, sense) and abstract model meet social
reality and the need for social protection. Polanyi's wartime
account of the original great transformation revolves around
the acquisition and loss, nationally and internationally, of the
balance between economic liberalism and social protection. Post-
war Western developments of the welfare state, the social market
and social capitalism readdressed this issue. Neo-liberal economists,
and politicians such as Margaret Thatcher and Ronald Reagan
who embraced their ideas, so shifted the balance in the 1980s
towards economic liberalism as to put in doubt the future of social
protection, but the economic policies and the periods in office of
Reagan and Thatcher terminated in the longest recession since the
1930s. The issue is back on the agenda (and Glasman is entitled
to ask why reformers in East-Central Europe have ignored the
enormously successful precedent of the German social market).

The Eastern Europeans have been unlucky with the timing of
change. The events of 1989 took place soon after the Western
economic boom of the mid-1980s had seemed to confirm the
efficacy of neo-liberal economics. Key figures in the transformative economics of East-Central Europe, such as Balcerowicz in
Poland and Klaus in Czechoslovakia, have very credibly been
called Thatcherites. Had the ascendancy of Gorbachev, or some
similar figure, waited a little longer, 1989 might have been, say,
1993, the nostrums of liberal economists might have seemed less
plausible, and economic transformation would have been attempted
as the world economy was coming out of recession instead of going
into it. At any rate, by 1993 the exaggerated expectations of rapid
economic transformation held by politicians, peoples and Western
economic advisers had been exposed as such. In a context
of rapidly rising unemployment, increased poverty, state health
and welfare services which cannot cope, falling voter turn-outs,
heightened nationalism (as in the dispute, over economic policy in

particular, which led to the dissolution of Czechoslovakia, and the dispute between Slovakia and Hungary over the Slovak diverted course of the Danube), and fears about migratory flows and other consequences of economic collapse in the former Soviet Union and elsewhere, the governments of East-Central Europe will have to search for new balances between economic liberalism and social protection appropriate to each of their countries. The issue at the heart of Polanyi's account of the great transformation will not go away (cf. Mareš, Musil and Rabusič in Chapter 5 of this volume; and Deacon, 1992).

In choosing to speak of transformation and not transition, we have signalled that we do not know where changes will end. We do suggest that Polanyi's issue has to be addressed, but whether it will be successfully addressed, and if so how, in the circumstances of each country, we do not presume to foretell. There are two other similarly inescapable issues to which we wish to draw attention. The first could be called the legacy of real socialism in an open future. It acknowledges that even when one takes into account the legacy of the past, one cannot be sure of its consequences other than disillusionment with all projects which promise transformation by grand design.

The feeling of living in a sham society was overwhelming in Eastern Europe before 1989. It was only natural to assume, as most intellectuals, including sociologists, did, that the 'socialist' social fabric, including its macrosociological properties, the artificial product of an imposed social order and an irrational economy, would vanish as soon as men and women were free to choose their own way. 'Socialist society' was treated as the temporary result of coercion, with little integrity of its own and little ability to sustain itself under normal conditions. It seemed to be composed of individuals and primary groups who would be willing, if not happy, to abandon whatever macrosociological categories they found themselves in under socialism in order to pursue their interests in a rational way and to regroup spontaneously in a 'natural' order with the middle class to the fore. It was this view of an amorphous and plastic society, distorted by the heavy hand of the communist party-state, that the Eastern European reformers had in mind as they worked out the details of their plans for reform. They took for granted that what was needed was to set people free by removing the economic and political impediments to the natural expression and articulation of individual interests. Accordingly, the core of the reform plans was *liberalization*, one might almost say *liberation*. The strategic goal of the reform plans was to transform the system; the tactical goal was to transform the system by enabling people to be their natural selves.

The Polish shock therapy, the first and the most successful radical reform in so far as the IMF expects 2 per cent growth in GDP in 1993 following a 19.5 per cent fall during 1990–91 (*Guardian*, 10 March 1993), was composed of powerful and carefully balanced macroeconomic measures. The first goal of the so-called Balcerowicz Plan was to stabilize the economy and especially to end hyperinflation. The main objective, however, was a radical change in the entire system; this goal was to be achieved by a complicated process of dismantling the instruments of state control over the economy, including mass privatization of the public sector. It was a sophisticated economic and political operation. On the other hand it largely neglected microeconomic considerations and failed to include a systematic programme to address the social dimension of reform – except for standard social policy measures dealing with such consequences of 'belt-tightening' as poverty and unemployment. That is to say the plan took into account problems of absolute economic deprivation, but not problems of, for example, relative social deprivation. It was simply assumed that newly released social energy would be used to maximize economic self-interest and thereby hasten establishment of a successful market economy. It was not anticipated that this energy would also be used, and effectively, to defend and enhance *social* group interests that, more often than not, block market mechanisms (cf. Mokrzycki, 1992; Tarkowski, 1992).

This episode casts doubt on the assumption that *homo economicus* is a natural being whose spontaneous appearance can always be relied upon once impediments to it have been removed. It would seem that at least some continuities of consciousness, interest definition and social relations are only to be expected in the short term and, maybe even in the medium and long term. Once freed to follow their own courses of action, men and women have both revealed attitudes and behaviours which communism suppressed or distorted and made choices which planners find perverse. There is a supreme irony in this. Spencer and other Victorian liberals used to argue against planning on the grounds that the unanticipated and unintended consequences of social action would always frustrate, and often overwhelm, the anticipated and intended. As Robert Burns more memorably put it, 'The best laid schemes o' mice an' men/Gang aft a-gley'. In so far as this applies, and Spencer and others underestimated what persuasion, agreement and informed collective commitment might achieve, it applies to capitalism by grand design as much as it does to socialist planning. Macroeconomics cannot substitute for micro-economics, and transformative economics cannot succeed so long as it is a project devised by technical experts and imposed on a population there to be manipulated for its own good. Continuity of continuities: a new self-proclaimed vanguard believes it can succeed where an old one failed forty years earlier! Or to make the same point as Dahrendorf does. What the closed system of communism has given way to is not the capitalist *system*, but an open society and an open future (Dahrendorf, 1990: 36). We cannot be sure what the outcome will be.

The third inescapable issue has to do with the search for an appropriate form for, and balance between, the state and civil society. Reflecting on the extraordinary events of 1989, Dahrendorf has again made the point well.

> 'We are the people' is a nice slogan but as a constitutional maxim it is a mirror image of the total state which has just been dislodged. If the monopoly of the Party is replaced by the victory of the masses, all will be lost before long, for the masses have no structure and no permanence.
>
> (Dahrendorf, 1990: 98)

Instead democratization has to combine the transmutation of the party-state into the liberal state and the transmutation of the people into a civil society. With respect to the state, the difficulty includes a legacy of both popular distrust of it and popular dependence on it. With respect to civil society, the difficulty includes a legacy of at best civil society *against* the state and at worst scant experience of civil society at all. In North America and Western Europe the flawed approximations of a society of citizens who are civil to one another regardless of differences of interest and sensibility, who are individually and socially self-reliant, and who are skilled in what de Tocqueville called the art of association, have always taken generations to form. East-Central Europe will have to have a measure of success much more quickly if democracy is to be secured. There is, as Tarkowski says, 'A dilemma which one can observe in all post-communist countries – how to reconcile the growing scope of freedom with obedience to the law, and how to explain to society that freedom also means responsibility' (Tarkowski, 1992: 146).

CONTRIBUTIONS TO THE ANALYSIS OF EAST-CENTRAL EUROPE

In this book the focus is on East-Central Europe: Poland, the Czech Republic, Slovakia and Hungary. After three years of reform, these countries are clearly ahead of other post-communist countries in terms of basic economic indicators, such as per capita GDP, and standard of living. It may be that a division is opening up between them and much of the rest of Eastern Europe – both Bulgaria, Romania and the republics of the former Soviet Union, and the special cases of Albania and the republics of the former Yugoslavia. Certainly they are sufficiently similar for informative comparisons to be possible between them. It is notable that all have had, and with the partial exception of Slovakia can be expected to continue to have, a Western orientation. They look West, not East.

When it comes to explaining the differences between them, how relevant is the radicalism and purity of economic reform? How important, too, are historical factors? Pre-war Czechoslovakia, for example, was a well-developed democratic country (albeit more industrialized in Bohemia and Moravia than in Slovakia). Claims that changes since 1989 represent the resumption of developments forcibly interrupted by communism have more plausibility there than elsewhere, but a shared memory of democracy and capitalism has not proved strong enough to prevent the division of the country into two. Then in Hungary there was the experience of goulash communism in the 1970s and 1980s and the development of much the largest second economy in all Eastern Europe, together with an informalization of social relations of production and distribution. Indeed according to Böröcz:

> informality constituted not a separate 'sphere' or sector of the economy but something of a 'systemic principle'. It saturated the most important processes of control, production and distribution of all levels of society, including the 'first' as well as the second economy, the workings of the ruling party apparatus, the state organs, and all major institutions. It is this combination of rigid formal rules with a set of informal provisions

ensuring the softness of the enforcement of those rules that has
made the Kádárist second period of state socialism into a clearly
recognizable, softer – 'winking-oppressive' – variant of state
socialism.

(Böröcz, 1993: 103–4)

What sort of legacy is that? Arato in Chapter 6 and Szalai in
Chapter 7 help towards an answer. And in Poland, of course, there
was the experience of an exceptionally strong and well organized
anti-communist social movement, Solidarity, in a society blessed
or cursed with two centuries' experience of opposition to state
authorities.

The chapters which follow do not offer definitive answers to
these or any other questions. They do, however, provide ample
argument and evidence that what is in train in East-Central
Europe is no simple and guaranteed transition to liberal democracy
and capitalism. Bauman opens the book by examining why those
who led oppositions before 1989 have so often been swept aside
afterwards. He also applies the concept of 'liminality' to current
circumstances in which anything may happen but little can be
done. His primary focus is on Poland but much of what he argues
is applicable to all post-communist societies. Cirtautas examines
processes of identity and interest formation in all four societies
and their relation to both party formation and historic Western
conceptions of democracy and citizenship. She expects the contest
between liberalism and nationalism to continue for the foreseeable
future without a decisive victory for either. Bryant prefers sociological realism to economic utopianism, notes that economic shock
therapies raise expectations and risk a backlash, and argues that
formation of a civil society and relegitimation of the state can only
take a long time. Mareš, Musil and Rabušic consider state welfare
provision in Czechoslovakia and the Czech Republic in relation to
the welfare principles of alternative types of political regime and
the historical practice of Czech corporatism. The contradiction
they describe between a strong demand for state welfare and an
empty treasury applies elsewhere too. Arato discusses system
change and revolutionary ideology in Hungary and assesses the
prospects for four projects of the radical right. By explaining how
and why the right constructs revolutionary claims in arguably the
least revolutionary society in East-Central Europe, he helps to
elucidate the character of transformative politics generally. Szalai
connects changes of elites in Hungary and the uncertain prospects

for civil society to the peculiar legacy of Kádárism. She stresses the need for the formation of a broad propertied class and notes the significance of the Democratic Charter movement. Duke and Grime set out the issues involved in different modes of privatization before describing and accounting for the differences in privatization policy, practice and outcome in Poland, Hungary and what was Czechoslovakia. Kowalik examines the experience of three years of economic reform in Poland and explains why agreement on privatization has proved hard to reach. He also considers whether there was an alternative way of proceeding. Glasman argues very forcefully that there was – a kind of social democracy cum social market anticipated by Polanyi in 1944 and subsequently achieved in the Federal Republic of Germany – but that it went unconsidered. As Lukes adds in a comment on Glasman, whether there was, is or could be an alternative to market utopianism is a question of the greatest theoretical importance and political relevance. No one could accuse Glasman of being someone *sine ira et studio*; on the contrary, the very passion of his argument will, we hope, remind readers in the West that it is not just a test of neo-liberal economic theory which we are asking them to consider but also the hopes, fears, experiences and lifechances of more than 64 million real live human beings.

We have not sought to advance any one line in the ideological disputes now current in East-Central Europe. Yet most of our contributors will probably be seen as left of the standard neo-liberal position prevailing in the region. The reason for this is clear: it is difficult, if not impossible, for a social and political scientist to refrain from criticism of a doctrine which disregards social, cultural and historical factors. Whatever the ideological dispositions of our authors – and they range from liberal criticism of neo-liberal economics to social democracy – all believe that the 'new great transformation' is a very complicated social process.

REFERENCES

Aron, R. (1967) *18 Lectures on Industrial Society* (French, 1961), London: Weidenfeld & Nicolson.
Ash, T. Garton (1990) *We the People*, Cambridge: Granta.
Böröcz, J. (1993) 'Simulating the Great Transformation: Property Change under Prolonged Informality in Hungary', *Archives européennes de sociologie*, 34: 81–107.

Bruszt, L. (1989) 'The Negotiated Revolution in Hungary', *Social Research*, 1990, 57: 365–87.
—— (1992) 'Transformative Politics: Social Costs and Social Peace in East-Central Europe', *East European Politics and Societies*, 6: 55–72.
Dahrendorf, R. (1990) *Reflections on the Revolution in Europe*, London: Chatto & Windus.
Deacon, B. (ed.) (1992) *Social Policy, Social Justice and Citizenship in Eastern Europe*, Aldershot: Avebury.
Kerr, C., Dunlop, T., Harrison, F. and Myers, C.A. (1960) *Industrialism and Industrial Man*, Berkeley: University of California Press.
Mokrzycki, E. (1992) 'The Legacy of Real Socialism: Group Interests and the Search for a New Utopia', in W.C. Connor and P. Płoszajski (eds), *Escape from Socialism: The Polish Route*, Warsaw: IFiS Publishers.
O'Donnell, G., Schmitter, P.C. and Whitehead, L. (1986) *Transitions from Authoritarian Rule* (5 vols), Baltimore: Johns Hopkins UP.
Offe, C. (1991) 'Capitalism by Democratic Design? Democratic Theory Facing the Triple Transition in East Central Europe', Paper presented to IPSA Congress, Buenos Aires, July.
Polanyi, K. (1944) *The Great Transformation: The Political and Economic Origins of Our Time*, Boston: Beacon, 1957.
Przeworski, A. (1992) 'The Choice of Institutions in the Transition to Democracy', *Sisyphus: Social Studies*, 1 (VIII): 7–40.
Ramet, S.P. (1991) *Social Currents in Eastern Europe: The Sources and Meaning of the Great Transformation*, Durham, NC: Duke UP.
Skocpol, T. (1979) *States and Social Revolutions: A Comparative Analysis of France, Russia and China*, Cambridge: CUP.
Stark, D. (1992) 'Path Dependence and Privatization: Strategies in East Central Europe', *East European Politics and Societies*, 6: 17–54.
Tarkowski, J. (1992) 'Transition to Democracy of Transition to Ohlocracy', *Sisyphus: Social Studies*, 1 (VIII): 139–49.
Theory: Newsletter of the Research Committee on Social Theory, no. 2 (1991).

Chapter 2

After the patronage state
A model in search of class interests

Zygmunt Bauman

Popular wisdom accuses revolutions of *infanticidal* appetite; it seems, however, that the charge of a *parricidal* inclination would be more to the point. Since revolutionary time runs fast, children turn into parents at a pace that defies the common view of generational change; in the short span of the revolution the parricide tends to be repeated many times over. Parricide becomes a 'permanent' mode of public life during the revolution; yet some revolutions reveal the parricidal bent more vividly than others. Whence the difference?

Revolutions are, as a rule, narrated by the victors or their more or less sycophantic court poets. No wonder, therefore, that good luck is painted as the intractable logic of forward-marching history, and past touch-and-go chances are promoted to the rank of historical inevitability. This is why, when thinking of revolutions, we are prompted to deploy the similes of germination, gestation, maturation: new life acquiring shape and clamouring to be let out, the alternative being suffocation of the embryo and the poisoning of the womb.

Translated into the language of politics, this is a vision of a new and invariably *better* (more just, more reasonable, more efficient, more enjoyable) form of life which the *ancien régime* arrested in its growth. More in tune with the jargon of political-scientific discourse, this vision is expressed in terms of a conflict between the interests of society and the increasingly self-centred and selfish elites of a jaded political regime which has outgrown its 'positive', 'enabling' capacity and otherwise outlived its time. Only when the revolution occurs are the social interests and the political realities, heretofore out of joint, brought into harmony; political forces thus far suppressed assume new political authority and re-shape the political frame to better fit their size and form. Today's rulers parade as the agents of yesterday's sufferers, and the regime over which they preside is said to vindicate interests hitherto thwarted.

Upheavals which follow the pattern of the 'Glorious Revolution' are adequately served by the above vision: outdated rulers are either chastised and forced to listen to the clamouring of new forces, or – if stubbornly sticking to their guns – replaced by alternative elites, able and willing to follow the call of the times; the laws of the realm are rewritten to respect interests up-to-now neglected. Recent history is full of such revolutions; the toppling of Greek generals or the disposal of the Franco or Salazar legacies offer the most obvious examples. It is not against revolutions like these, however, that the charge of parricide is lodged. Indeed, were an act of parricide to happen in their course it could only be seen as irrelevant to the 'logic of the revolution' – a step motivated by sibling rivalry, or caused by the regrettable temporary deregulation and brutalization of public life in the wake of revolutionary disturbance.

These, however, are not the only revolutions. Extrapolating from their experience may well serve the self-legitimizing needs of other revolutions, but would hardly account for their sharply different trajectory. Those other revolutions are marked by *the separation between the interests that brought the fall of the old regime and the interests which the new one serves or promotes*. They are, so to speak, two-step revolutions, with a void separating the two stages. In the first stage, the old regime is toppled; in the second, a new regime emerges, by fits and starts, from the ruins. In between there is little but ruins and their disoriented inhabitants. The latter are now formless, a raw mass yet to be worked upon and given shape. It is not for them to decide what form this shape will take.

IN THE VOID OF LIMINALITY

Many years ago the Dutch anthropologist Arnold van Gennep (1960) suggested a three-stage scheme to analyse *les rites de passage* – rituals that simultaneously produce, reflect, and announce the transfer of a person from one 'structured' position to another (say, age category, professional or power standing, sexual status). The first stage is one of 'separation', during which the person is stripped of all the trappings of his or her previous status; the last is 'aggregation', during which a new role is assigned/acquired and new rules come to guide the person's conduct. There is, though, an in-between stage, the stage of 'liminality' (*limen* means 'threshold' in Latin), an *unstructured*, formless condition, where neither the 'old' nor the 'new' rules apply, where existence is semiotically impoverished and the few symbols bandied around are conspicuously lacking in agreed meaning. Liminality is not determined; neither is it determining. It is, rather, a break in determination; a locale of unbound possibility; not a crossroad, but a desert where routes are yet to be drawn – marked out by the footprints of the travellers.

Van Gennep's insistence on the *unavoidability* of a mediating stage which separates the dismantling of the old from the aggregation of the new order is particularly eye-opening. In Victor W. Turner's rendition, liminality is 'necessarily ambiguous' – its conditions 'elude or slip through the network of classifications'; they are 'neither here nor there'; 'they are betwixt and between'; the state of liminality is 'frequently likened to death, to being in the womb, to invisibility, to darkness, to bisexuality, to the wilderness, and to an eclipse of the sun or moon'. The persons travelling from one position to another are, so to speak, 'on the loose' and devoid of socially enabling roles; for this reason 'their behaviour is normally passive or humble; they must . . . accept arbitrary punishment without complaint. It is as though they are being reduced or ground down to a uniform condition to be fashioned anew . . .' 'The ordeals and humiliations' to which they are as a rule submitted 'represent partly a destruction of the previous status and partly a tempering of their essense in order to prepare them to cope with their new responsibilities . . . They have to be shown that in themselves they are clay or dust, mere matter, whose form is impressed upon them by society' (Turner, 1969: 95, 103).

I propose that van Gennep's tripartite scheme may be usefully deployed in the analysis of the 'parricidal' brand of revolutions – with an important proviso, of course. Rites of passage assume a person moving between the stations of a fixed 'structure'; the *mobility* of persons is invested with meaning by the *fixity* of the positions between which they move. No such assumption can be made, however, if the 'passage' is the lot of a large group or the whole society. Here fixity and mobility cannot be visualized as separate conditions. The abandoned structure does not survive the movement; and the arrived-at structure is not in any real sense fixed before the movement starts. Its 'fixity' is but a sediment of mobility, and a contingent one at that. With this qualification, van Gennep's image is fully compatible with the experience of 'parricidal' revolutions. (From this point on, I shall use the term 'systemic revolutions' – as I have defined it elsewhere[1] – when referring to revolutions charged with parricidal proclivity.) Its (metaphorical) deployment allows us to make sense of phenomena which defy most alternative schemes. What the latter fail to predict – and thus explain away as deviations, corruptions or the poisoning legacy of the *ancien régime*) – appears as a regularity within an analytical framework derived from van Gennep's tripartite scheme.

Turner's vocabulary is strewn with references to purpose and function. This is well justified when liminality serves the reassertion of a relatively stable structure – its continuous reproduction over time. It is not permissible, however, in our extension to the passage of *societies* rather than their individual members. The decisive difference is that the end-structure to which liminality would eventually lead is 'given in advance', if at all, solely in the form of a vague utopia which more likely than not would bear little resemblance to the actual state of affairs established at the other end of the liminality ordeal. Unlike Durkheim's 'anomie', liminality has no specific normative system by which to measure its own normlessness; neither is it likely to end in the recomposition and reassertion of a temporarily weakened system. The underdetermination and ambiguity of the liminal condition cannot be said to serve any specific purpose, and even less a purpose deliberately set and pursued by the elite currently in charge. It is, rather, a combined outcome of the dissolution of past meanings and the nebulousness of promised new ones. Liminality is inherently ambivalent. It is a condition without clear time-span, obvious exit and authoritative guides.

The gist of our scheme is that in the systemic revolutions there is no direct road leading from the 'dismantling' to the 'aggregation' stage. The first process peters out in the quicksands of liminality, in which the more or less stable aggregations have yet to form and from which they must later extricate themselves. The moment society is sunk in the liminal condition; there is no way of predicting the shape of things to come. The forces that authored the dismantling of old societal forms are used up and exhausted;

they meet their demise the moment their task has been accomplished. In the formless magma into which they dissolve, new forces will eventually crystallize; but only the memorized symbols and hastily invented traditions will, retrospectively, provide their link with the past.

From the depth of Polish liminality there comes the sorrowful summary of Sławomir Majman:

> Three years after that June of hope and enthusiasm [June 1989 saw the establishment of the first *Solidarity* government], the post-Solidarity camp has compromised itself thoroughly through constant quarrels and retributions . . . After three years, the post-Solidarity camp is tired of power . . . Like all revolutions, this one is rapidly growing old . . . Why has blindness befallen people who used to fight together for a common cause? Why does something that began in exultation, end with the triumph of mediocrity?
>
> (Majman, 1992: 8)

Indeed, why? Three years ago Solidarity won: its enemy was toppled, the road to a new life wide open, the gruesome years of enforced negativity over. It was time to build anew. Today, the gallant heroes are occupied as much as anything with defaming and vilifying their brothers-in-arms of yesterday. In the eyes of the crestfallen nation, the parents of the Polish Revolution have already turned, as did their predecessors in power, into 'them'. A similar plight has befallen the Hungarian Free Democrats or Czech Civic Forum.

In May 1992 Adam Michnik, the unimpeachable voice of conscience of the anti-communist revolution, appeared on French television alongside the man he did more than anyone else to overthrow, General Wojciech Jaruzelski, who had come to Paris to launch the French translation of his reminiscences. Michnik and Jaruzelski talked to each other amicably, understood each other without difficulty, and seemed to agree on most points. The audience was shocked; some were furious with Michnik, their yesterday hero. What the shocked and the furious failed to comprehend was that Michnik and Jaruzelski were integral (though mutually opposite) partners of the same historical discourse; only together, in their conflict, could they gestate that discourse which led eventually to the dismantling of the communist legitimacy; and it was through that discourse that their historic meanings – nay, significance – were in turn gestated. The resolution of conflict was the end of that discourse; with the fall of communism, the discourse lost its subject-matter. For those who came after, it sounded as hollow as the credo of the yesteryear it exploded. Their past battles tied Michnik and Jaruzelski to each other more closely than Michnik's victory tied him to those who came later to share that victory's fruits.

Michnik and Jaruzelski, Solidarity and Polish United Worker's Party (PUWP), Free Democrats and the by now almost forgotten hapless reformers of the post-Kádárian party – all belonged to the *dismantling* phase of the systemic revolution. Some emerged from that phase as winners, others were defeated – but all entered the wasteland of liminality *homeless*. In that wasteland, the vision that brought about the downfall of communism found no solid ground in which to put down roots.

REFORM THROUGH SUICIDE

In Poland 'there is no section of society to which the government may direct its promises in the hope of stimulating economic activity' (Domański, 1992: 3). This, arguably, is the experience shared in varying degree by all post-communist societies; everywhere the anti-communist revolutions adopted the pro-capitalist label with few or no native capitalists to wear it and virtually no *Bürgertum* to covet it. All the *national* revolutions which brought about the collapse of communism were both indigenous and contrived. They were indigenous in so far as the communist nation-states were overwhelmed by dissent which they bred yet could not contain, and by demands which they promised to satisfy yet could not meet. They were contrived in so far as the disaffection which prompted them was informed by imported values, and its imputed causes were given, rightly, a foreign name.

Communism preached and practised the state monopoly of justice. Monopoly, however, meant unshared responsibility; anything conceived as injustice rebounded potentially as a complaint against the state; every disaffection turned into anti-state dissent. As a consequence, the communist state displayed an uncanny ability to attract diverse strands of grievance which would hardly combine in a type of society in which the satisfaction of desire is sought in the market-place. It allied dissenters with an awesome ease which the builders of rainbow coalitions in market societies could only envy.

Sooner or later, the mass of discontent had to transgress the system's capacity for accommodation and adjustment and force it on the road to self-cancellation. This process, however, was itself deeply paradoxical. Dissent bore the marks of its birth. It was prompted by the system's malfunction, more precisely by the feeling that the system does not function the way it should according to its own promises. Most groups opposing the practice of the state wished to press that practice closer to the ideal the self-same state had preached. At the height of popular disaffection in Poland, during the heyday of Solidarity and the years of its legal suppression, research after research found that a large (and growing!) majority of the population wanted the state to deliver more of its, specifically communist, promise. In 1985, for example, 62 per cent of those questioned emphatically stated their preference for the model of a 'caring' patronage state, and only 29 per cent preferred a society in which individuals themselves bore the responsibility for their own well-being; for that reason perhaps 50 per cent (against 27 per cent) considered capitalism to be a more unjust and exploitative system than their native form of socialism, and 55.7 per cent (a figure which went on growing with every successive opinion poll) approved of the introduction of martial law (Marody, 1988: 280–5).

Disaffection had to do not with the *content* of demands which jarred with the outspoken principles of the regime, but rather with the *volume* of demands that exceeded the performative capacity of a rigid, centralized system of production and distribution which cut the queues for jobs but only at the expense of ever stretching the queues for consumer goods. In the words of Claus Offe:

> In the European capitalist democracies, queues form in front of the job offices, while in the countries of 'really existing socialism' they form in front of butcher shops. In the first, there is a 'reserve army' of workers waiting to be employed (as well as a reserve army of commodities waiting for a customer), while in the second the managers wait for the workers and the workers wait for consumer goods.

> (Offe, 1989: 64)

Under the circumstances, the only hope of 'salvation' for the system was to lower the volume and intensity of anti-state discontent by shifting some of the 'caring responsibilities' of the state to the market and, more generally, to private or group initiatives (a method practised with great stabilizing effect by liberal democracies presiding over market-managed economies, and dearly wished, in vain, by the 'radical reformers' of the last stage of the old order such as Rakowski's team in Poland shortly before its electoral defeat). This was, however, a dubious means of saving the system; it amounted to a process of self-dismantling, one that only the most naive among the communist rulers could hope to contain and control once they had agreed to set it in motion.

In other words, the accelerating disintegration of the communist system was in a way an unanticipated outcome of demands the system itself gestated and styled. 'Objectively', and in the view of many protesters, the demands required a further strengthening of the managerial role of the state. But it was precisely that managerial role, already stretched beyond its capacity, which stood in the way of satisfying the opposition's demands. The truth of the matter was on occasions seen more clearly by the communist rulers than by their opponents; in their inchoate attempts at 'reform' (ceding the task of needs satisfaction to the market), the more far-sighted among the rulers found themselves deserted by the very forces of dissent whose demands the measures were meant to meet. Let us recall that the Jaruzelski/Rakowski plan of releasing the economy from pernickety governmental control was overwhelmingly rejected in a free referendum. Let us also recall that no side sitting around the Warsaw Round Table (and not merely for tactical reasons or fear of reprisal) voiced an intention to dispose of state ownership and to float the responsibilities of the patronage state. Blue- and white-collar protesters alike objected to the shabby existence meted out under the auspices of state-administered justice; but what they wished was more justice in state administration, not abdication of state responsibilities. It was far from clear at the time that they were prepared to trade off the state-guaranteed job security or social wages for the consumer joys they demanded.

Some of the protesters, in addition, were to be the first victims of revolutionary parricide. Polish workers who flocked under the banners of Solidarity were products of the absurd centralized system their protest was about to sap. It was the economic absurdity of the system that kept them in existence and supplied their livelihood. They were bound to go under together with the rulers they toppled.

To complete the paradox of the anti-communist revolution, the grievance that made the masses into the gravediggers of the communist system stood no better chance of rectification under the conditions that emerged after the collapse of the system. Neither the workers of the communist-built industrial dinosaurs, nor the state-tied farmers, got what they bargained for,[2] but they got much which they did not bargain for (including mass unemployment and the cancellation of state credits). Economically, most found themselves worse off than before their political victory. By well-settled habit they addressed their complaint to the state, now managed by yesterday's dissidents. This time, however, the powers that be refused to consider complaints as something they should address. The state stopped 'caring' before its wards stopped needing care. But like their predecessors, the new rulers could not devise a policy which would cater for existing interests. As for the policies they *could* devise, there were no interests in sight likely to feel enthused by them.

THE WANDERING STIMULUS AND ITS AVATARS

A few years ago Milan Šimečka complained that 'we here on the Eastern border of the West will just have to go on dutifully playing our roles as the victims and outsiders of history' (Šimečka, 1989: 161). History is narrated by the strong, historiography being the narrative of their victories and verbal display of their material power. The standards of history-telling have for some time now been set in the West ('In the Russian popular imagination' Tatiana Tolstaya recently wrote, 'the West, where the sun goes down, is a corridor to another world, a bewitched location . . . The line that divides East from West is a magic site where people are transformed' (Tolstaya, 1992: 25). Those left outside by the Western narrative cannot but agonize over their plight which they cannot conceive in any other form but that of deprivation. The deprivation was and is defined by what the 'West' currently stood or stands for, and what, accordingly, the 'East' felt or feels it is missing. In the time of Lenin and Stalin, it was electrification, steel works, tractors and technical skills. In the time of Gorbachev and Yeltsin, it is McDonald's, Woolco, Sun Holidays and Virgin Records.

Under 'Eastern' conditions, in the midst of post-communist liminality, the time for thinkers and artists to enjoy a post-modern freedom from social duty (or, as Philippe Genestier has recently put it, of 'disconnection of the registers of ethics and aesthetics' (Genestier, 1992: 90)) has not yet arrived. However reluctantly, the intellectuals must again take up the traditional role of 'Eastern' intelligentsia: that of the spiritual leaders, guides, teachers, prompters and animators of a 'people' deemed to be attached to obsolete values and resentful of 'progress'. As things currently stand, they must even, à la Havel or Gieremek, take up for a time the role of active politicians. Once more (like in the old bad times when belching factory chimneys were the intellectuals' good tidings and the object of poetic elation) they must tell 'the people' what is good for them and how to get there; and if talking brings no results, legislate them into the new and better world which they are reluctant to enter on their own. As Michael D. Kennedy (forthcoming) suggests – when lifted to positions of political authority on the wave of the revolution, the intellectuals 'by necessity return to their role in the beginnings of modernity: providing legitimation for the suppression of popular wants on the basis of knowing the public's true needs'.

Arnold J. Toynbee described the intelligentsia gestated along the *limen* that divides/connects the coveting civilizations from/with the coveted one, as the 'class of liaison-officers', or 'a transformer class'; 'captivated planets' of a 'pirate sun' (Toynbee, 1939: 154). The intellectuals of the *limen*, Toynbee suggested, 'were products and symptoms, not of natural growth, but of their own societies' discomfiture in collisions with an alien Modern West'. 'The Kerensky regime was a fiasco because it was saddled with the task of making bricks without straw: of making a parliamentary government without having a solid, competent, prosperous, and experienced middle class to draw on' (Toynbee, 1960: 185–7). We may say that in as far as modern liberalism was the form of life of the free bourgeois producer, and postmodern democracy is the form of life of the free bourgeois consumer, the 'Eastern' intelligentsia that preached and promoted these forms in generational succession has had to deputize for the non-existing 'historical subject' of the world it set about building until such time as the class interested in the world proclaimed by the current intellectual ideal of the 'good life' is brought into being.[3]

There is little doubt that the life of the affluent West, 'as seen on TV', holds a tremendous and unqualified attraction for 'the people' even if not briefed to this effect by the native intelligentsia.

What is not so clear is the form which the dreams, fed by that life, take. Most likely, it is the very plenitude and putative accessibility of material goods that arouses desire. But what about other things which go with them – that 'tyranny of opportunities' (Hannah Arendt), insecurity, uncertainty and risk-taking, the bitter after-taste of every choice made and perpetual nostalgia for choices not made, which are apparently undetachable accessories of consumer freedom? The consumers of the postmodern West seem to take such nuisances in their stride; presumably, the pleasures of con-sumer life are ample enough to outweigh the spiritual price to pay. This is not, however, the condition prevalent in the post-communist East, with its race between the fall in living standards and the rise in unemployment. There, the would-be consumer is asked to pay the full price of consumer bliss while the date of delivery of pre-paid goods has not been as yet even vaguely indicated. No wonder, then, that, as the Russian satirist Vladimir Voinovich found on his recent visit to his homeland, 'everybody there wants to be rich, but no one wants to earn money'.

Little wonder either that the brief, spectacular, carnivalesque honeymoon between the intelligentsia and 'the people' (so envied by the intellectuals in the West) is now by and large over throughout the post-communist world. Once more, things have fallen in line with the logic of life in the *limen* and are 'normal' again; intellectuals (whether in or out of ministerial office) are fast returning to their usual complaints against witless and mindless 'masses' unable to see what is good for them, while the 'masses' are back to their habitual half-wary, half-derisive view of 'those men with briefcases in the capital' who do not know and would not care anyway what real life is truly like.

The present breakdown of communication between the edu-cated elites and the 'masses' occurs at a time when the patronage state, fast disappearing from institutionalized reality, is far from losing its hold over popular imagination. As implied above, the popular revolt against the communist regime expressed (though in an oblique and perverse way) the deeply ingrained belief that the collective well-being ultimately depends on what the state rulers do – that *l'état peut tout* – and that for this reason it should remain the obvious address for collective complaints and hopes. The educated classes, however, joined the popular protest with a different motivation: they knew of the rapid discreditation of social engineering (particularly state-managed engineering) and the dramatic rise of neo-liberal philosophy in the West, and they believed that attempts to tinker with the 'natural course of affairs' by political means are futile and damaging.[4] In Poland, as Andrzej Koraszewski sourly commented, the intellectuals are busy curing *at home* diseases other countries suffer; they 'live by problems of a different reality'. 'The highest proof of competence in today's Poland is to move freely in the realm of problems experienced by countries at a different level of development' (Koraszewski, 1992: 69).

In all fairness, it is not just the collective squint of the educated classes in power that is to blame for the languages of 'intelligentsia' and 'the people' drifting apart. There is also a powerful external factor. Post-communist governments have little freedom to choose their policies, even if they wish to do so. A strict regime has been imposed by IMF, world governments and world bankers, none of whom brooks local initiatives gladly other than initiatives to make the locality hospitable for unbridled market forces. The elites presiding over impoverished post-communist economies have virtually no room for manoeuvre, though – suspended as they are between the devil of impatient population at home and the deep blue sea of the 'bitter medicine' purveyed by the world financial centres – they need it badly. There is little choice left even for those thoughtful and enlightened among the new elites who are aware of the dismal record of successive Western fashions when applied – each with the same arrogant self-confidence – to the periphery of the affluent centre; who know, or suspect, that 'wealthy countries destroy more than they create when they export their economic programmes and their values to the developing world' (Schwarz, 1992).

As Winicjusz Narojek observed in his brief, yet remarkably insightful study of the 'Post-Communist Utopia', the decline of the 'socialist welfare state' presents a truly grotesque spectacle, since

> the populist euphoria is to a large extent an effect of the official propaganda and the assertions of omnipotence of now demoted rulers, while the elites which embrace a large number of recent enthusiasts for socialist construction preach the abandonment of dreams to improve the world and of the hitherto practised forms of social organization.
>
> (Translated from Narojek, 1990)

The irony of the situation is, of course, that it is precisely the intellectual elite, lauding (by choice or by the lack of choice) the 'invisible hand' of the free market, which faces the need to *enforce* the change against the wishes, or at least without the active co-operation of, the 'masses'. At this stage, there are remarkably few takers for the current intellectualist offer of freedom from the state. The offer can count on the support of the creative intelligentsia, who read it as, first and foremost, freedom from censorship and state-enforced criteria of artistic propriety. It can also count on support of the small number of budding entrepreneurs, often merely a lenient definition of speculators and double-dealers, who read it mostly as freedom from vexing public scrutiny and excessive taxation. What the offer conspicuously lacks is a broad constituency able to enjoy the pleasures of consumer choice.

Full shops, if anything, make the situation still worse: to far too many people they show how pitiable are the gains so far and how exorbitant the price that has to be paid today, and for an indefinite period yet, in the name of future gains which are by no means assured. Ostentatious display of seductive affluence, if combined with the still vivid memory of the 'delivering state', bodes ill for the future of the one liberty undeniably gained – *political* freedom. It results already in the tendency of the rabidly nationalist-populist forces on one side, and the post-communist guardians of nostalgia for the defunct patronage on the other, to squeeze out the intellectual leaders and heroes of the anti-communist revolutions from freely elected parliaments.

As John Kenneth Galbraith pointed out recently, the astonishing feat of continuous (and, for a foreseeable future, secure) democratic approval of the kind of social order which pushes the differentiation of income, living standards and quality of life to ever greater heights, has been achieved in Western affluent democracies thanks to a novel political situation: the number of citizens who may reasonably expect a better deal from the free market than from any of its alternatives, and who are therefore averse to any political correction of putative market blunders, now exceeds (for the first time in modern history, and in large part thanks to the remarkable success of the welfare state) the number of those who cannot do well without state-managed corrections of the market. The first easily out-vote the second. The new 'contented majority' has vested interests in enhancing the sacred rights of individuals and maintaining political freedoms and the rule of an elected parliament; democracy as it is understood and institutionalized today throughout the affluent Western part of the globe is safe in its hands.

Before this new situation arose, the defence of inequality called for serious, often severe, curtailment of democracy in general and voting rights in particular (just remember the panic and the flood of dark forebodings among the English political and educated classes inspired by the two British Reform Bills of 1832 and 1867). In addition, non-exclusive democracy that entailed universality of political rights always resulted in the growth of state redistributive interference with incomes and capital gains, and sooner or later led to the creation and expansion of the welfare state (today, the most heinous of crimes in the eyes of world economic experts, and derisable populist pandering according to the ideological purists among native intellectuals). The prospect of combining universal political democracy with a state that cedes the task of social integration to blind market forces may once have seemed like squaring the circle. And it still does – unless, that is, the majority of people are content with the way the market attends to their livelihood.

In a recent article Alain Touraine (1992) forcefully restated the all-too-easily forgotten truth that in the West a very long period of brutal and cruel capitalism preceded the organized, and in the end successful, attempt to establish a degree of social control of the economy. The eventual exit from the initial savagery was made possible by the solidly established system of respected impersonal laws enforced by a strong state and sustained by a popular morality closely approximating Max Weber's worldly asceticism. None of these conditions are available in Russia, and (though in varying degree) all are in short supply elsewhere in post-communist Europe. A strong state and respected legal system seem so far to be remote prospects; but the most seminally missing is the last factor. Its lack is also the most daunting, as the countries in question enter their post-communist history prompted by the values of a world which underlies consumer values rather than those of gratification delay. (Having analysed the fall of communism from the perspective of the postmodern realities of the contemporary affluent West, Zdzisław Krasnodębski (1991) diagnosed the state of public consciousness in the post-communist East as 'waiting for the supermarkets'.) In this post-Weberian postmodern world, the communist regimes were the last bastions of the ethics of delayed gratification (though in a 'collectivised', or rather statized, form, significantly distinct from the orthodox Weberian variety). The combination of the absence of social control over the economy with the pressure of post-modern 'enjoyment now' ethics may well rebound, as Touraine says, in 'creating not a capitalist economy, but a free-for-all, where speculation, black market and criminal monopolies will hold the country to ransom while the production will continue to fall' (Touraine, 1992: 2).

THE MORNING AFTER

The revolutionary parricide can be interpreted in individual terms: the persons who stood at the cradle of the revolution are blamed for the rude awakening which is bound to follow the euphoria of political victory. But the parricidal tendency is also targeted against whole classes of people: the very same social forces whose wrath and stubborn refusal of obedience brought the old regime to bankruptcy and surrender are the first to pay the price of the implementation of post-communist utopia.

As *Gazeta Wyborcza* reported on 25 April 1991, 91 per cent of Poles did not attend a single political meeting throughout the whole period since 'the end of the revolution', whatever the latter may mean; that period, let us recall, included the first multi-party contest of local elections and a presidential campaign which was conducted in the full glare of the rapidly 'westernizing' media. The number of people who cared to cast their votes was derisively small by comparison with the massive commitment during the anti-communist explosion of popular activity which led to the change of the regime. New political parties arise in Poland almost every day (mostly through the astonishingly fissiparous tendency of the parties established the day before). And yet according to the same *Gazeta Wyborcza* survey, more than 90 per cent of Poles neither belong, nor intend to belong, to any of them; most do not even bother to make a note of their appearance, let alone acquaint themselves with their programmes.

According to every 'surface' observation as well as 'in-depth' surveys of political attitudes, the notorious 'us'n'them' posture emerged virtually unscathed from one of the most profound political shifts in recent history. Shortly after the change of state power, this posture turned against those who led and won the battle against the communist regime (the analysts agree that the chances of the erstwhile opposition leader Tadeusz Mazowiecki in the presidential contest against the political adventurer Tymiński were greatly – perhaps decisively – diminished by the 'stain' of his brief encounter with the practice of government). In the fashion in which the long rule of the patronage state trained the nation to think, the rulers are held directly responsible for all collective and individual sufferings; and the list of such sufferings has shown no sign of shortening since the day when the communists surrendered the administration of the state. Particularly painfully affected were the sectors of industrial labour which played a decisive role in the toppling of the communist regime (first and foremost, the staff of big state-owned industries).

As to the creative intelligentsia – the class more than any other group responsible for reforging diffuse popular dissent into the battering ram which crushed the communist fortress – it has its own reasons why the joy of newly acquired freedom of expression should be tainted with vague feelings of uneasiness. The first reason derives from the 'de-skilling' operation accomplished by the cultural wardenship of the state. The income of writers or actors used to depend on the job performed, not on its commercial success; nor was the chance of commercial success a decisive factor in publishing or repertory decisions. Writers never learned the complex art of churning out best-sellers. Learning the new art of commercial success also means drastically revising the criteria of artistic evaluation and self-assessment. The past masters in cheating the censors must yet learn how to lure the market-wise managers; they discover that negotiating the new *modus vivendi* entails its own measure of humiliating artistic compromise. It is not at all clear whether the established hierarchy of literary and artistic prestige will survive the advent of the new standards; and thus far there are few signs of new and younger literary and artistic figures of comparable merit replacing it.

The second source of anxiety is the possibility that the potential for artistic experimentation, though given a green light by the new cultural indifference of the once vigilant state, may still be rendered ineffective by the dearth of commercially viable outlets. The impoverished post-communist countries, with small and insecure *hautes bourgeoisies*, have no artistic market ready to absorb anything rising above the level of the customarily acceptable. Thus the danger that the commercialization of culture will 'level down' is much more immediate and realistic there than in the West, where it was staved off by the spectacular expansion of the prestigious (or snobbish) end of the cultural market. Cultural creators who had most reasons to resent state interference are finding out that they have exchanged the devil they knew for the deep blue sea they do not know how to swim in.

The third reason to worry, and the least likely to be offset by efforts at readjustment, is the redundancy threatening a large part of the creative intelligentsia given that it now faces a drastically reduced audience. It is improbable that levels of cultural consumption artificially inflated by lavish subsidies can be preserved once 'commercially viable' prices are charged for books, literary journals or theatre tickets. Suddenly, the country is finding itself lumbered with 'overproduction' of the intelligentsia.

To cap it all, there is something hard to pinpoint and still more difficult to admit, that most elusive of anxieties: a vague feeling that something of utmost importance, indeed something which used to give the intellectual existence its meaning, while tinting even the most gruesome of torments with joy and glory, has been lost. It is becoming transparent now that state censorship was an oblique recognition of the world-shattering potency of the word. Or was it, perhaps, the obtrusive and heavy-laden attention of the rulers which conjured up that potency? As one of Italo Calvino's characters put it: 'nobody these days holds the written word in such high esteem as do police states . . . Where it is the object of such attentions, literature gains an extraordinary authority, inconceivable in countries where it is allowed to vegetate as an innocuous pastime, without risks.' Relinquished by the state, rule over the cultural life of the nation did not fall into the hands of the intellectuals. As in the West, culture has instead become prey to the vagaries of commodity markets. It has been swiftly commercialized – long before the start of the promised privatization of state-owned industrial assets. As if to rub still more salt into the open wound, those among the intellectuals wishing to seek succour in the glorious memory of the recent past – when they, at high personal cost, laboured full-time for the liberation of the people – get little appreciation and fewer-still rewards for services rendered and find themselves among the favourite victims of the revolution's parricidal urge.

The impending generational change in the ranks of the intellectuals may take the form of bitter recriminations and pugnacious posturing – severe even by the usual standards of inter-generational change – in the course of which the most recent history of Eastern and East-Central Europe will become the subject of feverish argument from which it will emerge considerably re-evaluated and thoroughly rewritten. Though it would be unwise to bet on the direction which the triumphant version will eventually take, one outcome seems more likely than all others: the wisdom and the accomplishment of the spiritual fathers of the revolution will be subjected to close scrutiny in the light of standards *distinct* from those they themselves used to deploy. For one reason or another – for being excessive, misguided or half-hearted – those standards will stand condemned by the generation which will come to replace them.

SCENARIOS AND ACTORS IN SEARCH OF EACH OTHER

Polish journalists coined the expression 'political cabaret in the mangle' to denote the current reciprocal character massacre which has become the trademark of new political elites, the heirs of different strands of a once united Solidarity. ('The mangle' has sedimented in the public mind as the location where, before the arrival of laundrettes, housewives treated each other to the latest local gossip and with particular relish practised the art of neighbourly character assassination.)

Personal animosities and lack of parliamentary tradition, to which the unseemly conduct of political elites is commonly ascribed, offer but a part of the explanation. The causes of the unedifying spectacle reach deeper, and need more than a crash course in parliamentary etiquette before they can be rectified. The bitterness and venom of political life 'at the top' arises from the genuine quandary which the elites are facing: *there is a yawning gap between what the elites can offer and what their genuine or postulated constituencies want and expect*. Or, rather, there are few if any constituencies in sight for the 'realistic' programmes the elites put together, while potential constituencies still wait for feasible programmes which could forge them into real constituencies. If there is a view which the post-revolutionary political elites do share, it must be this: there is little hope that 'the masses' will agree with what has to be done to remake them into voters who will agree with what will then have been done; therefore, for some time to come, far-sighted rulers must brace themselves for a political practice that ignores what the 'masses', in their present form, think and feel.

One dangerous point about such a belief is that its holders (particularly when their confidence is boosted by authoritative Western words and deeds) argue themselves into the absence of any, except abstract and imagined, standards by which their actions may be judged and, if need be, corrected. Without due respect for democratic checks and balances, the fantasy, unlimited, may well go haywire – while mutual recriminations and backbiting may go on without bringing closer the day when the conflicts of opinion will be bindingly resolved. Another dangerous point is the political void stretching between daily preoccupations of the elites and the daily worries of the men and women who should be, but are not, their constituents; in such a void, particularly at a time when redundancy and poverty are the sole rapidly growing socio-economic indicators, the voice of the demagogues offering simple and guaranteed solutions (in most cases, combining rampant nationalism with the populist sentiment bred and left behind by the communist-run patronage state) tends to reverberate loudly and be resoundingly echoed. One further, and perhaps yet more dangerous, point is the endemic, protracted and prospectless weakness of the state: the fast dissipation of whatever was left of governmental prestige and authority; disdain for the law no one is able or willing to enforce becomes the popular way of life. The post-communist states live continuously in the situation of an incapacitating legitimation crisis. Under present circumstances, the preferred legal–rational legitimation is unlikely to make much progress. But the plight of contentious charismatic legitimations is not much better. Thus far, they wilt and fade as soon as they are born in a political atmosphere poisoned by the stench of disintegrating hopes.

The condition of liminality in which all post-communist regimes remain is one in which *everything may happen yet little can be done*; the absence of a strong government, and of well-rooted rules of political conduct leaves open a wide range of alternative scenarios while rendering ineffective the forces which might wish to pursue any of them with a degree of consistency. One model challenging all historical precedents (and least plausible, if precedents are anything to go by) is the conjunction of universal political freedom and parliamentary rule with the dismantling of what the French call *l'état providence*, the British *the welfare state*, and the Poles *państwo opiekuńcze* (caring state) in a situation in which relatively few members of the body politic can attend to their own survival using the impartial services of the consumer market. One of these ill-fitted factors must go. Yet all the internal pulls and external pushes militate against their separation.

The anti-communist revolution in the satellite countries was not set in motion by economic grievances alone. National self-determination was a most powerful mobilizing factor; it was also the first reward of victory. The patriotic euphoria has united classes whose interests would be otherwise hard to reconcile; it still holds them together, blunting the effects of economic conflicts – though its unifying power is progressively weakened by the blatantly differential impact of systemic change. The spirit-raising demand of Solidarity's unofficial anthem, 'we want Poland to be Poland', has been met, but what sort of Poland it is to be remains wide open. National sovereignty is, so to speak, 'model neutral'. It serves the preservation of the patronage state in Slovakia and its dismantling in Czechia. It offers a poor indication of the course each of the now sovereign states will take. With political sovereignty no more in danger, however, the spirit of patriotic sacrifice may not for long neutralize the impact of the clash of interests, and economic realities may decide the shape of post-communist politics. Reconciling political freedoms with the economic neo-liberalism of political elites may then prove as easy as squaring the circle.

NOTES

1 Compare Zygmunt Bauman (1992), ch. 7. The *systemic* character of recent revolutions in Eastern and East-Central Europe I argued there in the following terms: 'the social forces which led to the downfall of the communist power . . . are not those that will eventually benefit from the construction of the new system. Forces whose interests will gain from the working of the new system will need to be brought into existence in the process of system-construction' (pp. 157–8).
2 In his incisive analysis of the post-revolutionary plight of the Polish farmers, Andrzej Koraszewski (1992) wrote: 'In September 1989 the Polish village knew already not only that the new government had no agricultural policy, but also that it believed that the threat to the farmers' existence offers an excellent chance of slighting any demands coming from that occupational category' (p. 34).
3 In the current postmodern condition, the premonition of this need to deputize has manifested itself in the 'Eastern' intellectuals' predilection

for portraying 'społeczeństwo obywatelskie' or 'гра Данское о ество' (literally: 'society of citizens') – a distant travestation of Ferguson's *civil society* or Hegel's *bürgerliche Gesellschaft*, i.e. a society formed by free bourgeois producers and the site of political democracy – as a territory managed primarily by makers and distributors of ideas.

4 The philosophy behind the recent revival of (essentially right-wing) argument against the excessive ambitions of the state and social engineering in general, as Albert O.Hirschman (1992) found out, is twofold: sometimes the social world is viewed 'as a highly volatile universe, in which every move (in the sense of chess game) attracts numerous and unpredictable counter-moves'; at other times the social world is seen 'as remarkably stable, structured by immanent laws which human action is incapable of modifying' (p. 106).

REFERENCES

Bauman, Z. (1992) *Intimations of Postmodernity*, London: Routledge.

Domański, H. (1992) 'From Class to Class', *Polityka*, no. 24: 3.

Genestier, P. (1992) 'Grand projets ou médiocres desseins?', *Le Débat*, no. 70.

Hirschman, A.O. (1992) 'L'Argument intransigent comme idée reçue', *Le Débat*, no 69.

Kennedy, M.D. (forthcoming) 'Intellectuals, Intellectuality and the Restructuring of Power after Modernity and Communism'.

Koraszewski, A. (1992) *Wielki Poker*, Warsaw: PWN.

Krasnodębski, Z. (1991) 'W oczekiwaniu na supermarkety, czyli upadek komunizmu w wietle postmodernistycznej filozofii widziany', *Przełom i Wyzwanie: Pamiętnik VIII Ogólnopolskiego Zjazdu Socjologicznego, Toruń 19–22.09.1990*, pp. 146–52, Warsaw: PTS.

Majman, S. (1992) 'Beginning of Thermidor', *The Warsaw Voice*, no. 24(190): 8.

Marody, M. (1988) 'Sens zbiorowy a stabilność i zmiana ładu społecznego', in A. Rychard and A. Sułek (eds), *Legitymacja: Klasyczne teorie i polskie doświadczenia*, pp. 280–5, Warsaw: PTS.

Narojek, W. (1990) 'Utopia postkomunistyczna', *Głowne Problemy Dzisiejszej i Przyszłej Rzeczpospolotej*, pp. 274–9, Warsaw: University of Warsaw.

Offe, C. (1989) 'Ist der Sozialismus am Ende?', *Die Zeit*, 8 December: 64.

Schwarz, W. (1992) 'Beware the Rich Bearing Gifts', *Guardian*, 11 July.

Šimečka, M. (1989) 'Another Civilization? An Other Civilization', in G. Schöpflin and N. Wood (eds), *In Search of Europe*, Cambridge: Polity.

Tolstaya, T. (1992) 'Tsar of all the Answers', *Guardian*, 25 June: p. 25.

Touraine, A. (1992) 'Les deux tâches de la Russie postcommuniste', *Le Monde*, 3 July: p. 2.

Toynbee, A.J. (1939) *A Study of History*, vol. 5, Oxford: OUP.

—— (1960) *A Study of History*, abridgement of vols 7–10 by D.C. Somervell, Oxford: OUP.

Turner, V.W. (1969) *The Ritual Process: Structure and Anti-Structure*, London: Routledge & Kegan Paul.

Van Gennep, A. (1960) *The Rites of Passage*, trans. by M.B Vizedom and G.L. Cafee, London: Routledge & Kegan Paul.

Chapter 3

In pursuit of the democratic interest
The institutionalization of parties and interests in Eastern Europe

Arista Maria Cirtautas

The post-Leninist political landscape in Eastern Europe has erupted into a plethora of parties and political organizations all claiming to represent the interests of significant social groups. For example, over one hundred parties and organizations participated in the October 1991 elections to the Polish Sejm. Unfortunately, instead of reflecting or articulating the interests of social groups, the emerging party systems appear to be reflecting the faultlines, fissures and fads among political elites. Parliamentary debates in Warsaw, Budapest and Prague have begun to resemble closed dialogues conducted on a remote and distant plane, far from the everyday reality of social life in these countries. Whereas stable systems of representation are based on institutionalized relationships between the state, political parties and interest groups that allow for multiple channels of interest articulation and representation, the situation in Eastern Europe is characterized by the lack of institutionalized relationships between state bureaucracies, elected officials and socially based interests.

The process of dismantling Leninist institutions without a clear blueprint for replacing them has created a debilitating vacuum in which uncertainty about the rules of the game has come to represent the only certainty. Continuous friction over realms of institutional authority and jurisdiction in daily government operations is perhaps the most visible manifestation of the lack of established boundaries and rules of interaction between critical organizations. This vacuum is one of the most significant aspects, if not *the* most significant aspect, of the transformations underway in Eastern Europe. The political and economic future of the region may well be determined by the nature of the institutional arrangements that develop in response to the current situation. In order to assess the potential for the development of a system of representation conducive to liberal capitalist outcomes, this chapter will examine the articulation and representation of interests in Eastern Europe from a theoretical perspective.

In what follows, a preliminary framework for the analysis of the role played by interests and their representation in times of institutional breakdown and change will be offered. Essentially, I argue in this chapter that how interests are articulated in chaotic environments will depend on the way in which individuals constitute collectivities that solve the problem of identity. A system of political representation may then evolve to protect and represent an aggregation of interests mobilized according to one or another collective identity legitimating a specific relationship between the general interest and particular interests. Once established, such a system of political representation will foster the development of a system of social interest representation wherein particular or disaggregated interests outside the state are protected or promoted.[1] Out of this sequence of identity articulation, political aggregation and the rechannelling of social interests, emerge the institutionalized 'rules of the game' which the state, political parties and interest groups are expected to follow in their interactions with one another.

Eventually, the emerging systems of representation in Eastern Europe will stabilize in one of two directions. Either a liberal democratic representation of interests will emerge, or an ersatz representation of interests based on nationalism as an ideology that symbolically includes the nation in the decision-making process while substantively excluding the majority from participation will become entrenched.[2] In spite of the differences that divide Poland, Hungary, Slovakia and the Czech Republic, strikingly similar processes of articulating and aggregating interests are at work in all four countries that will have a profound effect on the institutional outcomes there.

The chapter will be divided into two sections. In the first section a theoretical framework will be introduced to illuminate the logic of interest articulation and representation in ideal–typical terms. The following section will then examine the developments to date in Central Europe in light of this theoretical appraisal of the goals to be attained and the obstacles to be overcome in pursuit of the democratic interest.

IDENTITIES, INTERESTS AND INSTITUTIONS

In a 1984 article March and Olsen point out that 'although self-interest undoubtedly permeates politics, action is often based more on discovering the normatively appropriate behavior than on calculating the return expected from alternative choices' (March and Olsen, 1984: 744). Action based on self-interest and action based on 'appropriate behavior' need not, however, be considered mutually exclusive or incompatible. In what follows, I will argue that collective identity provides the interpretive framework through which individuals assess the interests that determine their actions both in terms of cost–benefit calculations, and in terms of appropriateness.

Even if one conceives of interest articulation solely as the product of rational calculation, it becomes obvious upon closer examination that the process of determining one's interests is never self-evident or neutral. A choice must be made not only between various goals, but also between a multiplicity of competing and mutually exclusive means to achieve these goals. How these choices are made will be determined by the interpretive framework through which individuals assess their interests – a framework that is directly related to the question of identity.

On an individual level, interests are determined by the needs we deem critical for our personal security and well-being. To the extent that we feel affected by certain outcomes or circumstances, we may take actions to protect or enhance these interests. Interests cannot, however, be automatically derived from social or economic conditions. As Suzanne Berger points out, although socio-economic structures can and do shape interests by providing 'points of opportunity around which groups may organize' and mobilize, these structures do not provide 'an unequivocal answer to an individual's (or group's) problem of identity' (Berger, 1981: 12). When faced with multiple and mutually exclusive claims on participation and organization such as a national party, a regional movement, or an occupational association, how an individual perceives her needs will determine how she chooses to articulate her interests, and which group or organization she chooses to join. This perception, in turn, is governed by the way in which an individual identifies herself, or locates herself in the social, economic and political landscape. Identity, in this sense, provides not only the standards by which one defines one's needs, but also the criteria by which one judges what is the correct or appropriate course of action to satisfy those needs. Because one's identity merges a conception of what is right with a conception of what is expedient or necessary for the satisfaction of one's needs, it becomes a critical and powerful factor in choosing 'with which group one's fate and fortunes lie' (ibid.: 12). In other words, identity provides the interpretive framework within which the rational calculation of interests can take place. Identity is not, however, a primordial psychological entity, rather it is a socially and culturally constructed category of collective membership.

In an established and stable system of representation, social identities and the articulation of interests derived from them tend to reinforce, or at least not threaten, the overall institutional structure. Because this overall structure represents the concretization of a collective identity that legitimates a specific relationship between the general interest of the nation and the particular interests of the people comprising that nation, it provides a set of constraints within which identities can be mobilized and interests can be organized. For example, to pursue an analogy provided by Berger, a Corsican winegrower must first define his identity in order to choose the best vehicle to represent his interests. A winegrowers' association, farmers' union, Corsican regionalist movement or a national political party all provide potential means of expressing his interests. The winegrower's decision does not, however, have an impact on the overall institutional structure in France. Certainly, Corsican winegrowers acting collectively in any of the organizations mentioned may have an impact on the institutional arrangements within the overall structure, but it is highly unlikely that they would succeed in redefining the collective identity that underlies the overall structure.

However, in the absence of such an overall structure, or when existing structures have decayed past a certain point, the choice of identity can have critical consequences for institutional stability. The choices made by Slovakian manufacturers in the recent elections provide graphic evidence of the fact that in turbulent times the mobilization of identities and interests has a decisively different impact on institutional outcomes. Without the constraints provided by an established overall institutional structure, groups will attempt to mobilize followers around collective identities that provide both a vision of the general interest that they believe should animate such a structure, and of the way in which particular interests should be addressed. In other words, interest articulation in times of institutional breakdown and change will inevitably be oriented toward the aggregation of interests according to conceptions of the general interest. This will include defining how the state, as the embodiment of the general interest, should protect the interests of all under its jurisdiction, as well as how the state should establish the ethnic and/or territorial boundaries of that jurisdiction. These conceptions of the general interest will determine which groups are able to represent their particular interests as claims on the state. Seen from this perspective, it becomes clear why in Poland, for example, political parties persist in presenting vague platforms addressing the nation at large rather than directly representing the interests of specific socio-economic constituencies.[3] In a situation where not just political power exercised through the state but the very definition of the state itself is at stake, the identity of Poland as a whole must be addressed before particular interests organize within the framework of that collective identity.

This explains why it is premature for analysts to assume that an East European 'middle class' created by the privatization of state assets, for example, would automatically articulate their interests within a liberal democratic identity. While one can hope that privatization will produce property owners acting in accordance with liberal capitalist norms, there is no automatic correlation between property ownership and democracy – as the history of the Weimar Republic shows. Members of the middle class in Eastern Europe could easily choose an authoritarian nationalist identity as the appropriate interpretive framework for the articulation of their interests.

In short, times of institutional breakdown are characterized by the prevalence of competing collective identities. In such environments the ability to mobilize and to aggregate fragmented and unorganized interests in the service of a particular collective identity becomes critical. Only if a core elite animated by a collective identity succeeds in organizing a committed followership capable of monopolizing political power for a crucial period of time can a stable system of political representation emerge.[4] This system will then delineate the lines of authority determining the relationship between the various organs comprising the state, and the relationship of political parties to the state. During this period of monopolization competing collective identities are marginalized and decisively undermined, since access to the state and its resources is granted only to interests articulated according to the dominant form of collective identity. Subsequently, after a dominant form of collective identity has been established, social interests can be rechannelled in order to represent particular constituencies within a system of interest representation. Without such a period of successful monopolization, interests will continue to be articulated within mutually exclusive collective identities that make long-term compromises difficult. Since each identity contains a claim on the definition of the state itself, as well as a claim on the state's resources, a situation of chronic political instability ensues.

Furthermore, the development of economic institutions oriented towards production rather than redistribution is rendered difficult, if not impossible, in this situation. Without a dominant collective identity that can establish a stable balance between the general interest of the nation and the particular interests comprising that nation, there is no basis upon which any particular interest can legitimately be subsumed to the general interest. Without the ability to legitimate and to enforce institutionally outcomes that are preceived to be in the long-term interests of the nation, while being to the short-term disadvantage of particular interests, political elites will not be able to break through the myriad claims on the state to redistribute economic resources. Based on this analysis, two questions become critical in determining whether or not political institutions support or hinder economic development. Firstly, a core elite must be able to monopolize political power in the service of a specific collective identity that can lead to the creation of a stable balance between general and particular interests. Secondly, the nature of the collective identity itself must be assessed in order to determine the extent to which economic development is compatible or incompatible with the given vision of the general interest.

In the case of liberal capitalist development, liberal elites were able to create successfully institutional arrangements that reflected their collective identity. In spite of the undeniable differences, the democratic systems of representation that have emerged in the United States and in Western Europe are all based on the common collective identity articulated by liberal elites in the seventeenth and eighteenth centuries. At the core of this identity is the concept of national citizenship. Before and during the American and French revolutions, liberal elites developed a new vision of the relationship between the general interest and particular interests. The nation, as it developed during the age of absolutism, was accepted as the repository of the general interest, but the interests legitimately comprising that nation were decisively recast. Instead of the corporate collectivities characteristic of hierarchically organized estate societies, the individual citizen became the sole legitimate bearer of interests and rights in the polity. Furthermore, the collective will of these individual citizens was held to determine what was in the general interest of the nation.

During the period in which liberal elites monopolized political power (mainly by limiting the franchise, although coercion also played a significant role) this abstract collective identity was concretized into a specific form of government. Since liberalism is based on the principle that all citizens comprising the nation have the right to be fully represented in its governance, the means of representing these individuals had to be developed. Clearly, it was no longer possible to apply ancient models of democratic government to large and populous states. The authority vested in every individual citizen to determine and judge the policies of his government had to be delegated to a small number of representatives. Moreover, since citizens in large nations could no longer conduct the affairs of state themselves, state officials had to be entrusted with the implementation of government policies. Simultaneously, however, limits had to be defined for the authority exercised by both representatives and officials on behalf of citizens in order to protect against tyranny and abuse.

On the basis of these premises, a sovereign source of authority was created that provided for a stable balance between general and particular interests. According to Lipset, 'democratic stability requires that the source of authority be out of reach of any of the contending parties, which should aspire to become the agents of authority, not its creators' (Lipset, 1963: 313). In other words, the national interest, or general interest, must have ultimate authority over the state. In the United States, for example, the Constitution provides this source of authority, legitimating not only the balance of power between the various organs comprising the state but also setting the limits of state powers in general. The creation of this sovereign source of authority, as mandated by the liberal identity, has provided the institutional means whereby particular interests can legitimately be subsumed to the general interest – thereby fostering the development of production-oriented economic institutions. Furthermore, the liberal belief that individuals have the ability and the right to determine, pursue and represent their interests is highly compatible with capitalist economic development since these individual rights abolished all hereditary and ascriptive rights that had previously channelled economic resources into redistribution rather than production.

Although Eastern Europe was exposed to liberal capitalist institutional forms such as parliamentary government and private property in the interwar period, these forms did not lead to 'political democracy, a capitalist market economy, and a society based on equal rights'. Instead, 'they resulted in a bureaucratic polity, a pseudo-market, and a neo-corporatist society in which rights continued to be commensurate with social function, while social function was less frequently assigned by merit than by heredity' (Janos, 1982: 92). Because the political elites monopolizing power during this period were animated by a nationalist as opposed to a liberal collective identity, Western-style institutions operated as façades and did not result in the types of behaviour characteristic of liberal institutions in Western Europe. Since the traditions, customs and conventions comprising the national heritage were considered the appropriate foundation for institutional arrangements, rather than individually based rights, the hereditary and ascriptive rights of the feudal era were not supplanted or eradicated. In many ways, the hierarchical, segmented and corporate nature of feudal society was simply replicated – but under conditions of considerable socio-economic, political and cultural strain as Eastern Europe was exposed to a changing global environment.

In this context, the attempt made by political elites to animate Western institutional forms with a nationalist collective identity did not succeed in legitimating a stable balance between general and particular interests. The removal of monarchical authority, traditionally the ultimate source of authority, left a vacuum which rule by aristocratic elites could not successfully fill. Since these elites equated their particular interests with the general interest, no sovereign source of authority curtailed the powers of the state. Although constitutions, for example, did exist they did not generate the constraints on political behaviour typical of West European constitutional arrangements. Moreover, the *raison d'être* of the state was not to protect individual rights and to represent all citizens but to protect and represent the privileges of besieged classes and status groups 'against the vagaries of the market, and, as a last resort, [to] provide the bankrupt landowner security of employment in its bureaucracy and political institutions' (Janos, 1982: 66) As these claims were combined with the political elite's own desire to extract economic resources for its purposes (either for national prestige, or to satisfy status privileges), a heavy burden was placed on the economy. In Eastern Europe, this burden resulted in economic stagnation and underdevelopment prior to the Second World War.

Although the imposition of Leninist institutions after the war did achieve a stable balance between general and particular interests, these institutions and the collective identity that animated them led to a radically different kind of political and economic development in Eastern Europe than that carried out under liberal auspices. Under the influence of Lenin and Stalin, a collective identity was articulated before and during the Russian Revolution that did away with the Western bourgeois notion of citizenship altogether. This identity, emerging in explicit opposition to liberalism, legitimated a relationship between the general interest and particular interests that was based on the conception of a national party dictatorship.

In this conception, the sole legitimate bearer of interests and rights in the political community was the party acting on behalf of the proletariat as the embodiment of the general interest. With Stalin's proclamation of 'socialism in one country', the political community that Marxism originally defined in internationalist terms became restricted to the nation, thereby adding the national element to Lenin's prior conceptualization of the party dictatorship. Based on this collective identity, the party elite succeeded in creating political institutions that, through force and coercion, dominated and marginalized the status-based identities inherited from feudal society.

The party's position as the sovereign source of authority in the polity did allow for a stable balance between general and particular interests that fostered economic development for a certain period of time. As long as the party could organizationally suppress the particular interests of its members that subverted the Leninist general interest, as well as insulating itself from social claims for the redistribution of economic resources, it was able to create economic institutions that forced a rapid pace of industrialization. In the post-Stalin era, however, as widespread corruption began to erode the party's ability to resist redistributive claims both from party members and from social groups, its ability to support continued economic growth eroded as well, bringing the era of rapid economic development to an end. By the late 1970s, declining rates of economic growth and social mobility created an environment in which counter-elites questioning the existing political elite's claim to represent the general interests of the nation began to acquire a stronger voice and a greater resonance among the populations of Eastern Europe.

Subsequently, the demise of really existing socialism during the revolutions of 1989 again placed the goal of liberal capitalist development on the agenda in Eastern Europe. In the effort to achieve this goal, the obstacles to be overcome are not simply related to the well-known difficulties of eradicating the legacies of Leninism, but are also related to the capacity for resisting a repetition of the region's nationalist past. The ease and rapidity with which former communist leaders have become nationalist leaders in the Republics of the former Soviet Union testifies to the potential strength of a nationalist collective identity fused with the dictatorial institutional arrangements of these formally defunct Leninist regimes. The pursuit of democratically defined interests during this period of institutional change and transformation clearly represents a tremendous challenge to the nations of Eastern Europe.

IN PURSUIT OF THE DEMOCRATIC INTEREST

According to the theoretical framework presented above, the emergence of a system of representation conducive to liberal capitalist outcomes is dependent on the existence of a core elite representing a liberally defined collective identity that can successfully monopolize political power for a crucial period of time. In what follows, recent developments in Poland, Hungary, Slovakia and the Czech Republic will be analysed with reference to the probability of such outcomes.

At present no collective identity has succeeded in dominating these East European polities. The political landscape is, therefore, characterized by a multitude of competing collective identities seeking to aggregate interests according to different conceptions of the general interest. In spite of this complex situation, one can observe certain trends that do not bode well for liberal outcomes.

Three trends in particular deserve our attention. First, a debilitating stalemate is emerging between competing collective identities that does not appear to be amenable to solution via negotiated settlements or reformed institutional arrangements. As will be seen below, conflicts between the Presidency and the Parliament exemplify this situation. Second, nationalism is gaining strength throughout the region and may well be the only collective identity capable of breaking through the current political log-jam. Third, although liberals and liberally oriented parties do exist, they are substantially weakened by the way in which the conception of liberalism has been articulated in Eastern Europe.

As one East European observer has noted, there has been a general failure in all post-communist states 'to establish satisfactory political institutions with their competencies adequately defined and . . . to submit . . . willingly to the rule of law' (Sajo, 1992: 45). This is an obvious indication that no political group has as yet succeeded in firmly establishing its vision of a collective identity as the basis for an institutionalization of a system of representation. Moreover, the unwillingness to submit to the rule of law indicates that a sovereign source of authority as embodied in a Constitution, for example, has also not been established. What has instead developed is a stalemate between competing political elites that are now firmly entrenched in partially reformed political structures. Clearly, this is not a situation conducive to the development of economic institutions geared towards productive rather than redistributive goals. In the absence of a breakthrough capable of generating institutional change, Eastern Europe may well face a future of political instability and economic stagnation since redistributive claims on the state cannot be subordinated or suppressed under the existing circumstances. Without an accepted soverieign authority that can mandate a stable balance between the general interest of the nation and the particular interests comprising it, it is not possible to enforce outcomes that work to the short-term disadvantage of particular interests. While some Western analysts assume that a viable Constitution establishing a sovereign source of authority can emerge out of a process of negotiation between these political elites, or that reformed electoral arrangements can effect positive changes, the current situation in Eastern Europe casts doubt on this assumption.

Negotiations or reforms that proceed on the basis of competing collective identities will not have the power to enforce a sovereign source of authority such as a Constitution, and will, therefore, not have the ability to legitimate a permanent balance of powers between political institutions such as the Presidency and the Parliament. Furthermore, without an enforceable sovereign authority, political parties and government officials will always perceive themselves as the potential creators of a new, overarching authority, and will not submit to existing institutional constraints. As long as there is a perception that the Presidency can be occupied by an 'alien' force embodying a different collective identity, or conversely that Parliament and the Cabinet can represent the 'wrong' collective identity, no stable division of authority will result regardless of Constitutional agreements. Conflicts between agents of authority will take on a zero-sum nature wherein any Presidential initiative, for example, is perceived in Parliament as an intolerable encroachment on parliamentary sovereignty. This is an understandable reaction, given the assumption that any increase in Presidential authority means an increase in the ability of that office to create a new balance of power that would diminish Parliament.

To date, numerous conflicts in Poland, Hungary and the former Czechoslovakia over the appropriate division of authority between the office of the Presidency and parliamentary governments provide ample evidence of this zero-sum mentality. Moreover, in the absence of an accepted sovereign authority, almost every political conflict between these political institutions brings fundamental constitutional issues into play – regardless of whether or not a formal Constitution exists. Such conflicts, therefore, have taken on greater significance than, for example, the ritualized wrangling between the American President and Congress.

In Poland nothing less than control over the army was at the root of a recent controversy between Wałęsa and the Minister of Defence appointed by former Prime Minister Olszewski. While the Constitution existing at the time of this controversy gave the Presidency greater authority over the military, that Constitution was easily assailable as a product of the communist era, amended to serve the Presidency of General Jaruzelski. Moreover, the notion of allowing Wałęsa, whom all sides of the political spectrum had painted as a potential dictator along the lines of Piłsudski, greater control over the military was profoundly disturbing to all members of Parliament. Possibly this contributed to the environment of fearmongering and the escalation of rhetoric that even included accusations by the Minister of Defence that Wałęsa had formulated plans for a martial law take-over of the country.

In Hungary, a controversy flared up in 1992 over whether the President or the government was to have the ultimate power of appointment over the government-controlled media organizations. In the absence of a media law, which was still being drafted, and in the absence of a clear Constitutional division between the Presidency and the Cabinet elected by Parliament, both President Göncz and Prime Minister Antall felt they had the right to control appointments. These rights were hotly and bitterly contested given the perception that control over the media would represent a partisan victory for whichever political party won the battle – either Antall's Democratic Forum or Göncz's Free Democrats.

In the case of the former Czechoslovakia, the conflicts between the President and the Federal Parliament over the future of the federation resulted in defeats for President Havel, arguably the most popular and respected leader in Eastern Europe. Parliament remained unconvinced by Havel's plea for co-operation after he had asked the public to support his efforts to maintain the federation:

> Unlike some deputies, I did not understand this support as unacceptable pressure on parliament, but rather a thoroughly justified expression of the voters' will, which ought to have served as an important signal to parliament, an impulse to its work and an aid to all of its members who feel, as do their constituents, the necessity for an early agreement on the manner of our existence as a state.
> (Quoted in *The Eastern European Reporter* (March–April 1992): 5)

Currently, a debate over the role and scope of the Presidency in the new Czech Republic is again taking shape in conjunction with the preparation of a new Czech Constitution. Predictably, President Havel is in favour of a strong, popularly elected presidency while Prime Minister Klaus is less than enthusiastic about this plan. Although this debate may well be resolved in favour of the type of presidency Havel has proposed, it is doubtful whether the new Constitution will prevent future conflict between the two realms of authority. This case presents a particularly clear-cut example of competing collective identities attempting to negotiate a new constitution. Havel represents the most liberal and civic elements in the Czech Republic, while the newly elected Parliament has been polarized between the socialist left and the nationalist right. Prime Minister Klaus's government, although moderately right, will have to lend an ear to the more radical right-wing nationalist groupings (like the Republican Party) in order to strengthen his hand against the ex-communist left. The disappearance of the political centre has left him without any other coalition options. Given this political constellation, it is doubtful that a renewed Havel presidency, even if endowed with greater formal authority, would face anything but the most sustained and bitter opposition from the dominant nationalist forces in the Parliament, opposition that would again result in the negation of all of his initiatives.

Seen from this perspective, the conflicts mentioned above are not simply indicative of problems institutionalizing a dual executive system (wherein a popularly elected President serves with a Prime Minister elected by Parliament) that will disappear once new constitutions are negotiated and implemented. These conflicts reflect a fundamental competition between political elites proposing decisively different collective identities. Moreover, these elites are attempting to create institutional bases for the monopolization of power. Since past means for monopolizing power, such as limiting the franchise or coercion, are no longer readily available, the choices now revolve around the Presidency and the Parliament. Both institutions derive their authority from the popular or general will, yet those elected to these institutions claim that their office is the sole legitimate manifestation of that will – as the quotation from Havel illustrates. Havel's direct appeal to the people, an appeal which he felt he had the sole authority to undertake, was considered by parliamentarians to be an illegitimate infringement on *their* prerogatives as the sole representatives of the people. Support for a strong Presidency or for absolute parliamentary sovereignty in this context represents an effort to monopolize and limit power in the service of a particular collective identity. Neither institution is inherently more democratic in the liberal sense. The decommunization laws proposed in Czechoslovakia, Poland and Hungary in 1991 and 1992 are all examples of the anti-liberal tendencies parliaments are capable of. In Hungary and Poland the proposed laws were deemed unconstitutional upon judicial review. In Czechoslovakia, however, the Screening Law passed without incorporating President

Havel's proposals which would have provided greater protection for individual rights.

What matters more than institutional forms is the collective identity animating institutional development. The most liberal democratic institutional forms will not produce liberal democratic behaviour, if people are acting on the basis of collective identities that are not compatible with these forms. Political stalemate and chronic instability are the predictable outcomes of this tension between institutional forms and behavioural content. However, once people's interests are aggregated according to a collective identity that attains a dominant position the stalemate will be resolved. This is nowhere more evident than in Slovakia where political elites under the leadership of Premier Mečiar are in the process of forming a new state on the basis of a cohesive nationalist identity. Not surprisingly, therefore, *The East European Constitutional Review* reports that the constitution-making 'process in Slovakia has been less problematic and better co-ordinated than in the Czech Republic' (*EECR*, Summer 1992: 3). Although the regime emerging in Slovakia promises to be profoundly anti-liberal, it is a regime based on a dominant collective identity and as such has broken through the institutional stalemate generated by competing elites elsewhere in Central Europe.

Under the charismatic leadership of Mečiar, diffuse and frag-mented interests were aggregated and mobilized in support of the nationalist identity he articulated in the course of the June 1992 elections. Although opinion polls taken in the months before the elections indicated that a majority of Slovaks were uncertain about dissolving the federation, by June Mečiar had succeeded in mobilizing a substantial portion of the population around his pro-Slovak banner.[5] Combining an ideology of national supremacy with socialist economic orientations, Mečiar's party, the Movement for a Democratic Slovakia, succeeded in creating a strong social and political base. Given the unreconstructed nature of the socio-economic structures inherited from Leninism, parties protecting the interests of workers and other occupational groups embedded in these structures will find a natural constituency.

This fusion of nationalism and socialism has provided Mečiar with a strong political base since both the ex-communist party and the nationalist parties became willing coalition partners. Such an uncontested power base will give Mečiar the ability to institutionalize a new system of representation protecting two central principles – the absolute primacy of the Slovak people, and the right to work. Needless to say, this system will not be hospitable to capitalist economic development, and economic stagnation will be the most likely outcome. At that point, it is likely that Mečiar, who already has a propensity for secret police activities, will use coercive measures to stifle any manifestations of discontent.

This dismal trajectory was not, however, a foreordained conclusion. Civically oriented political elites did exist in Slovakia, as for example in the Public Against Violence, but their failure to come to terms with the exercise of political power paved the way for Mečiar's victory. The intellectual leadership of Public Against Violence found it difficult to accept organizational changes that would have turned the movement into a more viable political party. As one member stated, 'a collection of friends had been transformed into an organization of employees wearing pin-stripe suits' (quoted in *The East European Reporter*, 1992 (January–February): 67). This distaste for the more routinized tasks of political life contributed to the fact that few efforts were made to create and maintain organizational linkages to the public. A potentially liberal or civically minded social constituency was, therefore, not cultivated or mobilized. Instead, Public Against Violence restricted its political activities to the government and to parliament. The resulting gap between the intellectuals and the public was readily exploited by nationalist parties that could build on the traditional popular distrust of the power elite.

The failure of Public Against Violence is illustrative of a general failure throughout Central Europe of civically oriented elites to move beyond the limited articulation of a democratic collective identity to a broad mobilization and aggregation of interests in order to consolidate a power base within the population. Essentially, the reasons for this failure lie in the way in which this democratic identity was articulated, and in the nature of the social group that did the articulating. Upon being elected, civic elites not only assumed that the general interest was to be defined in liberal capitalist terms, but also that particular interests legitimately comprising that vision did not yet exist. Leninist socio-economic structures had not produced liberal citizens or capitalist entre-preneurs, therefore, these elites concluded that the 'natural' social constituency for liberal parties was not yet present. In defining the appropriate political strategy to cope with this situation, civic elites have clearly preferred parliamentary activity over building strong social constituencies within the existing circumstances. Since these elites were predominantly drawn from the ranks of the intellectuals, the character of this social group played a significant role in determining which strategy was emphasized.

Both the first Solidarity governments in Poland (1989–91) and the political party Fidesz (the Young Democrats) in Hungary provide examples of the disinclination to mobilize and to organize potential social support in favour of an almost exclusive focus on parliamentary activity. This limited and rather passive strategy is all the more surprising given the democratically oriented social activism that characterized Solidarity and Fidesz in earlier years. In both groups, however, former dissident intellectuals are attempting to accept the new responsibilities and burdens of parliamentary leadership while resisting the routinizing effects of political organization. As a result of this dynamic, they have developed an almost dogmatic adherence to pragmatic expertise and the rule of law in order to meet the demands of responsible political leadership. Simultaneously, there has been an attempt to retain small groups, even within larger political parties, as the preferred form of political organization, instead of forging linkages with the population that would require an organizational format characteristic of mass parties.

While a rigid adherence to the rule of law and a distaste for social mobilization under the auspices of a mass party are under-standable given the experience with Leninist parties, this has proved to be a dangerous combination in the post-Leninist era. As the fate of Prime Minister Mazowiecki's government in Poland illustrates, it was not enough to assume that people would automatically abide by the rule of law after having experienced years of government-sanctioned abuse of the law. People needed to be convinced that it was in their best interests to do so, and this would have required a mobilization of popular support that Mazowiecki refused to undertake. Mazowiecki's government, therefore, became vulnerable to charges of elitism and political insensitivity to people's demands for justice *vis-à-vis* the former rulers. Wałęsa subsequently used these charges to undermine Mazowiecki's government and to galvanize the population in support of his own presidential campaign in the fall of 1991. Whatever one may think of Wałęsa's tactics, to a certain extent his charges were justified. The Solidarity leadership *was* elitist in the sense that they hoped to rule by example, to set an example of virtuous civic leadership that would inspire the Polish population with trust, and a desire to emulate this civic virtue. Unfortunately, the assumption that the rest of the population was not yet ready or capable of behaving democratically led to a tendency to create a new liberal capitalist social constituency by fiat, decree or reform, instead of aggregating and mobilizing existing social interests on behalf of radical reform.

The fact that the Solidarity leadership assumed an implicit monopoly over civic virtue prevented them from taking the necessary steps to fulfil completely the potential inherent in their monopoly over political power. To date, the first Solidarity government under Mazowiecki's leadership remains the only case in Central Europe of an elite animated by a civic–democratic collective identity coming to power with substantial room to implement institutional changes. Indeed, the reforms associated with the Balzerowicz Plan were successfully implemented. Unfortunately, however, by not broadening political activities to include the organization of social interests on behalf of a liberal or civic collective identity, the door was left open for competing elites with different collective identities to engage the population, and subsequently to achieve the electoral successes that have resulted in the current stalemate in Poland. The same fate would appear to be imminent in Hungary where Fidesz's strategic choice of restricting itself to parliamentary activity may mean that there is no strong civic alternative to the governing coalition's growing nationalist tendencies. As a Hungarian commentator has warned:

> competence displayed at the level of elite politics will not guarantee electoral success for any party. The party which wins the next election will be the one that can win people's confidence and stir society at the grass-roots level. The successful party will need to think and act in a social dimension and not just a political one.
>
> (Bozóki, 1992: 72)

The fact that nationalist parties have been more successful at achieving a balance between the social and political dimensions is less a testament to the primordial strengths of nationalism in the region than a reflection of the effective way in which these parties have taken advantage of the largely self-inflicted organizational weaknesses of the liberally oriented parties. Nationalist parties such as the KPN in Poland may be small, but they are also well organized and capable of sustaining organizational linkages to the grass-roots level. Moreover, these parties are now competing with the ex-communist parties for the support of workers and other social groups negatively affected by the current efforts to dismantle Leninist socio-economic structures. As Mečiar has demonstrated in Slovakia, this can be a very successful strategy.

To replicate Mečiar's success, however, nationalist parties elsewhere would have to overcome conflicting tendencies within their ranks. Nationalist political forces are currently divided over how to define an appropriate collective identity. The two central groups, historically based nationalists and morally based nationalists, disagree over how to define the particular interests that can legitimately comprise the nation. For the historically based nationalist groups, legitimacy is conferred by virtue of ethnic membership and cultural heritage. For the morally based nationalist groups, usually associated with the Catholic Church, only those who are free of contamination from the past regime can legitimately have a place in the polity. This latter position is clearly articulated by Stefan Niesiolowski, chairman of the parliamentary caucus of one of Poland's Catholic–nationalist parties (the ZChN), in a statement he gave in support of Prime Minister Olszewski's proposed decommunization resolution:

> Once this resolution is implemented, Poland will be another country. This will be a country where the border line between the tormentor and his victim, between good and evil and between truth and duplicity will be definitely delineated.
>
> (Quoted in *The East European Reporter* (July–August 1992): 7)

To assign good and evil on moral grounds, instead of on the more traditional ethnic–cultural grounds, was not acceptable to the KPN, whose own leader came under suspicion of having been an agent for the former regime. Not surprisingly, the Catholic moral agenda has, therefore, kept these nationalist forces apart in Poland. In Slovakia, however, Mečiar's more traditionally oriented nationalism would appear to have successfully marginalized the alternative nationalist identity articulated by former Prime Minister Czarnogursky (leader of the Christian Democratic Movement).

The presence of a competing nationalist identity based on moral rather than ethnic purity has created a more complex situation today than in the interwar period. Whereas traditional, ethnically based nationalism was not necessarily hostile to capitalist economic development and allowed for the forms of liberal government to be established before the Second World War, the position of today's morally oriented nationalists towards Western institutions is decidedly more hostile. As Czarnogursky has stated unequivocally:

> Liberalism threatens the necessary balance between different groups in society . . . promotes a culture of artificial consumption . . . promotes an environment which divorces the individual from values of morality and the articles of the true faith . . . [and] . . . allows the individual to do everything, but forgets that the devil is present in the human soul.
>
> (Quoted in *The Eastern European Newsletter* (3 Feb. 1992): 8)

This type of nationalist identity, were it to succeed in establishing political control over state institutions, is unlikely to produce even the bureaucratic polity, the pseudo-market and the neo-corporatist society characteristic of Central European development prior to 1945. Although the political groups articulating this identity are small, they are linked to the Catholic Church which has a strong institutional presence in Poland, Slovakia and Hungary.

From this brief overview of the political parties currently competing for power in Central Europe, it becomes clear that one cannot adequately assess the role played by interests and parties during this period of institutional transformation without an understanding of how these parties are attempting to articulate collective identities. The fact that political parties are addressing themselves to the nation at large instead of limiting themselves to the representation of socio-economic interests is not a sign of political immaturity; rather it is an indication of the turbulent nature of the post-Leninist environment. In such an environment, it is not just political power exercised through the state but the very definition of the state itself that is at stake. The identity of the nation as a whole must be addressed before particular interests can organize within the framework of that collective identity.

As we have seen, efforts to define the nation in terms of a liberal collective identity have been hampered by the way in which civic elites have articulated that identity and by the organizational choices they have made. An elitist orientation and a disinclination to foster the development of broadly based democratic political parties have largely prevented the organization and mobilization of social interests in support of radical reform. While political elites advocating an alternative nationalist identity have not manifested these kinds of organizational weaknesses, they have been less successful than in the interwar era due largely to the split between morally and ethnically based nationalists.

Although one cannot preclude the possibility that either liberal or nationalist forms of representation will emerge from this situation, it is highly likely that the current stalemate in Central Europe between these competing collective identities will continue for the foreseeable future. Efforts to institutionalize any new system of representation will thereby be rendered extremely tenuous and subject to vehement opposition both on the part of disaffected social groups and on the part of opposing political elites. In this case, the pursuit of the democratic interest will, unfortunately, have given way to a cycle of political and social instability combined with frustrated economic development.

ACKNOWLEDGEMENTS

Research for this article was supported in part by a grant from the American Council of Learned Societies. I would also like to thank my colleague Stephen Hanson for his critical comments, and for his careful reading of the text. The views expressed are, however, my sole responsibility.

NOTES

1 For a different, albeit complementary, approach to the same pheno-mena, i.e. the dynamics of post-revolutionary politics, see Ralf Dahrendorf (1990).
2 I am indebted to Kenneth Jowitt for this definition of nationalism.
3 For an elaboration of this tendency in Poland from a different theoretical perspective, see Jadwiga Staniszkis (1991).
4 In using the term 'elite'. I am referring to 'the best or most powerful of anything considered collectively, e.g. of a group or class of persons' (*Random House Dictionary*, 1980). I do not mean to imply that this group must always come from the privileged echelons of the social structure taken as a whole.
5 Although opinion polls continue to indicate ambivalence in Slovakia over the coming separation (which will go into effect in January 1993),

support for Mečiar in the 1992 elections was given on the basis of his pro-Slovak position. Either within the federation or in an independent state, it was assumed that Mečiar would be able to provide strong leadership in support of Slovak national interests.

REFERENCES

Berger, S.D. (ed.) (1981) *Organizing Interests in Western Europe*, Cambridge: CUP.

Bozóki, A. (1992) 'Shifting to the Centre', *The East European Reporter*, 5(3): 69–72.

Dahrendorf, R. (1990) *Reflections on the Revolution in Europe*, New York: Random House.

The East European Constitutional Review. Edited by D. Franklin. Chicago and Prague: Centre for the Study of Constitutionalism in Eastern Europe (University of Chicago) and the Central European University.

The East European Reporter. Edited by J. Sunley. Budapest: Twins Kiado es Tipografiai Kft.

Janos, A. (1982) *The Politics of Backwardness in Hungary 1825–1945*, Princeton N.J.: Princeton UP.

Lipset, S.M. (1963) *The First New Nation: The United States in Historical and Comparative Perspective*, London: Heinemann.

March, J. and Olsen, J. (1984) 'The New Institutionalism: Organizational Factors in Political Life', *American Political Science Review*, 78: 734–49.

Sajo, A. (1992) 'The Arrogance of Power', *The East European Reporter*, 5(3): 45–47.

Staniszkis, J. (1991) *The Dynamics of the Breakthrough in Eastern Europe: The Polish Experience*, Berkeley: University of California Press.

Chapter 4

Economic utopianism and sociological realism
Strategies for transformation in East-Central Europe

Christopher G.A. Bryant

INTRODUCTION

In East-Central Europe today they would have, and quickly, a new great transformation from state socialism, or better 'real socialism', to liberal democracy and a capitalist market economy. Such a transformation would be every bit as great as that original great transformation, described by Polanyi (1944), which gave rise to a market economy and liberal democracy, in that order, in Western Europe in the eighteenth and nineteenth centuries. Many sociological commentators are disturbed by the excessively high expectations after 1989, among people, politicians and Western economic advisers, of what could be achieved quickly. Using a title that echoes the conservative, Burke, that self-styled radical liberal, Dahrendorf, has argued in his *Reflections on the Revolution in Europe* (1990) that Poland, Czechoslovakia and Hungary might get an initial agreement on a democratic constitution in six months, but would need six years before liberal economic reforms showed much benefit and sixty years before both a democratic constitutional order and the social framework of a market economy were safely rooted in a robust civil society. True, he soon backtracked from the rhetorical flourish of sixty years for a civil society – but only to two generations. What de Tocqueville called the art of association is only slowly perfected.

Scepticism at the proposed speed of change apart, sociologists have so far found it hard to theorize the lineaments and course of the would-be great transformation. Indeed, they have spent more time on what led up to the changes than what they might lead to – whence the changes, not whither. Who can listen to those who have nothing to say? In times of upheaval, it is those who speak authoritatively who command attention (cf. Hankiss, 1990). Neo-liberal economists spoke with great assurance, filled the vacuum, and advised the new regimes in Poland, Czechoslovakia and Hungary that a *rapid* transition to capitalism was feasible. Three years later this is far less plausible to all concerned; in particular, it is all too obvious that economic shock therapies have failed to deliver all they promised. The moment is therefore opportune to consider again what is happening and what is possible, and this time it is imperative that sociologists be heard.

In what follows I shall indicate why I agree with Stark (1992a) and Murrell (1992) about the utopianism behind the application of neo-liberal economics to East-Central Europe, paying attention to the criticisms of sociologists, and, occasionally, dissenting economists. As Sztompka recalls of 1989–90, 'Neither the masses, nor even the intellectuals, in their utopian optimism were ready to admit that the "valley of tears" lies ahead' (Sztompka, 1991: 306). I shall then turn to more realistic scenarios for the trans-formation of Poland, the Czech Republic, Slovakia and Hungary.

UTOPIA, SHOCK THERAPY AND THE RISK OF A BACKLASH

In a remarkable paper written in 1990, Weitman (1992) theorizes the revolutions of 1989 in terms which have proved prescient. One of his working hypotheses proposes that 'The revolutionary tendency by the new government to try and liberate many domains simultaneously and in short order – rather than doing so piecemeal and gradually – is more likely to retard than to promote regime liberation' (p. 16). Economic liberalization, for example, may be expected greatly to widen social inequalities, and lead to demands for redress in the form of state intervention in the affairs of non-state formations; economic liberalization could, perversely, lead on to the re-empowerment of the state. In similar vein, Weitman suggests that revolutionary attempts to change everything quickly generate 'an acute state of anomie throughout society' whose consequences include 'spectacular rises in rates of so-called "social problems" – pervasive corruption, violent crimes, drug addiction, truancy, juvenile delinquency, alcoholism, prostitution, suicide, mental illness, and the like' (p. 17). These too can lead to demands for a restoration of law and order and re-empowerment of the state. Other writers, such as Dahrendorf, are more relaxed about the general prospect of some re-empowerment, but fear that it is hard to get the balance right. (Dahrendorf adds that Popper, the advocate of the open society and piecemeal reform, is a safer guide for the new regimes than Hayek, the closed-minded systematizer, who seems to have captured the imagination of many who advise them.)

Weitman argues, in effect, that it is utopian to try to do too much too quickly. However comprehensive the rejection of state socialism, and however desirable the idea of liberal democracy and a market economy, there are not credible steps whereby these can be secured in the short term, and to pretend otherwise is to invite failure and risk a backlash. By 1992 this seemed all too possible as disillusionment and despair at economies which have failed to grow as liberal reformers promised played their part, not just in lower voter turn-out in elections throughout Eastern Europe, but also in the resurgence of ex-communists (with Lithuania the extreme case), the rise of right-wing nationalists and the reappearance of anti-Semitism. The insistence of Václav Klaus, the Czech prime minister, on neo-liberal economic policies was also a factor in the break-up of Czechoslovakia. (Slovakia has proportionately more giant industrial plants and defence plants which cannot survive without state subsidies and which cannot easily be privatized.) I shall make the record of the Balcerowicz Plan introduced in Poland on 1 January 1990, however, a central feature of my comment.

Influenced by the Harvard celebrant of free market forces, Jeffrey Sachs, the Balcerowicz Plan scrapped the gradualist approach to transformation agreed in the spring of 1989 in the Round Table negotiations which led to the change of regime in favour of shock therapy and the big bang (Sachs, 1990; Kowalik, 1991; Hutton, 1992). The plan made the standard neo-liberal economic assumptions that people are everywhere the same regardless of culture and society, and that only the heavy hand of the state holds people back from rationally maximizing their self-interest (cf. Mokrzycki, 1991–92). It assumed that free enterprise is natural and communism an aberration. One component of the plan, the stabilization programme, had the immediate objective of ending hyperinflation; the other, the liberalization and privatization programme, had the short- to medium-term objective of establishing a successful market economy. Encouraged by the World Bank, the IMF, the US Department of State, Sachs, the

Thatcherite new-right policy institutes in Britain, and international banks, the Polish Government abandoned planning, committed itself to privatization, freed most prices including those of foods and energy which had hitherto been heavily subsidized, greatly reduced subsidies to firms, made the zloty internally convertible, and began to provide for the market allocation of resources – including labour (Beksiak *et al.*, 1990; Etzioni, 1991). The plan's proponents warned that times would be hard during the transition but its success would be evident to all within two years. Once the restrictive apparatus of central planning was removed, market mechanisms would start working spontaneously and the natural processes of economic development would assert themselves. Sachs simply assumed, without empirical reference to Polish economic life of the kind sociologists routinely make, that there were copious 'unleashed energies in the East' waiting to be tapped and that suitable entrepreneurship, management and labour commitment would materialize spontaneously (Sachs, 1990: 23). He also neglected what sociologists since Durkheim have known as the non-contractual elements in contract. Yet as Hare (1991) has pointed out in an introduction to the microeconomics of transition in Eastern Europe, none of these could be taken for granted.

The Balcerowicz Plan was much more drastic than the measures adopted immediately after the change of regime in Hungary (partly because economic reforms in the 1980s made the need for a big bang more questionable) and in Czechoslovakia (partly because of the absence of hyperinflation and partly because of differential public support for such initiatives in the Czech and Slovak Republics) – but the assumption that free market economics are *natural* and spontaneous and that communism is an unnatural diversion found favour in those countries too.

Three years later we can ask whether the shock therapy has worked within the time-scale its apologists claimed for it. The answer has to be negative. True, inflation has been hugely reduced (though it remains high), street traders have appeared in all the big cities trading first from suitcases and now from market stalls, and there is scope for old second economy private businessmen and women to become new first economy, rather larger, business-men and women if they can be persuaded to pay taxes. But, according to Mokrzycki, industrial output fell 38 per cent in the first two years, unemployment rose from next to nothing to 12 per

cent, most state enterprises have done little to adapt to the ways
of a market economy and are close to bankruptcy, private agriculture cannot compete with Western imports despite tariff protection, the state is in fiscal crisis, and the education and health
services are near to collapse (Mokrzycki, 1991–92: 131). (Many
firms do not face effective competition and have found it easier to
cut production and raise prices than become more efficient.) By
the end of 1991 privatized firms were still responsible for less than
25 per cent of industrial production (compared with more than 80
per cent in domestic trade) (ibid.: 131). Of course the loss of the
Soviet Union as a market and a source of cheap energy, and the
world recession, have impeded Polish economic reconstruction,
but they are marginal rather than central to Poland's difficulties.

What does Sachs have to say about this? Berg and Sachs (1992)
claim that official statistics overstated the decline by under-
recording private sector trade. They also argue that output fell as
hoarding was no longer necessary and inventories were run down,
that 'the efficiency of the economic response has been reduced by
the prevalence of socialized ownership, especially in the large
industrial sector' (p. 120), and that the sharp fall in real wages did
no more than wipe out the rise in real wages in the late 1980s. In
short, things were not as bad as official statistics suggested or the
people believed. Instead of the official decline in GDP from 1989
to 1990 of 12 per cent, Berg and Sachs estimated a decline of 5 per
cent. What they cannot deny is that GDP and real wages were
down, and unemployment and prices were up. Additionally, fear
of unemployment in a society with inadequate unemployment
benefits, bewilderment at the declining asset values of industrial
plants as evidenced by the lack of foreign interest in buying all but
a few of them, and shock at the newly revealed scale of industrial
pollution, all contributed to a despair which Berg and Sachs
acknowledged but seem not to have expected.

The IMF regards Poland as a success story of sorts. The fall in
GDP bottomed out in 1992, growth of 2 per cent is expected in
1993 and over half of output now comes from the private sector.
But there remains a downside.

Unemployment is rising inexorably towards 3 million, or 16%
of the labour force. A third of the population may be living in
poverty, with no immediate sign of relief. Basic industries
like shipbuilding and coal have yet to feel the ice hand of

rationalisation. Plans to privatise 600 large firms by handing over the shares to people are held up in Parliament by opposition amendments.

(*Guardian*, 10 March, 1993)

Reconstruction of the Polish economy is going to be a much more protracted affair than the heady rhetoric of the winter of 1989–90 suggested, and the patience of the Polish people is going to be tested.

Answers to what has gone wrong represent variations on the theme that many aspects of the legacy of real socialism cannot be superseded as quickly as neo-liberal economists with delusions of frictionless change imagine, or as quickly as local populations were told by their politicians and by Western advisers. This has now been conceded by two of the economic reformers concerned, Reynolds and Young, in a devastating report published by the Adam Smith Institute in 1992 – and by the Polish privatization minister, Lewandowski, in its foreword. Writing about Eastern Europe as a whole, Reynolds and Young argue that enormous sums of money from Western sources have been wasted on projects that do not work and cannot work as intended because the economic theory that shaped them took no account of the real local economic, social, cultural and political conditions of their implementation. Their catalogue of (anonymized) examples is enough to make one weep. The trouble, as they see it, is that macroeconomic reforms, such as price liberalization and currency stabilization, have been implemented but microeconomic market reforms and privatization all too often have not.

> Under current rates of progress, it will take an average of 28 years for Hungary, Poland and The Czech and Slovak republics to privatize only 50% of their state enterprises; longer for other countries. However, within five years from now, over 60% of remaining state enterprises are likely to close, causing unemployment to rise above 40%, which would be politically unsustainable.
>
> (Reynolds and Young, 1992: 131)

Eastern Europe, they claim, is on the brink of a catastrophe.

Reynolds and Young present their sorry stories with an air of surprise, and a recommendation that it is time now to heed microeconomists. But none of what they have to say about economic projects in the real economies and societies of Eastern Europe would come as any surprise to sociologists (whose advice would have been obtainable for a pittance by comparison). Podgorecki, for example, refers memorably to the 'miasmatic overhang' of totalitarianism (Podgorecki, 1991: 96). I will review just some of the elements of the legacy of real socialism which Kowalik (1991), Podgorecki and Mokrzycki have discussed with respect to Poland, and Etzioni (1991) with respect to all Eastern Europe, in connection with infrastructure; banking, accountancy, law and taxation; capital and capital assets; management; and labour, culture and values. I shall add some comparisons with Czechoslovakia and Hungary.

Infrastructure

Poland has to revolutionize its telecommunications, improve its transport and equip itself with more business hotels. If it wants inward investment to include foreign managers, it will also have to address its appalling environmental pollution; as it is, investors can usually find healthier places to invest and live.

Banking, accountancy, law and taxation

Poland has to effect major reforms of its banking, accounting, property and commercial law, and fiscal systems. Hare and Révész comment that

> Throughout Eastern Europe priorities are extensive retraining of bank staff (especially those in lending departments), computerization, and development of the most basic services taken for granted in the west. Both firms and banks need to introduce Western accounting conventions for business.
>
> (Hare and Révész, 1992: 251)

Reforms made in the 1980s have, however, given Hungary a head start. (For a list see Hare and Révész, 1992: 233.)

Capital and capital assets

There is not much investment capital in the country. It has been estimated that total national savings are only equivalent to 10 per cent of the notional value of assets to be privatized. It is also not clear whether there is much worth investing in. Certainly government and people have overestimated the asset value of industrial plant. What is an obsolescent plant making unmarketable goods in a polluted environment worth? A quip attributed to Lewandowski says it all: 'privatization is when someone who doesn't know who the real owner is and doesn't know what it's really worth sells something to someone who doesn't have any money' (in Stark, 1992b: 39). In Hungary there have been complaints that some firms have been sold to Western investors for much less than they are worth (Burawoy and Lukács, 1992: 154), but the disappearing asset value of plants is the commoner experience in East-Central Europe. It is also worth noting that the principal reason why the integration of the former GDR into the FRG is proving much more expensive than expected is that far more East German plant is having to be written off than was anticipated at the time of unification in 1990.

Management

Senior and middle management with the skills and competencies of managements in G7 countries (the seven largest Western economic powers) is conspicuous by its absence. Who knows which of the new street traders will be capable of running a big business in ten or twenty years' time, but there are none now and it was foolish in the extreme to suppose that their appearance confirmed that Poland was well supplied with the right entrepreneurial talent. Etzioni quotes with disbelief *The New York Times* of 3 March 1990 as saying that '. . . what is going on here is precisely the kind of capitalist initiative and competition that Finance Minister Leszek Balcerowicz and other officials hope will bring prices down and renew the economy' (Etzioni, 1991: 3). But by that token Kathmandu would be a major centre of international capitalism.

Part of the problem of unsatisfactory management has to do with the survival of the former *nomenklatura*. Many former party placemen and socialist factory managers have manipulated legal and other changes (beginning before 1989 in Hungary and Poland) to acquire effective control, and sometimes ownership, of former state firms. There are two objections to this. One is that the former dominant class is merely reconstituting itself in the new capitalist order – the so-called 'soft landing'. How much these people are reviled is best illustrated by the lustration process in Czechoslovakia.

When Lech Wałęsa called for 'acceleration' in his campaign for the presidency in 1990, accelerated displacement of the former *nomenklatura* was one thing to which he was referring. The other objection is that they have the wrong management experience and skills. Beksiak *et al.*, for example, argue that they 'usually know very well how to plead persuasively in party committees, ministries, state agencies, banks, etc., for new subsidies, tax relief or cheap credits' (Beksiak *et al.*, 1990: 14) but these are not now the skills required. Some of the old *nomenklatura*, however, do at least know something about how to run large organizations; also some of the former officials in economic ministries and some of the state factory managers have experience of market demands in Western Europe and North America and of the expectations of prospective Western business partners. There may be times when tainted know-how is better than no know-how, even if the long-suffering populations of these four societies do not see it that way. Hostility to the old *nomenklatura*, incidentally, can in one respect merely transform what it seeks to destroy; there has been a tendency in Poland to make new appointments on Solidarity or other anti-communist credentials rather than on competence – a sort of alternative anti-communist *nomenklatura*.

Labour, culture and values

Worker organization, whether in Solidarity, or in workers' councils, is sometimes a factor which cannot be as easily disregarded as liberal economists would wish given the part played by Solidarity in effecting the changes in Poland and beyond; it has to be won over. In addition, Mokrzycki refers to the persistence of *homo sovieticus* – the attitudes and habits of passivity, welfare dependency, poor labour discipline, disrepect for the law, etc. – but argues that this opportunistic being will disappear along with the command economy which provided the opportunities. I would like to believe this but doubt whether the habits of a lifetime can be changed so easily. Etzioni's list includes working slowly, aversion to taking initiatives and responsibililty, diversion of work time for private purposes, and barter of work time and materials for other favours. (There is a wonderful account of the diversion of employers' materials in Kenedi's *Do It Yourself: Hungary's Hidden Economy* (n.d.).) I would add that it will take a long time to establish Western ideas about giving a service. It should also be noted that the geographical mobility of labour is limited not just by the custom of staying near to one's extended family and community of origin but also by the shortage of housing. Etzioni notes how in Eastern Europe the right to work and to job security are very important values (also see Rabušic *et al.*, 1991: 5–6, on Czechoslovakia), and how there are reports from Hungary of enterprise managers cutting sweetheart deals whereby Western investors buy their firms for artificially low prices in return for guaranteed jobs and pay (Etzioni, 1991: 8).

None of this should be taken as implying that Poland, the Czech Republic, Slovakia and Hungary have no chance of transforming their economies. All do have some capital assets, some inward investment and joint ventures, some products for which demand is strong internationally, and relatively well-educated labour forces. The possibilities for tourism are obvious. Some labour values, too, may yet prove helpful; Burawoy and Lukács (1992), for example, emphasize how flexible and resourceful workers have had to be on the floors of the Hungarian machine shop and steel works they studied in order to make the rates under adverse conditions. Even so, reviewing economic, social and cultural factors of production, Kowalik, Podgorecki and Etzioni are all highly cautious, if not plain pessimistic, about the prospects for rapid socio-economic change; and Rabušic *et al.* (1991) report polling data from Czechoslovakia which confirms that respondents expected positive change within two to three years.

Mokrzycki is more optimistic and in this I think he is in error. He is as clear as everyone else that 'The assumption that the key to the development of Eastern Europe was the release of economic initiatives blocked by the communist system of central planning turned out to be false' (Mokrzycki, 1991–92: 136). It is false, however, only because it did not take into account the need to overcome the real obstacle to reform – the existing structure of group interests. All social groups want to keep the privileges they derived from the distributive policies of the socialist state.

> Workers as a class benefitted from forced industrialization, farmers from the economy of shortages which guaranteed unlimited demand for food irrespective of quality, intellectuals from the patronage of the state and the 'soft financing' of science, culture, etc., and the hounded private sector from the lack of competition and the second economy.
>
> (Mokrzycki, 1991–92: 135)

(Back in 1974, incidentally, Matejko gave similar reasons why the state socialist system was more stable than one might otherwise have expected.) In so far as supersession of the structure of group interests may now be about to happen, Mokrzycki argues, it will be the occasion of bitter conflict – especially in heavy industry – but it will also belatedly open the way to rapid economic advance.

Mokrzycki sociologizes Balcerowicz. He shares the assumption that free market forces are natural but believes they have been suppressed not only by central planning and the state ownership of firms but also by the structure of group interests. He denies that culture and values are to blame, or that *homo sovieticus* could survive beyond the conditions which gave rise to him. No cultural revolution is thus needed. I think this is wrong on both counts. There is nothing natural about *homo economicus* (cf. Polanyi, 1944), and his/her absence from much of contemporary Poland cannot be remedied without a cultural revolution whose completion will be protracted and uncertain (cf. Inglehart (1990) on culture shifts in advanced industrial societies).

REAL STRATEGIES, ARCHIPELAGOS AND *BRICOLAGE*

By 'real strategies', I mean simply the identification of means to medium- or long-term ends which are 'realistic' in so far as they take account of real social and cultural conditions, stocks of knowledge and agential dispositions (cf. Crow, 1989).

Kowalik notes how 'Lech Wałęsa . . . accepted Balcerowicz's plan in advance, even before its details were known, apparently convinced that control of "our" government was unnecessary' (Kowalik, 1991: 42). No attempt was made to explain its consequences to the people. Instead the impression was given that apolitical technical experts were masterminding a process, which, however painful at the time, would quickly enable Poland to close the gap with the market economies of Western Europe. The 'return to Europe' was assured. That it did not happen had much to do with the defeat of Prime Minister Mazowiecki in the presidential elections of November 1990; Wałęsa's ambiguous slogan of 'acceleration' also suggested that the transition to a market economy and prosperity could be speeded up. Western European governments, too, have encouraged thoughts of economic convergence by supporting the goal of Polish, Czech(oslovak) and Hungarian membership of the European Community by the end of the century – even though Greece, with a per capita GDP four times that of Poland has had to be exempted from some of the convergence requirements of the Maastricht Treaty of December 1991. The foreign minister designate of the new Czech Republic said in London on 1 December 1992 that he sought to negotiate full Czech entry to the EC by the end of the decade (*Guardian*, 2 December 1992). Expectations of what could be done in two years were too high; now expectations of what can be done by the year 2000 are too high.

How could a more gradual transition be accomplished? True to his alternative approach to economics (1988), Etzioni answers as follows:

(1) If one could keep expectations low, so that results would be fulfilling rather than frustrating;
(2) If the rewards of the transition could be kept high compared to the pain, which a 'pull' strategy seems to offer; and
(3) If the moral case for the new regime could be strongly made, which is easier to do for the more humane and less brutal transition.

(Etzioni, 1991: 11)

By a 'pull' strategy, Etzioni means credit and fiscal concessions for new private businesses with realistic business plans, rather than the Balcerowicz 'push' strategy which removes subsidies from state firms, invites them to adjust to new market conditions but only succeeds in driving them into bankruptcy. These new businesses would then attract the ablest managers and the most skilled workers and would be the best placed to obtain new technologies. As the new businesses grow in size and number, the old (ex-)state firms would lose more of their subsidies and wither on the vine. The transition would be protracted, but it would also, he thinks, be less dislocative, more humane, and more assured of success. If he is correct, it would also leave fewer desperate people prey to the overtures of old communists or the new forces of the nationalist and anti-Semitic extreme right.

Etzioni's 'pull' is a variant of what could be called an archipelago strategy. What are needed are successful new businesses which also serve as demonstrations to others. Western investment, provided it is coupled with Western management, might also provide islands in the archipelago. In the Polish case, in particular, there may also be scope for diaspora capital and returnee capitalists.

One interesting example of a demonstration business is the McDonald hamburger restaurants in the Russian rouble economy. Hutton (1993) has also suggested that 'big bang crash programmes of impossibilist technical reform' are increasingly discredited in Russia, and that instead, Yeltsin should look to the example of Peter the Great in the early eighteenth century and import foreigners to teach Western skills, establish commercial enterprises and create a Russian business class. The key to reform, he argues, are the 'pilot islands' for privatization currently under discussion by G7.

In his critique of 'cookbook capitalism', Stark argues that 'Capitalism cannot be introduced by design in a region where the lessons of forty years of experimentation by a rational hand have made the citizenry cautious about big experiments' (Stark, 1992b: 19). Instead institutional legacies make themselves felt and transformations are more a matter of *bricolage*, making the best of whatever comes to hand. In similar vein, Murrell sets out the characteristics of utopian and piecemeal approaches to policy in general and privatization in particular and, shades of Popper, favours the piecemeal (Murrell, 1992: 13–14). Interestingly the economists, Hare and Révész, have argued that Hungary laid the foundations for a market economy in the 1980s and that a gradual transition there, taking up to two generations, is more likely to secure the popular support and social peace indispensable to success than any big bang policy. Of course Hungary saw in the 1970s and 1980s not just economic reform but also the development of very large grey and second economies. What remains to be seen is how smoothly grey and second economy practices – which, in addition to initiative and resourcefulness, include the particularisms of corruption, connections, favours, theft of materials, diversion of paid time and tax evasion – give way to the universalisms of the lawful first economy.

PROTO-CIVIL SOCIETY AND THE DELEGITIMATED STATE

I want now to return to political change and the quest for liberty. Weitman argues that crucial to the prospects for regime liberalization are the 'social and cultural infrastructures without which formal liberties . . . have little chance of being enshrined into actual liberties' (Weitman, 1992: 17). His list includes independence of spirit, self-reliance, organizational skills and habits of co-operation, a synergetic rather than zero-sum attitude to others, a pragmatic willingness to find a *modus vivendi*, an ethic of responsibility, a willingness to horse-trade and find honour in compromise, an avoidance of intransigent last stands, and respect for rules and mistrust of those who cynically bend or ignore them. He surmises that, for the most part, these have either never existed in Eastern Europe or were destroyed by 'the totalitarian State under the old regime' (ibid.: 18). In this context it is worth noting Musil's use of survey findings derived from Inglehart (1990) and Mareš *et al.* (1991): 'In the Netherlands, Great Britain, Belgium and Luxembourg 88 to 90 percent of respondents stated that "people can be trusted"; in Czechoslovakia, the number was only 30 percent' (Musil, 1992: 192). As he says himself, it will take time and patience to heal so serious a 'social disease' (ibid.).

I prefer to speak of the need for a civil society in the sociological sense which runs from the Scottish Enlightenment through de Tocqueville to Gouldner (1980) and beyond (Bryant, 1993). It affirms the self-organization of society, rejects the state dependency of citizens, and treats civil society as an entity in its own right which is irreducible to economic structures. There is, however, a danger in critiques of the state that the decoupling of civil society and state will go too far. Solidarity and the Polish case all too easily prompted the notion of 'civil society against the state' (Arato, 1981), which makes sense as an oppositional strategy to the party-state but is unhelpful in conditions of democratic reconstruction. Frentzel-Zagórska avoids this: she treats civil society 'as a structure of the self organisation of society, located outside, though not disconnected from, the institutional framework of the state' (Frentzel-Zagórska, 1990: 760). I would add that civility, in Scottish and English usage, bespeaks a common standard within which a multiplicity of ways of living, working and associating are tolerated. It underwrites pluralism; it demands that in all life outside the home we afford each other certain decencies and comforts as fellow citizens regardless of other differences between us. It is, it should be noted, a cool concept. It does not require us to like those whom we deal with civilly, and as such it contrasts strongly with the warmth of communal, religious or national enthusiasms.

Frentzel-Zagórska compares the civil societies of Poland and Hungary. She argues that

In Poland the emergence of a self-organised civil society preceded
(by eight years) the attempts to adjust conditions for its official
functioning. In Hungary, on the contrary, these conditions
(whether adequate or not) were created by a reformist leadership ahead of the self-organisation of society.

(Frentzel-Zagórska, 1990: 761)

Like Szelényi (1988), she holds that 'the stress on economic
activity versus self organisation of society around basic values and
political and social goals constituted one of the essential differences
between Hungary and Poland' before 1989. (Frentzel-Zagórska,
1990: 773). The Hungarian reformers encouraged a kind of
embourgeoisement. Managers have proved to be one of the
best-organized groups in Hungary, and, whilst their counterparts
in Poland were active in Solidarity, elite workers in Hungary
were, and are, part-time entrepreneurs inside or outside public
enterprises (Bruszt, 1992: 63, n.16; Burawoy and Lukács, 1992:
part 2).

In both cases the result after 1989 is what might be called a
'proto-civil society'; the germ of a civil society is there but it has
yet to develop. Poland has experienced society against the state
(arguably for the last two centuries); even in the case of Solidarity
this largely took the form of mass protest or recourse to primary
relations and personal networks. The Polish Roman Catholic
Church, too, made, and makes, universal claims. In other words
citizens exist as a mass and as atomized individuals but they do
not yet associate in the Tocquevillean sense; the legitimate pursuit
of sectional interests within a framework of law is not yet established, and as one consequence political parties which secure the
support of large sections of the electorate have yet to crystallize.
Hungary experienced elements of non-oppositional economic
advancement on the part of individuals and groups. It is possible
that the consequent differentiation of economic interest is providing
a better basis for the legitimate pursuit of sectional interests within
a framework of law. Certainly Wesołowski contrasts the organizational forms of the opposition before 1989 – the all-national
movement Solidarity in Poland and various political groupings in
Hungary (Wesołowski, 1991: 89). Although forty parties contested
the April 1990 elections in Hungary only six won seats in parliament in contrast to the extreme fragmentation of the vote and
consequent parliamentary representation in the October 1991

elections in Poland. The germ of a civil society may thus be stronger in Hungary.

Sztompka argues that the key to the future is the restoration of civil society and the closure of the chasm which opened up under real socialism between the public and the private sphere. This, he continues, requires the completion of three tasks. First, there is the development of a 'pluralistic network of voluntary associations, interest groups, political organizations, and local communities' intermediate between state and family (Sztompka, 1991: 309). Second, there is 'the creation of an economic market and a representative democracy as institutional arrangements permanently asserting and demonstrating the link between individual interests and the public good, personal choices and the public welfare' (ibid.: 309). The third has to do with the formation of active and informed citizens able and willing to engage with the new institutions for their own benefit and society's.

Sztompka cites Dahrendorf's estimation that establishment of a civil society will take sixty years – and he has little to say about how it might be done. One could add that how it is done is not separable from a fourth task which he omits altogether: reform of the state. The problem is not just how to cut the state down to size but how to secure respect for it. It is particularly severe in Poland where there has been scant experience of legitimate political authority for the last two centuries. Politicians in the Czech Republic and Slovakia, too, have hardly won trust and respect by dividing the former Czechoslovakia in two against the apparent wishes of the majority of citizens in each of its constitutent republics. Bruszt has commented that there are supporters of a strong state version of economic and political transformation – such as Staniszkis – and supporters of a strong civil society version – such as Arato (Bruszt, 1992: 60, n.11). The dilemma, as I see it, is that *none of the countries of East-Central Europe has a strong state or a strong civil society.* So what can be done? Electoral laws which prohibit representation in parliament for parties obtaining less than a threshold percentage of the vote would encourage social and political co-operation. Reform of civic education might help. The supply of, and support for, enlightened leaders is a chancier business – as the case of Václav Havel illustrates. For the moment what East-Central Europe presents are proto-civil societies and state structures without authority because the delegitimation of the state consequent upon its association with state socialism did not, and could not, come to an abrupt end in 1989. Real strategies to secure civil society and reform the state can only take time. Avoidance of economic programmes which threaten destabilization by promising more than they can deliver is therefore imperative.

CONCLUSIONS

I have argued that the communist legacy in East-Central Europe – the structural and cultural 'overhang', to mimic the language of economists – precludes quick establishment of a market economy, liberal capitalism, a civil society and a reformed state. Instead post-communist societies may turn out to constitute a distinctive social type for which new concepts and characterizations will have to be found. One such is that of 'proto-civil societies' to which I have already referred. Another might be the 'tri-world capitalism' which they can be expected to continue to display, with some firms comparable in their operations and culture to those of the First World, some whose operations and culture retain obvious continuities with those of the erstwhile Second World, and some economic concerns from poor smallholdings to street traders more akin to the developing Third World. There are already worrying signs that the elusiveness of economic prosperity for the majority provides political opportunities for ex-communists and for the nationalist and anti-Semitic right (which are sometimes one and the same). In addition the state remains responsible for a large public sector, and for welfare provision, but is unable to discharge its responsibilities effectively because it lacks the necessary tax revenue and public trust.

Too often in the Western media and in East-Central Europe itself, the terms of debate seem to present a false choice between just two options. First, there is liberal economic and political reform which must be done quickly if it is to be done at all. Second, there is a slowing down of reform which is all too often a euphemism for preservation or restoration of as much of the old order as possible. In practice a great deal of what happens is neither of these. The goal of privatization, for example, is still endorsed, but privatization programmes are delayed. Even more importantly, very many of the citizenry know they are worse off, are unsure why or what can be done about it, and retreat into political apathy. I want to suggest a third choice. I do not mean by this some halfway house between state socialism and capitalism, or people's democracy and liberal democracy, because there is not one – although the capitalisms of North America, Britain, Germany, Sweden, Japan, Taiwan and Brazil, to take but a few examples, do provide enormously varying models. Rather, I mean slow but deliberate progress towards capitalism and liberal democracy – using the archipelago strategy, educational reform, gradual reconstructions of the professions, *bricolage* and whatever other piecemeal steps towards those goals one is able to take. That means tempering talk of a return to Europe (Taiwan might be of greater economic relevance anyway) and no more references to membership of the EC by the year 2000.

That exceptionally shrewd observer of East-Central Europe, Garton Ash, immediately in the aftermath of the 'revolutions' of 1989 sketched a prospect 'in which the post-communist future looks remarkably like the pre-communist past, less Central Europe than *Zwischeneurope*, a dependent intermediate zone of weak states, national prejudice, inequality, poverty and *Schlammassel*' (Garton Ash, 1990: 155). He does not regard this as inevitable and neither do I. But it does seem to me the likely outcome of trying to do quickly what cannot be done quickly. For better or for worse the economists have had their big bangs and their shock therapies: for better, in so far as currencies have been stabilized; for worse, in so far as the hopes of many for economic prosperity were raised only to be cruelly dashed. It is time now for sociologists to try to lower expectations and fortify resolve for the long haul.

ACKNOWLEDGEMENT

I presented an earlier draft of this chapter at the the ISA Social Theory Research Committee meeting on 'Theoretical Lessons of the Transition from Communism: Convergence Theory Revisited' at SCASSS, Uppsala (Sweden), in June 1992. I am very grateful to colleagues for their comments in Uppsala and subsequently.

REFERENCES

Arato, A. (1981) 'Civil Society Against the State: Poland 1980–81', *Telos*, no. 47: 23–47.
Ash, T. Garton (1990) *We the People*, Cambridge: Granta.
Beksiak, J., Gruszecki, T., Jedraszczyk A. and Winięcki, J. (1990) *The*

Polish Transformation: Programme and Progress, London: Centre for Research into Communist Economies.

Berg, A. and Sachs J. (1992) 'Structural Adjustment and International Trade in Eastern Europe: The Case of Poland', *Economic Policy*, no. 14: 115–73.

Bruszt, L. (1992) 'Transformative Politics: Social Costs and Social Peace in East-Central Europe', *East European Politics and Societies*, 6: 55–72.

Bryant, C.G.A. (1993) 'Civil Society and Pluralism: A Conceptual Analysis', *Sisyphus: Social Studies*, 1(8): 103–19.

Burawoy, M. and Lukács, J. (1992) *The Radiant Past: Ideology and Reality in Hungary's Road to Capitalism*, Chicago: University of Chicago Press.

Crow, G. (1989) 'The Use of the Concept of "Strategy" in Recent Sociological Literature', *Sociology*, 23: 1–24.

Dahrendorf, R. (1990) *Reflections on the Revolution in Europe*, London: Chatto & Windus.

Etzioni, A. (1988) *The Moral Dimension: Toward a New Economics*, New York: Free Press.

—— (1991) *Eastern Europe: The Wealth of Lessons*, Washington, DC: George Washington University.

Frentzel-Zagórska, J. (1990) 'Civil Society in Poland and Hungary', *Soviet Studies*, 42: 759–77.

Gouldner, A.W. (1980) 'Civil Society in Capitalism and Socialism', ch. 12 in A.W. Gouldner, *The Two Marxisms: Contradictions and Anomalies in the Development of Theory*, London: Macmillan.

The Guardian (1993) 'IMF Gives Poland Credit for Reforms', and 'Say Poles for Progress' (leader), 10 March 1993.

Hankiss, E. (1988) *East European Alternatives*, Oxford: Clarendon Press.

—— (1990) 'In Search of a Paradigm', *Daedalus*, 119: 183–214.

Hare, P. (1991) 'The Assessment: Microeconomics of Transition in Eastern Europe', *Oxford Review of Economic Policy*, 7: 1–15.

—— and Révész, T. (1992) 'Hungary's Transition to the Market: The Case Against a "Big-Bang"', *Economic Policy*, no. 14: 227–64.

Hutton, W. (1992) 'Selling the Capitalist Miracle', *The Guardian*, 2 March 1992, p. 21.

—— (1993) 'Western Spin Doctors' Writings Ignore the Real Needs of Russia', *The Guardian*, 29 March 1993, p. 11.

Inglehart, R. (1990) *Culture Shift in Advanced Industrial Society*, Princeton, NJ: Princeton UP.

Kenedi, J. (n.d.) *Do It Yourself: Hungary's Hidden Economy*, London: Pluto.

Kowalik, T. (1991) 'Socio-economic and Cultural Limits of Market Economy', *Sisyphus: Sociological Studies*, 7: 41–51.

Mareš, P., Musil, L. and Rabušic, L. (1991) 'Sociální změna očima česke veřejnosti', *Sociologický Časopis*, 27: 702–14.

Matejko, J. (1974) *Social Change and Stratification in Eastern Europe: An Interpretive Analysis of Poland and Her Neighbours*, New York: Praeger.

Mokrzycki, E. (1991–92) 'Eastern Europe After Communism', *Telos*, no. 90: 129–36.

Murrell, P. (1992) 'Conservative Political Philosophy and the Strategy of Economic Transition', *East European Politics and Societies*, 6: 3–16.
Musil, J. (1992) 'Czechoslovakia in the Middle of Transition', *Daedalus*, 121(2): 175–95.
Podgorecki, A. (1991) 'A Concise Theory of Post-Totalitarianism (Poland – 1989/1990)', *Polish Sociological Bulletin*, no. 2: 89–100.
Polanyi, K. (1944) *The Great Transformation: The Political and Economic Origins of Our Time*, Boston: Beacon Press, 1957.
Rabušic, L., Mareš, P. and Musil, L. (1991) 'Social Change in Perception of the Czech Population One Year After the Revolution', Paper presented to the Conference on Social Change and Macroplanning, IUC, Dubrovnik, April 1991.
Reynolds, P. and Young P. (1992) *Eastern Promise: Privatization Strategy for Post-Communist Countries*, London: Adam Smith Institute.
Sachs, J. (1990) 'Eastern European Economies: What is to be Done?', *The Economist*, 13–19 January: 23–8.
Stark, D. (1992a) 'Introduction' to 'Transforming the Economies of East Central Europe', Special number of *East European Politics and Societies*, 6(1): 1–2.
—— (1992b) 'Path Dependence and Privatization Strategies in East Central Europe', *East European Politics and Societies*, 6: 17–54.
Szelényi, I. (1988) *Socialist Entrepreneurs*, Madison: University of Wisconsin Press.
Sztompka, P. (1991) 'The Intangibles and Imponderables of the Transition to Democracy', *Studies in Comparative Communism*, 24: 295–311.
Weitman, S. (1992) 'Thinking the Revolutions of 1989', *British Journal of Sociology*, 43: 1–24.
Wesołowski, W. (1991) 'Transition to Democracy: The Role of Social and Political Pluralism', *Sisyphus: Sociological Studies*, 7: 79–94.

Chapter 5

Values and the welfare state in Czechoslovakia

Petr Mareš, Libor Musil and Ladislav Rabušic

In this chapter we shall consider cultural factors influencing the development of the welfare state in the Czech Lands after the 'Velvet Revolution' of November 1989. First, we shall offer general information on the character of current social change. Then, we shall identify relatively stable characteristics of the culture of Czech society which, within the framework of the current process of social change, operate as factors of continuity. Finally, we shall hypothesize about the influence of these stable cultural factors on the probable course of development of social policy in the Czech Republic.

Let us stress that we shall concentrate more on the situation in the Czech Lands than in Czechoslovakia as a whole. The reason is simple. Developmental trends in the Czech and Slovak Republics after 1989 have showed that, due to their respective cultures, Czechs and Slovaks have diverged considerably in their understandings of the goals which their societies should pursue (see Mareš *et al.*, 1992). These cultural differences have proved incompatible since the June 1992 national elections. At the time of writing (September 1992), it seemed very likely that this incompatibility would lead to a 'velvet divorce', i.e. the breakup of the Czechoslovak federation into two independent states. We do not presume to anticipate the results of complex and difficult negotiations between Czech and Slovak political representatives; rather, our focus on the Czech Republic is indicative of a certain confusion about the situation in Slovakia which we, as Czechs, are not able to resolve at present.

INTRODUCTION

The more time has elapsed from the *annus mirabilis* 1989, the more it has been apparent that revolutions are deceptive. The

Czech and Slovak public may have realized already that revolutions are just melancholy moments of history, brief gasps of hope which then become submerged in misery and disillusionment (Dahrendorf, 1990). Perhaps it is clearer now that the change of the regime is only a beginning, and that completion of the economic and social changes will take a long time. The longer we live under the new political system, the more clearly we can confirm what political scientists have long averred: revolutionary change is completed only after a cultural change. Students of cultural change know that

> a culture cannot be changed overnight. One may change the rulers and the laws, but changing basic aspects of the underlying culture will take many years. Even then, the long-run effects of revolutionary transformation are likely to diverge widely from revolutionary visions and to retain important elements of the old pattern of society.
>
> (Inglehart, 1990: 19)

Or as Inglehart sums up, there is always a great deal of institutional and cultural inertia working against change.

These 'old patterns of society' are above all internalized value structures and codes of behaviour which have to be restructured and redefined under new political, economical and social conditions. We agree with observations made by several Central and East European sociologists (see, for example, Hankiss, 1990) that struggles over discrepancies between cultural values and the needs of their economies are the crucial problems in the transformation of all post-totalitarian countries. In all of them 'governments, ruling parties, parties of opposition, experts and expert committees are desperately searching . . . for a new paradigm, a new social and economic model with which to launch these countries onto a new course of dynamic development' (Hankiss, 1990: 183).

That discrepancy between the value systems and the needs of liberalized economies should create tensions comes as no surprise. In Czechoslovakia (as in other countries of Central and Eastern Europe), there have already been three generations socialized (about three-quarters of the current population) in settings where there was no market, no private property (Czechoslovakia, together with the former USSR, was the only country with practically no private sector at all), no civil society;[1] not only the economy but also human destinies were centrally planned and controlled literally from cradle to grave. These huge masses of people went only through the socialist educational system, worked under the conditions of socialist economics, and lived the way of life which had emerged as a reaction and adaptation to state paternalism. This population considered it normal that elements of 'real socialism' (e.g. the emphases on egalitarianism achieved in everyday life by complicated redistributional mechanisms, on social homogeneity, and on the duty to work interpreted officially as the right to work,[2] all reinforced by a Marxist-Leninist ideology presented and enforced as the only one possible) have become a part of the lived world. Incomes were levelled off and were not, basically, dependent on one's performance or qualification. According to Večerník (1991a), the extent of income equalization in Czechoslovakia was one of the greatest of all the European communist countries. Jobs were lifelong jobs, the labour market did not exist and one's life was stripped of any dynamics and individualized authentic decision-making. Seemingly positive was the fact that deep poverty did not exist,[3] and unemployment was not a threat – indeed there was a shortage of labour force. The communist state became the only social assistance provider after doing away with the market and destroying all independent social assistance institutions (see also De Deken, 1992).

This milieu of state paternalism has been systematically eroded after 1989 by liberal interventions into the economic mechanism. Price supports were eliminated and prices increased rapidly after economic liberalization in January 1991: the consumer price index rose 184 per cent in the Czech Republic and 193 per cent in the Slovak Republic between 1989 and 1992. (Price increases in the Czech Republic from January 1989 till June 1992 were 166 per cent for meat and meat products, 275 per cent for milk and dairy products, 158 per cent for textile goods and 221 per cent for shoes.) Inflation hit an alarming 54 per cent in 1991. The unemployment rate has reached, for the time being, 7 per cent (3 per cent in Czech Lands and 12 per cent in Slovakia)[4] and the standard of living declined substantially. The reaction of the public was immediate. As early as 1991, which was the first year of market reform, about a quarter (26 per cent) of the population began to perceive themselves as poor (Večerník, 1991b). According to the social survey of Matějů and Řeháková (1992), 93 per cent of the Czech and Slovak population claimed that inequality had increased after November 1989 and perceived this as socially unjust.

The decline in the standard of living in Czechoslovakia has increased fears and worries about the further course of economic reform; it has also lowered people's optimism with regard to the near future and has even moved a relatively large part of the population to express some nostalgia for the 'good old days' of social stability and security.

The overall decline of optimism in the Czech Lands can be illustrated by the data in Table 5.1 from our three consecutive surveys on representative samples of population in Brno (the capital of Moravia, with a population of about 400,000).

Table 5.1 The Brno population's attitudes towards development in the next 5 years of Brno (April 1990, November 1990 and November 1991)

	Definitely fearful	Rather fearful	Rather hopeful	Definitely hopeful	Don't know	Number
April 1990	9%	14%	29%	38%	10%	510
November 1990	12%	34%	31%	20%	3%	1,024
November 1991	15%	34%	34%	15%	2%	1,023

Source: Hopes and fears of Brno population, data sets I, II, III.

This syndrome is common to all post-communist countries. According to a cross-cultural survey in Hungary, Poland and Czechoslovakia, carried out by the Freedom House Foundation in April 1991, there were large proportions of people who then regarded their current situation as worse in comparison with that of the past regimes: 60 per cent in Hungary, 48 per cent in Czechoslovakia (37 per cent in the Czech Republic and 67 per cent in the Slovak Republic). In Poland, the figure was only 16 per cent at the time (Lamper, 1991). However, a year later a Polish opinion poll, the results of which were published in *Rzeczpospolita*, recorded 30 per cent of respondents who would not object to the return of the past regime.

Despite the fact that in April 1992 51 per cent of Czechs and 64 per cent of Slovaks maintained that the development after November 1989 has brought them big dissatisfaction (Boguszak, 1992), the June 1992 national election results suggested that the proportion of people supporting rapid and determined pace of economic restructuring was not small. In the Czech Republic, 56 per cent of voters balloted for right-wing parties (in Slovakia only 24 per cent), thus expressing their will to continue the neo-liberal economic reform. Nevertheless, various social surveys showed that the Czech public was willing to accept difficulties connected with the reform only if they would achieve prosperity soon. The public also believed, according to the surveys, that the economic changes would not threaten substantially their living standards.[5] Strategists of the reform therefore must assess very carefully what the population can bear. Various polls reported that there had been a sudden and significant shift of opinion towards dissatisfaction and fear of the future in a large part of the population immediately after the price liberalization in January 1991. According to Hiršl's (1992) calculations, about 7 per cent of Czechoslovak households (about 1.4 million people) were below the poverty line at the beginning of 1992. Janáček's (1992) estimate suggests that about 30 per cent of households in Czechoslovakia will be at the risk of poverty at the end of 1992.

It should now be obvious that a necessary condition for a positive development of Czech society will be the willingness of the public to bear patiently the hardships brought about by the economic transformation. Naturally, this patience has its limits.

According to a Western analyst, Czechoslovakia can be regarded as 'a shining example of how to make the postcommunist transformation work. It has taken itself to the point of economic turnaround, and done so with no violence, no serious conflict, not a single strike' (Jackson, 1992: 26). We do not share such optimism. It is clear that the 'legacy of real socialism' (Mokrzycki, 1991) and the culture of the 'totalitarian socialism' have influenced everyone to a much higher degree than they are willing to admit.[6] It is more and more evident that one of the crucial factors determining the course of development in the Czech society will be 'social peace' or 'social consensus'. According to the public discussions of many politicians, economists and trade unions representatives, social peace can only be maintained by appropriate state social policies.

If we take all these facts into consideration, it is evident that *the existence of the welfare state in Czechoslovakia* (and in other post-communist countries) *becomes the crucial condition for the success of all initiated changes*. Logically, there emerge questions such as: 'How can the processes connected with establishing the welfare state in post-communist countries influence changes in the value preferences and codes of behaviour of their populations?' And conversely: 'How will the existing value structures and codes of behaviour established in the context of a centrally directed economy and state paternalism influence the content and form of the Czech welfare state?' The significance of the welfare state for keeping social peace and legitimizing the economic restructuring in post-communist countries is given by the necessity to prevent anomie in the society. Should anomie develop and last, 'it is an invitation to usurpers to impose a false sense of order' (Dahrendorf, 1990: 164–5).

PERSPECTIVES FOR THE WELFARE STATE IN THE CZECH SOCIETY

Socialism was a specific attempt to create a welfare state of some kind. From a typological point of view, the socialist welfare state of Central and Eastern Europe was characterized by De Deken (1992) as 'Leninist', in which elements of various 'welfare-regimes' – in Esping-Andersen's (1990) sense – have been combined. Important features of the Leninist type were that it was not based on citizenship and that it was not, despite its protestations, universalistic in the real sense of the word, because entitlement to social benefits depended upon being a loyal worker or employee of the state. Thus, employment in the public or co-operative sector, rather than citizenship, was the key criterion for the entitlements to social benefits and social programmes (De Deken, 1992).

In our thinking about the possible forms the welfare state could take in the Czech Lands, we are mindful of historical developments in the welfare state in Western Europe during the 1940s and 1950s. The growing role of the modern state in securing the social rights of citizens in the second half of the twentieth century was, as is generally known, a reaction to fluctuations of the market and to the events of the Second World War (Titmus, 1969). When the state became a guarantor of the social rights of citizens after the Second World War, differences emerged between efforts to restore the confidence of citizens in the social effectiveness of the market economy on the one hand, and a tendency to rebuild the industrial society altogether on the other hand. Some countries have focused on regulating the social impact of market economy, while others have tried to replace market mechanisms with a rationally designed and socially justified redistribution of resources, goods and services within the whole national economy. Czech society followed the second strategy after the communist take-over in 1948 and carried the traditionalist Slovakia along with it. It did so partly because Czechoslovakia entered the sphere of influence of Stalin's USSR after the Second World War, and partly because of autonomous developments in a Czech population which has traditionally favoured leftist, paternalistic and egalitarian tendencies. In 1989, the road to the promised communist heaven ended in total collapse and the Czech public, despite its traditional support of the idea of equality, made manifest their rejection of communist-style economic and ideological paternalism.

Revival of the market is, in terms of securing the social rights of citizens, undoubtedly the crucial turning point in the Czech Lands. The social impact of the re-emerging Czech market economy will have to be regulated according to principles whose legitimacy goes much deeper than the past cultural adaptation of the population to conditions of 'real socialism'. It will be very important to analyse how the public faces two key dilemmas: the dilemma of equality of results (achievements) versus equality of opportunities (see Flora and Heidenheimer, 1987) and the dilemma of civic solidarity versus status-specific solidarity (see Esping-Andersen, 1990). A probable solution to these dilemmas is encoded in the cultural traditions of Czech society. These traditions will probably determine the future design of the Czech welfare state to a much greater extent than the contemporary wave of pro-liberal euphoria born in the Czech Lands in the autumn of 1989.[7]

PATERNALISM AND EQUALITY OF RESULTS

The legitimacy of state activities in the sphere of the social rights of citizens is based, among other things, on the respect the public has for two key values of the welfare state: equality and security. Perception of these two values in the Czech society was influenced by the events of the 1930s and the Second World War. The experience of existential insecurity associated with the economic depression of the 1930s and the Nazi Protectorate of Bohemia and Moravia led to a desire for a fundamental restructuring of the society which would provide the achievement of existential security for everyone. The fluctuations of the market and the risks of free enterprise are synonymous with insecurity in the eyes of the Czech public. By contrast, principles of equality and security have been articulated in conscious rejection of liberal values and institutions. This attitude towards the key values of the welfare state has persisted in the second half of the twentieth century due to two circumstances: (1) the communist state systematically liquidated the traditional carriers of liberal values of self-reliance, i.e. small businessmen and middle-class people; (2) communist propaganda has endlessly stressed that in socialism, contrary to capitalism, there is neither unemployment nor the insecurity and poverty resulting from it. So, by a deliberate change in social stratification (equalization of incomes and compulsory labour participation) and by permanent ideological manipulation with threats of unemployment and poverty, the communist power elite managed to keep the public convinced about the basic incompatibility of the values of equality and security on the one hand and the principles of competition and self-reliance on the other.

Only a part of the public in the Czech Lands appreciates that in the Western cultural tradition the concept of equality has two different meanings. One is a major component of the socialist ethic, often called equality of results, and it implies an equalization in the disposal of resources, commodities, and services, and their redistribution according to personal needs. The other, the major component of the liberal ethic, is equality of opportunity. It is most relevant in the field of public education (Flora and Heidenheimer, 1987) and is based on merit.

Choice between these two concepts of equality influences the general orientation of social policy in any country. In the first case, where equality of results is preferred, social legislation is focused primarily on establishing various kinds of national minima which are represented by poor relief, a minimum wage, national pensions, compulsory education, etc. (Flora and Heidenheimer, 1987). As a result of this, the relationship between the existential security of citizens and the functioning of the market is loosened. From a citizen's point of view, then, security against market fluctuations is created and individual motivation to compete is weakened.

When a system of social legislation based on equality of opportunities is preferred, the state becomes above all a guarantor of equal access to education and employment. Young people have relatively open possibilities to acquire occupational qualifications and educational degrees. Their use is determined by market mechanisms. The relationship between existential security and the market is relatively close. A citizen knows that he or she is able to compete and is not protected from market forces.

Both approaches can be, and to some extent are, combined in their practical application. Nevertheless, this combination has its limits. A high degree of security against the effects of the market weakens the willingness and capacity of individuals to compete. Equality and security exclude each other to a certain extent and it is necessary to choose one or the other as the guiding principle of social policy.

A large part of the Czech public does not understand the dilemma of equality of results versus equality of opportunities. They have become accustomed to the idea of the equality of results as a natural principle of the welfare state. This attitude is documented by various social surveys. For instance, Matějů and Řeháková (1992) found that the relationship between performance and income is only vaguely understood by the Czech population. According to the authors, it is so because of the past influence of egalitarian ideology and redistributive practice. It is no coincidence that a substantial part of the Czech population perceives current social changes as a loss of former securities and privileges and also as a narrowing of life chances. We have recorded the same attitudes in our November 1991 social survey among the population of Brno. For 25 per cent of respondents, the current course of the development of society means personal loss.

We think that a welfare state organized on the principle of equality of opportunities would hardly be acceptable for the majority of the Czech population, who favour paternalism. The 'ideology of individualism' which underpins the American welfare state would be incomprehensible to it.

From the point of view of the 'ideology of individualism', a direct state guarantee of existential security is not a solution in the case of an individual's economic failure. On the contrary, as Higgins (1981) puts it, welfare support in the form of income and services would only exacerbate the situation by making the individual more dependent on outside support. His or her character faults (such as unwillingness to work, lack of diligence and perseverance) would only be deepened.

The Czech public seems to understand the concept of 'social policy' in terms of the above mentioned 'welfare support in the form of income and services'. The majority of people take this type of social support not only as granted in the case of their contingent existential difficulties, but also as a quite normal part of their everyday life. State subsidies of food, energy and rents, state-financed means of transport, state-financed maternity allowances and child benefits, state provision of special loans to newly-weds, state-built apartments – these state-funded social and population policy measures have been and still are customary elements of the short-term as well as of the long-term economic strategies of Czech citizens.[8] Therefore, they would hardly accept social legislation based on the philosophy of self-reliance. Unfortunately, cohorts of people who are now in their middle and old age have found themselves in a hardly enviable situation after 1989. Many of the new life strategies demanded from the whole population can be successfully adopted only if applied from the very beginning of one's adulthood, like, for instance, mortgage on a house or apartment.

All things considered, it is not very likely that 'the liberal welfare state'[9] could be politically successful in the Czech Republic. In the Czech cultural milieu, it would seem likely that movement towards a residual welfare state could be enforced only with great difficulties. The future Czech welfare state will most likely keep many features of universalist social policy.

BRANCH IDENTITY AND STATUS-SPECIFIC SOLIDARITY

If we accept the assumption of such universalistically oriented social policy in the Czech Lands, then we can expect that the Czech welfare state will gradually assume features of one of the continental models of welfare-state regimes. Esping-Andersen (1990) identified 'corporatist welfare state' and 'social democratic regime-type' in the European continent.

According to Esping-Andersen, it is typical for the *corporatist welfare state*, the prototype of which is the German 'social-market economy', that status differentials are preserved, and individual rights are attached to class and status.

> This corporatism was subsumed under a state edifice perfectly ready to displace the market as a provider of welfare; hence, private insurance and occupational fringe benefits play a truly marginal role. On the other hand, the state's emphasis on upholding status differences means that its redistributive impact is negligible.
> (Esping-Andersen, 1990: 27)

The corporatist welfare state is 'strongly committed to the preservation of traditional family-hood . . . Family benefits encourage motherhood . . . the state will only interfere when the family's capacity to service its members is exhausted' (ibid.).

The social-democratic regime-type was created by Social Democrats and its prototype is the Swedish 'state of social services'. The Social Democrats tried to build

> a welfare state that would promote an equality of the highest standards, not an equality of minimal needs as was pursued elsewhere . . . [in which] services and benefits be upgraded to levels commensurate with even the most discriminating tastes of new middle classes . . . the equality be furnished by guaranteeing workers full participation in the quality of rights enjoyed by the better-off . . . All benefit; all are dependent; and all will presumably feel obliged to pay. The ideal is not to maximize dependence on the family, but capacities for individual independence.

> (Esping-Andersen, 1990: 27–8)

De Deken (1992) pointed out that the corporatist welfare state is based on status-specific or intra-class solidarity. The social-democratic regime-type relies on civic or inter-class solidarity.

In April 1992, the then Czech Minister of the Health Service, Martin Bojar, published the following ideas in Czech newspapers:

> I think that a country as poor as ours cannot afford to break the principle of general solidarity . . . I regard it as moral that healthy people with higher incomes contribute more by certain percentages into the Fund of General Health Insurance and thus also to those who earn less and are not healthy . . . There is a danger that a such small and poor fund of General Health Insurance will be divided into many funds.

> (*Narušíme*, 1992: 1)

His statement was a reaction to the fact that enterprises and companies with much higher income than the average wanted to single themselves out from the system of general health insurance. We present this quotation as a proof that the dilemma between status-specific and universalistic solidarity is quite vital and topical in contemporary Czech society. It is logical, then, to ask which of the two types of solidarity will influence the future form of Czech welfare state.

Our observation, together with the analysis of De Deken (1992), leads us to believe that a *corporatist welfare state based on status-specific solidarity will be preferred in Czech society*. De Deken maintained that the choice between the universalistic and status-oriented models is not only a question of economic presumptions. but is also (indeed more) a matter of political will. This will is determined in Czech society by the fact that the communist power elites (or the 'Leninist regimes' in De Deken's words) totally discredited everything connected with socialism. They also discredited values like 'collectivism' and 'solidarity'. On the other hand, the Leninist principles 'From each according to his work' (which was supposed to apply for a socialist phase of development), and 'To each according to his needs' (promised to be true in communism) advertised to the population by communist governments, conformed to the ideal of fair resource distribution. Departures from these principles have been perceived by the Czech population as a betrayal of social justice and fundamentally correct principles. Neo-conservative policies, elements of which are now being implemented in the Czech Lands, can therefore be understood as a method of practical realization of the principle *'To each according to his or her work'*. In these circumstances, then, it is very likely that the social-democratic type of the welfare-state regime does not have a chance of succeeding in the Czech Republic. Indeed, according to De Deken (1992), it has no chance anywhere in Central Europe. It seems probable that Czech social policy will lead to a corporatist welfare state.

Such a hypothesis can be supported by other arguments. The system of social security that has been developed in Czech society during the last decades is compatible to a high degree with the principles of the corporatist welfare state. Key roles in the current situation are played by two elements: national economy and family (with its kinship networks).

The policy of so called 'social planning' introduced centrally in Czechoslovakia in the 1970s reproduced the principle of 'preservation of status differentials'. The centrally controlled distribution of planned production costs, production investments and investments into social services, at both the branch and enterprise levels, reflected the 'bargaining' of leading representatives of the various branches of the national economy over the financial resources of the state budget. The amount of resources allocated to social services for employees was therefore dependent on the power and influence of a particular branch of the economy over central decision-making. The easiest way for a worker or employee to increase his or her share in state social expenditures was to take a job in one of the better-funded branches, for instance in mining, heavy industry, the army, the police, or in the higher ranks of the Communist Party and state administration. People having these jobs had access to better-equipped recreational and health resorts or to privileged shops, and they were accorded special bonuses above salaries, etc. At the opposite end of the job market there were occupations in textiles, education, health-care, culture and social care.

This whole system of a branch-differentiated distribution of state social expenditures had in itself an encoded mechanism of self-reproduction. Those branches which could claim a larger part of the state budget could offer to their labour force higher earnings and better social services. They could therefore accept higher plan targets because they could attract labour of good quality and not suffer any shortage of workers. Following fulfilment of higher plan targets, they could also successfully bargain for a larger allocation of resources in the state budget for the next fiscal year, and so on. Gradually, in the course of 'our socialist buildup', the branch-differentiated distribution of social investment has been established. The quotation of ex-minister Bojar points to the fact that many Czechs favour maintenance of this status-differentiated structure of social care even during the social transformation of the post-totalitarian society.

The distribution of social care was bureaucratized at an 'official' level. There was also, however, the unofficial, hidden structure formed by socialist networks of kin (see Možný, 1991 or Šrubař, 1991). Families learned how to mobilize and use their social capital in keeping their welfare. In such circumstances, people can easily accept the principle according to which 'the state will intervene when the family's capacity to service its members is exhausted'. Such 'principle of subsidiarity' is regarded by Esping-Andersen (1990: 27) as one of the most characteristic signs of the corporatist welfare state.

The role of the family in welfare distribution is regarded by the Czech population as very important. After all, the social policy of the Czechoslovak socialist state was oriented towards strong family and population policies which co-determined the 'Czech ways to marriage' and motherhood.

The Czech society is culturally very closed and ethnocentric. Survey data speak about deep intolerance against everyone who is somehow different from the population majority. According to the AISA's survey carried in 1991, 72 per cent of Czechoslovak population would not want to live next door to gypsies, 54 per cent to homosexuals, 33 per cent to refugees and 30 per cent to persons of a different race. Because of this, social programmes for the gypsy minority (its size is estimated between 250,000 and 600,000) often become a target of public criticism. That could be taken as an indication that a welfare state based on broadly understood civic solidarity could meet with resistance if its clients or targets group were to include members of other racial or ethnic groups, immigrants or political refugees. Incidents of such hatred have been recorded lately in localities where camps for political refugees had been set up. Preconditions for universal civic solidarity are missing in Czech society due to one of the legacies of real socialism – lack of interpersonal trust,[10] trust in authority, trust in social institutions and last, but not least, trust in the possibility of common action (Možný, 1991). In addition, the possibility of civic solidarity is undermined by a special Czech (and Slovak as well) phenomenon, envy.[11] It is therefore probable that the aversion of Czechs to gypsies or other racial groups can be easily transformed into an aversion against homeless people, drug addicts, the mentally handicapped or the long-term unemployed.

CZECH CORPORATISM AND ITS HISTORICAL ROOTS

The future evolution of the Czech welfare state will to some extent be determined by the fact that the branch of the economy in which employees worked was one of the crucial factors of their social status. As we mentioned above, the correlation between branch identification on the one hand and social stratification on the other has been a consequence of central redistribution of social costs through the system of centrally directed branches. This system was destroyed after 1989. But its cultural consequence – the strong status-specific solidarity of various branches – has remained. Czech attempts to (re)establish a market economy generate the question: 'What system of social cost distribution is able to satisfy the seemingly paradoxical attitude of people who do not prefer massive redistribution on one hand and who (at the same time) wish to be protected against the uncompromising market on the other?'

The most probable solution of this 'paradox' is an institutional network of status-segregated insurance funds, which is compatible with the corporatist model of the welfare state (Esping-Andersen, 1990). The capacity of this type of state social policy to displace the market as a provider of welfare and to give guarantees for social security against the fluctuations of the market, and, at the same time, to limit massive redistribution, seems very important in Czech conditions.

With great simplification, we can say that a Czech citizen confronts the dilemma of civic and status-specific solidarity with the attitudes of an individualist imbued with paternalism habits: 'Let everyone take care of himself on his own but I want to have my standard secured'. It means that the designers of Czech social policy will have to draft social legislation which would guarantee all citizens their usual standard of living and which would not require an extensive redistribution of income through high taxation and payments into general social funds. The political elites of the Czech Republic could lose their legitimacy at the moment when the Czech public senses an extreme exposure to the arbitrariness of the market. They could also lose their legitimacy, however, when the people realize that they do not have the living standard to which they feel 'entitled' due to having to support other social groups by their taxes.

We believe the requirement to be protected against the vagaries of the market and the idea of the automatic entitlement for 'my standard of welfare' can be combined in universalistic social legislation which will guarantee everyone's social status and at the same time facilitate the financing of social provisions on the basis of status-specific solidarity. Were such a concept acceptable to the Czech public, it would amount to a corporatist social policy based on social entitlements clearly guaranteed by the authority of the state. This combination of paternalism, with the principle of self-reliance of various social strata, is not a simple consequence of the development of Czech society during the past forty years. It has much deeper historical roots.

The similarity of the hypothesized Czech form of the corporatist welfare state to its German prototype is not coincidental. The rise of civil society in the Czech Lands was strongly influenced by German and Austrian culture and education in the second half of the eighteenth and the early nineteenth centuries as pointed out by Urban (1978) and Střítecký (1990). Both argue that the modernization of state administration and the educational system, as well as the liberalization of economic legislation, resulted from the political actions of absolutist rulers. According to Urban and Střítecký, the development of both German and Czech civil societies was strongly influenced by 'modernization from the top down'. This course of development corresponded with the Enlightenment rationality which had penetrated Czech territory through German culture and education. The linguistic and national differentiation of the German and Czech communities which followed was only a secondary process that did not play a key role in initiating the rise of German and Czech civil societies.

The tendency of the Czech public to expect a guarantee of social rights from a strong central state seems to be supported by their historical experience of 'modernization from the top down'. After the Second World War, top-down modernization helped to legitimate the replacement of the market by the decision-making of a strong, 'socially oriented' political centre. Trust in such modernization has led the Czech public to accept economic and social planning as practised by communists, and it is also a source of contemporary Czech corporatism.

CONCLUSION

Czech social science has not yet elaborated on Czech corporatism. It is therefore very likely that Czech politics does not have a clear conception of the social policy the Czech public would willingly support. In this chapter we could only outline the basic features of this phenomenon. We are aware that our hypothesized trend of the development of the Czech welfare state can lead into blind alleys. It will be some time before consensus on legitimate forms of social policy is reached. However, the current uncertainty cannot last long since social peace among all social strata and groups is essential for further development in the Czech Republic. Nevertheless, to accommodate such contradictory factors as the empty Czech treasury, the mentality of a populace which demands social provisions, and the efforts of the government to introduce neo-liberal mechanisms will be very difficult.

ACKNOWLEDGEMENT

We would like to acknowledge our gratitude to our colleague Ivo Reznicek of Washington Catholic University for his valuable remarks and comments.

NOTES

1 'Really existing socialism' had many features of a traditional society. According to Šrubař (1991), in socialism, rational arrangements of society, i.e. a publicly controlled state (with a parliamentary system and the rule of law) and market economy, were turned upside down. The state was privatized by the ruling Communist Party, and the means of production were nationalized. Naturally, this has influenced the sphere of social relations. The Communist Party penetration of all levels of management and administration by means of the *nomenklatura* led to further state privatization, the last stage of which was quasi-personal appropriation. This created conditions for corruption and client–patronage networks which made the uncontrollable behaviour of party bureaucrats possible. Thus, acquired political capital was transformed into economic capital with which one could enter the 'socialist market' where goods and services were not sold but exchanged. The access to political power was rewarded by economic privileges. As Šrubař stresses, the socialist market was not the market of competing producers but the market of competing customers. The planned socialist economy was a *shortage economy* where one of the main problems was not how to sell goods but how to obtain them. Since there was no supply and demand mechanism operating in the centrally planned economy, and since the state distributive networks were no substitute for it, consumers had to organize their access to commodities by themselves. Thus, hunting out or chasing up goods was a typical activity of 'really existing socialism'. That meant, of course, that money lost its power and priority: much more important was information on where the hunted goods were available. Naturally, such conditions were hotbeds for 'socialist relations': kinship networks, client–patron networks and the system of 'knowing the right person at the right place'. These networks were the logical outcome of 'really existing socialism'. Though they were socialist networks, they were not open to everyone. Entry was possible only to those who were able to offer goods or services to be exchanged.

2 To be more precise, though rather ironic, the right to work under the conditions of the suppressed performance principle could be called the right to be physically present at work.

3 According to Večerník's (1991b) calculations, the 7 per cent figure of poor households in Czechoslovakia in the mid-1980s was really quite low in comparison with EC countries and was comparable with Belgium with its 5 per cent of poor households, the Netherlands (8 per cent) and FRG (9 per cent). However, Večerník rightly maintains that the meaning of these cross-cultural statistical comparisons is problematic, for they say nothing about the general nature of poverty and non-poverty in Western and former communist countries.

4 Very likely, unemployment in the Czech Lands is so low only temporarily. The present demographic situation is the opposite of that in the countries of the EC, where, 'in the 1990s and beyond, the prospect is for the number of young people entering the labour market

each year to decline' (*Unemployment*, 1990: 30). In Czechoslovakia, the irrational and even controversial population policy of the previous regime led to about 400,000 'excess' children being born in the period of 1973–7. This represented about 5 per cent of the working force in 1987 (Rabušic, 1990). From 1992 to 1997 the labour market in Czechoslovakia will have to absorb a large influx of young people each year, better educated and anxious to exploit the opportunities of the post-totalitarian society. It is clear now that demand for labour will be much lower then its supply. The full employment that had existed in Czechoslovakia up to 1990 was maintained only at the cost of underemployment. The market mechanisms will definitely remove many of these unneeded jobs, thus reducing the labour force enormously. Such a situation would be critical in any society. Unluckily, in Czechoslovakia, at the same time, we will have the 1970s' baby-boomers entering the labour market and demanding jobs.

5 Mokrzycki (1991) noted that resistance against liberal economic reform in post-communist countries was an expression of efforts of social groups to defend their wealth (no matter how modest the wealth was) and their long-term-built small privileges.

6 For instance, 55 per cent of respondents in the Czech Republic and 35 per cent in the Slovak Republic manifested liberal attitudes in a national survey carried out in September 1991. Also, 59 per cent of Czechs and 50 per cent of Slovaks preferred freedom to equality (EVSS, 1991). On the other hand, in an April 1992 opinion poll to choose the three most important rights (Boguszak, 1992), only 42 per cent of Czechoslovak respondents chose freedom of speech, 20 per cent chose the right to free elections, 8 per cent freedom of the press and 6 per cent freedom of association. Rights to social benefits – the right to free medical care, to work, and to minimum welfare – were clearly preferred by large percentages.

7 The same neo-liberal euphoria was also recorded by Edmund Mokrzycki (1991) in Poland and Rudolf Andorka (personal communication, 1991) in Hungary. By the way, our social surveys of a representative sample of the population of Brno carried out in 1990 and 1991 revealed that hidden and latent paternalistic codes of behaviour were covered by manifested liberal attitudes (Mareš, *et al.*, 1991).

8 Rabušic (1990) and Možný and Rabušic (1992) maintain that the Czechoslovak (pronatalist) population policy of the past communist regime has had many latent functions and unintended consequences. One of them was that it successfully lured young people (at the age of 20–22) into getting married and having a family through the various subsidies which made births of second and third children advantageous, through long maternity leaves, advantageous marriage loans (extremely low interest rate and partial loan forgiveness after the birth of the first child), etc. They also pushed them into parenthood by high taxation of childlessness and, perhaps most effectively, by the practical impossibility of getting an apartment for unmarried and/or childless couples – and single persons as well (Možný and Rabušic, 1992).

9 The liberal welfare state was characterized by Esping-Andersen (1990: 26) as 'a regime which minimizes decommodification effects, erects an order of stratification that is a blend of relative equality of poverty among state welfare recipients, market-differentiated welfare among the majorities, and a class-political dualism between the two'. According to him, in such welfare-state regimes means-tested assistance, modest universal transfers, and modest social insurance plans predominate. Benefits cater mainly for clients of low income, and entitlement rules are associated with stigma.

10 In the Netherlands, for instance, the level of interpersonal trust measured by Eurobarometers has been quite high for more then a decade: about 90 per cent of people say that they can generally trust other people. In Czechoslovakia, however, it is quite low: about 25 per cent in the Czech Republic and 20 per cent in the Slovak Republic (EVSS, 1991).

11 As Šrubař (1991) explained, one's social status and one's social role in socialism were not only determined by one's performance but also by one's connections with social class and effective networks. They formed one's social background and identity. Such a situation has had an important implication: the self-definition of the individual could hardly be based on self-confidence and reliance on one's own abilities. The existence of social networks contributed to differences between 'them' and 'us'. 'Them' were not confined to those in Communist Party structures, but included all of those whom one did not know and who were potentially one's enemies. This also had another negative consequence. A higher standard of living was perceived with suspicion and often regarded as immoral, for it was either the outcome of political privilege, in which case it was not due to one's merit, or it was due to connections with right networks, in which case it was not legal. We can expect that in the transitional period, the mechanisms of socialist networks will still exist. The questions for the future are these: after the privatization of economy stratifies society by income and wealth will social inequality be perceived by the public as legitimate and will it be accepted? The accumulation of capital has either happened already in the old socialist days, or it is going to happen as former family property is recovered. In both cases, Šrubař predicts, the capital gained will be regarded as undeserved or illegal, as something that is not the consequence of one's own abilities and performance.

REFERENCES

Boguszak, M. (1992) 'Než začne kampaň' (Before the Campaign Starts), *MF Dnes*, April 29.

Dahrendorf, R. (1990). *The Modern Social Conflict*. Berkeley and Los Angeles: University Press.

De Deken, J. (1992) 'Sociální politika a politika solidarity' (Social Policy and the Politics of Solidarity), *Sociologický časopis*, 3: 351–68.

Esping-Andersen, G. (1990) *The Three Worlds of Welfare Capitalism*, Princeton, NJ: Princeton University Press.

EVSS (*European Value System Study data set*), Prague 1991.

Flora, P. and Heidenheimer, A.J. (eds) (1987) *The Development of Welfare States in Europe and America*, New Brunswick and London: Transaction Books.

Hankiss, E. (1990) 'In Search of Paradigm,' *Daedalus*, Winter, pp. 183–214.

Higgins, J. (1981). *States of Welfare. Comparative Analysis in Social Policy*, Oxford: Martin Robertson/Basil Blackwell.

Hiršl, M. (1992) 'Chudoba a nouze v Československu' (Poverty and Indigence in Czechoslovakia), *Demografie*, 2: 137–42.

Inglehart, R. (1990) *Culture Shift in Advanced Industrial Society*, Princeton, NJ: Princeton University Press.

Jackson, J.O. (1992) 'Can This Marriage Be Saved?' *Time International*, 6 July: pp. 24–6.

Janáček, K. (1992) 'K vybraným sociálním efektům transformace československé ekonomiky' (Some Social Effects of Economic Transformation in Czechoslovakia), *Sociologický časopis*, 3: 386–93.

Lamper, I. (1991) 'Nejhorší nás teprve čeká' (The Worst Can Be Only Expected), *Respekt*, 27 May – 2 June.

Mareš, P., Musil, L. and Rabušic, L. (1991) 'Sociální změna očima české veřejnosti' (Social Change by Eyes of Czech Public), *Sociologický časopis*, 6.

—— (1992): 'Vox Populi, Vox Dei?' (Czechoslovakia 1992), Paper presented at the First European Conference of Sociology, Vienna, 26–9 August.

Matějů, P. and Řeháková, B. (1992) 'Od nespravedlivé rovnosti ke spravedlivé nerovnosti? Percepce sociálních nerovnostíca sociální spravedlnosti v sončasném Československu' (From Unjust Equality to Just Inequality? Perception of Inequality and Social Justice in Contemporary Czechoslovakia), *Sociologický časopis*, no. 3.

Mokrzycki, E. (1991) 'Dědictví reálného socialismu a západní demokracie' (Legacy of Real Socialism and Western Democracy), *Sociologický časopis*, 6: 751–7.

Možný, I. (1991) *Proč tak snadno?* (Why so Easy?), Prague: Slon.

—— and Rabušic, L. (1992) 'Unmarried Cohabitation in Czechoslovakia', *Sociologický časopis*, 5.

Narušíme princip solidarity? (Shall we Break the Principle of Solidarity?) (1992) Lidová Demokracie, 85: 1.

Rabušic, L. (1990) 'Manifestní a latentní funkce čs. populační politiky' (Manifest and Latent Functions of Czechoslovak Population Policy), *Demografie*, 3: 234–8.

Šrubař, I. (1991) 'Společnost a sítě' (Society and its Networks), *Přítomnost*, no. 2: 13–15.

Střítecký, J. (1990) 'Die Tschechische nationale Wiedergeburt: Mythem und Denkanstösse. *Bohemia*, 31(1): 38–54.

Titmus, R.M. (1969) *Essays on 'The Welfare State'*, Boston: Beacon Press.

Unemployment in Europe 1990, Luxembourg: Office for Official Publications of the European Communities, 1990.

Urban, O. (1978) *Kapitalismus a česká společnost* (Capitalism and Czech society), Prague: Svoboda.

Večerník, J. (1991a) 'Distribuční systém v socialistickém Československu: empirická fakta výkladové hypotézny (The System of Distribution in Socialist Czechoslovakia: Empirical Data and Explanatory Hypotheses), *Sociologický časopis*, no. 1.

—— (1991b) 'Úvod do studia chudoby v Československu' (Introduction to the Study of Poverty in Czechoslovakia), *Sociologický časopis*, no. 5.

Chapter 6

Revolution and restoration
On the origins of right-wing radical ideology in Hungary

Andrew Arato

INTRODUCTION

The idea of the 'self-limiting revolution' represents one of the major contributions of recent East European thought and action to political philosophy.[1] And yet from the outset, from the times of the first Solidarity, this idea was scornfully rejected by would-be radical revolutionaries, largely but not exclusively from the nationalist right. Of course, as long as the geopolitical reasons for strategic self-limitation, rooted in an intact Soviet imperium, continued to apply, it was not fully apparent that a minority of intellectuals and movement militants also promoted a self-limiting radicalism on historical and normative grounds. Given the strategic reasons, there was no apparent need to argue fully a case that would have contributed to ideological divisions within the opposition – divisions that were pragmatically unnecessary.

With the happy collapse of the geopolitical context of self-limitation, the idea of radical revolution has clearly reappeared at least among some intellectuals and politicians. And yet, as the continued use of adjectives like 'peaceful', 'velvet', 'gentle', 'quiet', 'bloodless', 'negotiated', 'legal', and 'constitutional' indicate, there has been, at least for a time, a reluctance, on a wide variety of grounds, to define or interpret the East European transitions as revolutions in the classical sense of the modern revolutionary tradition.

In what follows, I will first give reasons for retention of the notion of self-limiting revolution; and then consider why, mainly in the form of revolutionary restorationism, radical revolutionary ideology is nevertheless experiencing a revival among political forces even in Hungary, perhaps the least revolutionary of East and East-Central European societies. I will point to the present

political weakness of this revival, as well as the normative complex
from which, even so, it may continue to draw its energies.

SYSTEM CHANGE OR REVOLUTION?

The most common term Hungarians use for their political changes
is *rendszerváltás*, literally 'exchange of systems'. The term has
endured in spite of the prime minister's, and subsequently
his party's, the MDF's, stated preference for *rendszerváltozás*,
'change of system'. One exchanges horses, not systems, Antall
liked to say. Possibly the MDF's one-time defence of a slower, less
radical model of change was originally responsible for this preference. Equally likely, the introduction of the first term by the
rival SzDSz, championing rapid transformation in its famous blue
book, played a major role in the terminological conflict (SzDSz,
1989).

Change of system and subsystem

The idea of a change of systems without a global subject behind
this process seems particularly appropriate for Hungarian conditions. While in all the other countries of East and Central Europe
one can register the decomposition of old structures and the
neutralization of old systems in co-ordination, it is in Hungary that
one can speak most of the emergence of new subsystems, as well
as an overarching social system, even if the processes are hardly
completed. Instead of a single party political system based on the
nomenklatura model of selection, Hungary has a multi-party
political system largely based on free elections at both national
and provincial levels. Even if the exact nature of the party system
is not yet determined (polarized, mildly polarized via two rival
coalitions, etc.), it certainly seems as stable as new party systems
introduced elsewhere in post-war Europe – thanks in part to a
viable electoral law and fairly well established parties. Moreover,
in spite of attempts to re-establish old forms of dependence and
central control, Hungary already has a more autonomous system
of local administration than some Western European countries
whose model the ruling coalition could not impose because of the
pressure of the opposition.

Turning to the cultural system, instead of a model based on
political constraint and strong mechanisms of censorship and

self-censorship, the country now has a dynamic and active public sphere in spite of government pressures to instrumentalize the press and the media. The ability of the public sphere to fight these pressures has been remarkable. While the legal system is by no means fully altered, and the independence of the courts is still at issue, the constitutional court (the most successful in the region) has come to enjoy an entirely new independence, representing thereby an important stepping stone to constitutionalism. Compared to only a few years ago, a remarkable number of independent associations has emerged; and, if their input into big politics has been limited, their sectoral and local role, expressed in part through the national media, should not be underestimated.

Perhaps most importantly of all, Hungary has gone a long way in the economic sphere from command structures or even the co-ordinating primacy of informal regulation towards the primacy of market forms of co-ordination – despite the slowing down of the privatization of the state sector and attempts to restatize some industries which had earlier enjoyed a large measure of manager-led decentralization. Most crucial in this context has been 'indirect privatization': in other words the vast increase of new forms of private enterprise, using both domestic and foreign capital, thereby displacing the overall weight of ownership and employment in the direction of purely market-oriented forms – although this too has slowed down from late 1991 (Petschnig, 1992). To be sure, one cannot fully determine on this level whether the threshold between a primarily state-owned, redistributive, command economy, based on soft budgetary constraints and a market economy has been definitively passed. Based on what has happened in the related political subsystem, one can only say that the chances of Hungary passing this threshold relatively soon, though not independent of policy choices, remain rather good.

The rate of change in the various subsystems is of course not the same. There is some consensus that while the political system change is more or less completed, the economic system change lags far behind. And yet, in my view at least, the foundations for new central institutions and systems of co-ordination are laid down in all subsystems with the possible exception so far of the state administration which continues to control the larger part of the national economy. The statism of the ruling coalition has indeed reinforced this type of continuity, which, significantly, has been registered for the great revolutions by some of their foremost students, beginning with Tocqueville. To evaluate the meaning of this continuity, however, one must look at the system as a whole within which it persists.

While it remains controversial how to define the principle of organization for the societies of the Soviet type, I continue to stress in this context the general social primacy of a political prerogative or discretionary power (Arato, 1982). In the Hungarian case this organizational principle, in my view, has been replaced by that of a liberal democratic rule-of-law state, even if it has not yet been securely established. The counter-evidence for an exchange of systems is that many of the same people continue to occupy important positions in political, economic and cultural life. This argument exaggerates, however, both the centrality and the number of those who have managed to convert their earlier power and position into new forms. More importantly, it also confuses the issue of replacing structures with that of replacing individuals. Those who state it are not deterred by the parallel between their own proposals and earlier communist purges; in their view the historically cumulate effect of the old regime's purges and *nomenklatura* can be reversed only by new forms of social purification. The lustration laws of the Czech and Slovak Republics indicate that the problem is hardly a Hungarian one alone. And yet the focus on persons and elites may once again displace the real issue relevant to rapid system change: the transformation of institutions and the patterns of social interaction (Szabó, 1992).

To be sure one need not support quasi-revolutionary blacklists and purges to argue that little has changed in Hungary outside the political system narrowly defined – the top of the social pyramid as it were (cf. Teller, 1992, who in any case seeks a remedy in the promotion of the countervailing power of the self-organization of civil society). This alternative argument focuses on the survival of old elites, perhaps identifying this sociological category (rather than persons and job-holders individually) with structures and institutions against which the liberal opposition always concentrated its fire. But even this distinction is wrong. Even elites can survive and play a very different historical role in the context of changes of institutions and mechanisms of co-ordination. In the case of state-socialist societies, the complete transformation of hitherto hegemonic political systems can leave nothing else intact even if other changes lag behind.

Of course the persistence of the same office-holders, many of whom now owe their jobs to democratic national, and even more local, elections can be extremely repulsive to those who have suffered. It is in this context that some radical fighters against the old regime now affirm their radical revlutionary intentions (cf. Sükösd, 1992). Undoubtedly, their radicalism feeds on the missing or disappointed subjective components of revolutionary transformation.

The absence of revolutionary experience

The term *rendszerváltás* is peculiarly appropriate for Hungarian conditions not only because of what it says, but also because of what it is silent about. It is a strangely colourless term capable of inspiring little passion or enthusiasm. It expresses the fact that many Hungarians, whenever they refer to the transformation as a revolution, feel obliged to add not only constitutional and negotiated, peaceful and bloodless, but also quiet and sad. At times these last adjectives are even applied to *rendszerváltás*, doubling the effect. And indeed compared to other countries – Poland with the history of Solidarity as a mass movement; East Germany, Czechoslovakia, Bulgaria, and even Russia at the time of the attempted putsch, with their popular movements – Hungary's population was strangely quiescent through the radical changes. There were, to be sure, key events in the transition, but these were either well-organized peaceful demonstrations set in limited time-frames, or events in which elites encountered other elites. The petition campaign on the presidency in November 1989 was only a partial exception to the trend. Subsequently, increasingly low electoral participation also showed that Hungary's revolution was hardly joyful.

Evidently many leading politicians preferred a quiet non-revolutionary transformation in 1989 and 1990. More than just strategic geopolitical reasons were involved. Prime Minister Antall does occasionally use the term (peaceful or quiet) 'revolution' for public consumption. In his own circle, however, he is known for his rather spiteful remark to critics, apparently a rationalization of his statist conservatism: 'You ought to have made a revolution.' Gáspár Miklós Tamás, a leading voice of the conservative-liberal wing of SzDSz, did affirm the revolutionary nature of non-reformist system change as part of a polemic against others in his own party still insisting on a Polish-type radical reformism. But the idea of a social revolution filled him with horror, and he soon stopped speaking about any kind of revolution except in negative terms. Finally, the core of the democratic opposition, originally advocates of a Polish-type radical reformism, though the first to realize that the geopolitical reasons for self-limitation were disintegrating, nevertheless adhered to a strategy of self-limitation throughout the transition. While they were no longer ready to offer institutional concessions to the communists, as was Antall's MDF almost till the bitter end, they tried to defeat such concessions only through a completely legal loophole, allowing referenda on even constitutional issues. Their normatively based opposition to radical revolution continued even as the strategic reasons for self-organization evaporated, as they were the first to recognize. They posited, moreover, the avoidance of reprivatization, political justice, and campaigns against job-holders as the necessary tokens of self-limitation that could not be sacrificed, for reasons of fundamental principle, to any mass revolutionary sentiments.

The strategy of course affected the labelling. At the time of the key negotiations of 1989, almost no one (Tamás was the one exception I know of) spoke of the transition at hand as a revolution. After the 'German' and 'velvet' revolutions, some Hungarian authors and political actors began to occasionally use the term, as it were retrospectively, but always with the adjectives already mentioned. Social scientists remained consistently sceptical. They too preferred the term *rendszerváltás*, and if they needed a substitute they borrowed 'transition' from Latin American discussions, 'great transformation' from Karl Polanyi, or the half-serious 'refolution' (even *'reforradalom'*) from Garton Ash (Bozóki, 1992). The one significant exception is Bruszt (1989) who referred to Hungary's 'negotiated revolution'. Many would agree with Akos Szilágyi who commented that the most revolutionary event in all Eastern Europe was the avoidance of revolution (Szilágyi, 1992).

Even those who tended to use the term 'revolution' in Hungary with various qualifying adjectives had at first no interest and even less ability to make up for the missing experience admitted by all. But the case of the FKgP (the Independent Smallholders' Party) is interesting. After the first decision of the Constitutional Court rejecting the reprivatization only of land in October 1990, members began to speak openly of the impasse of the bloodless revolution and the beginning of the counter-revolution. These characterizations were meant to mobilize a given constituency behind the programme of reprivatization, which after the first relevant court decision, now denounced as counter-revolutionary, could no longer supposedly be achieved through a bloodless revolution or exchange of systems. Were the speakers promoting a violent second revolution? Not yet openly, it would seem. At most, members of the FKgP called for a new constitution or the abolition of the Constitutional Court or both. But the indirect reference declaiming the end of the bloodless revolution is revealing enough.

In 1991 and 1992 the populist wing of the MDF, too, got into trouble with some of the key (as it were counter-majoritarian) institutions of post-communist Hungary – the press, the presidency, and the Constitutional Court which would not give parliament a free hand against these other institutions. The Court in particular continued to interfere with the reprivatization plans of the coalition, as well as its attempts at political justice. It was in this context that some of the leading figures of the MDF, such as István Csurka, Gyula Fekete and Imre Kónya, discovered that the arrangements in whose negotiation they had played a major part amounted to a 'stolen', or 'betrayed' or 'embezzled' revolution. These adjectives, as well as the thinly disguised call for a second revolution, belong, of course, to the classical vocabulary of the great revolutions. 'It seems that there is a great price to pay for the bloodless character of the peaceful revolution, when the street is not possessed by the revolutionary people . . . is it a revloution at all?' (Fekete, 1992: 9). In the Hungarian context this tirade is directed against those who insisted on keeping the rules of the game agreed at the round tables, and later between the two major parties, MDF and SzDSz. It is also directed against the supposed beneficiaries of these rules, office-holders in the press and the media who have not come round to the celebration of the coalition government.

How can a revolution that has not happened be betrayed? The revolution did not happen because the elites betrayed the people and deprived it of its possible experience of victory, argued a leader of one such elite, the most important one. Power remained in the hands of old power-holders claimed the party controlling the new governmental power. Curiously their argument was supported by some who considered the round table agreements, the electoral law, and the monopolization of the political field by merely six parties as betrayal from the outset. On the one hand they denounced the dictatorship of parties in parliament; on the other they declared their support for 'this government, this parliament . . . if they too are in opposition to the Communism organised among us and above us' (Zsille, 1992: 199–200).

Relationship to the revolutionary tradition

The advocates of a second revolution are thus not sure if they wish for a revolution of civil society from below, or a state-led revolution from above. This dilemma is, of course, inherent in the Jacobin–Bolshevik tradition. Hungary's new Jacobins reject this tradition all the same, even if their rhetorical devices – like Csurka's constant talk of national and international conspiracy, Kónya's implied distinction between the empirical and the authentic people, and the very different calls for a real or second revolution – very much resemble intellectual devices of that tradition. But in Hungary, after forty years of a Bolshevik or neo-Bolshevik regime, any positive references to its heritage remain off limits. This effects the semantics of key actors. No one describes himself or herself as a revolutionary, nor are actions, institutions, events or processes so described. The semantical revival inherent in the talk about conspiracy, enemies, and counter-revolution remains partial. The young activists of Fidesz who eschew all such terminology are far more characteristic of the population than the populist demagogues who selectively use it. All the same, even the selective use is striking given that the most revolutionary rhetoric comes from the most determined anti-communists.

One explanation lies in the fact that Hungary has another revolutionary tradition, symbolized by the dates 1848 and 1956, which indeed belongs to the central symbolic core of national politics. The power of their interrelated heritage is by no means exhausted. Every Hungarian regime since the Compromise of 1867 has tried to use the symbols of 1848 for its own legitimating purposes. The commemoration of its initiating events on 15 March has been an important contested ritual from the nineteenth century to the communist regime (which de-emphasized the holiday) to the dissidents of the 1980s (who tried to revive it) (Hofer, 1992). Similarly, even small demonstrations on 23

October and 16 June, two central dates commemorating 1956 and its bloody defeat, were important for the opposition when it sought to delegitimate the Kádárist regime. The official redefinition of 1956 as a national uprising, and the national reburial of Imre Nagy and his comrades on 16 June 1989, completed this process of delegitimation.

Nevertheless, reference to the heritage of 1848, and even more to 1956, has not been easy (Pomogáts, 1992). To an extent, they both belonged to the classical tradition of revolutions and attempts to redefine them within the context of the new East European politics of self-limitation have not been particularly convincing. Kossuth and his collaborators were not 'constitutional revolutionaries' since there was no modern constitution whose rules they could use for change, and they sought to overthrow the heritage precisely of estate Hungary (Hofer, 1992: 38). Nor was the idea of revolutionary dictatorship far from their minds once they were in open war with foreign invaders. Similarly, while it may have been technically correct (and politically understandable in 1986) to make the workers' councils after the second Soviet intervention of November 1956 into forerunners of the self-limiting revolution of Solidarity, the parallel remains artificial and selective given the whole context of 1956 (Kis, 1989). Neither 1848–49, nor especially 1956, can be made sense of within a model of non-violence. Moreover, in 1989 no important political force was willing to revive crucial aspects of the political programmes of 1956, especially the elements of direct and industrial democracy and of dual power. The influence of the radical democratic ideas of Istvan Bibó, the leading political philosopher of 1956, was negligible in 1989 in spite of his great importance for both the populist writers and the democratic opposition of the 1980s.

Most importantly, both 1848 and 1956 had the character of *national* struggles of *liberation*. The domestic enemies of the revolutions had in both cases overwhelmingly powerful foreign supporters. In 1989 on the other hand the international context only facilitated a transformation whose internal enemies had no significant foreign support. Indeed the late Kádárist regime helped to destabilize dramatically the sources of whatever support they could have had (in the GDR for example). This points to the fact that the transformation of 1989 did not even have major, readily identifiable, internal enemies. The reformist Kádárist regime, and especially post-Kádárist regime, managed to the end to avoid a scenario in which 'we' the people arrayed against 'them' the power structure (Bruszt, 1989).

The tradition of the extremely short-lived 1956 revolution provides absolutely no guidance or framework for those who seek to act in the present. Indeed one can derive entirely opposite models from it, street violence or self-limitation, party pluralism or council democracy, alliance with reform communists or utter hostility to them, etc. In addition, the context for the revival of the traditions of 1848 and 1956, to the great chagrin of some veterans of the latter, is entirely missing in 1989 and after. The symbolism and the commemoration of those revolutions could be, and were, used to delegitimate the Kádárist regime without providing anything like positive symbolic identifications, let alone strategic guidance, to the actors of 1989. If it is true, as Hofer argues, that the peaceful demonstrations were meant to and did frighten the regime by recalling the spectre of 1956, there is little evidence that the option of open rebellion in the streets was any less frightening to the majority of the population. In this context, 1956 represented a negative scenario for both sides, regime and opposition. The shared positive scenario was a negotiated and legal transfer of power, following both the actual Polish model as well as all major oppositional programmes.

Hungary's population was in a conservative rather than revolutionary mood in 1989 (Tamás, 1992). The victory of the MDF, originally promising a slow transition with a soft landing, was built upon this premise. Elements of the ruling coalition, notably the Christian Democrats and the group around the prime minister, sought to channel the conservative mood in the statist-traditional, anti-secular and anti-republican direction they favoured. The disappointment of some veterans of 1956 had to be great, but, given the prevailing mood, they could do little to revive their cause – especially since the most radical forces for system change, the radical liberal SzDSz and Fidesz, were willing to integrate only those '56ers who accepted the programme of a self-limiting, peaceful, and above all fully legal, exchange of systems. More radical would-be heirs of 1956 were to come up against the last of these limitations; ambitions fuelled by memories of open and violent conflict with the communists were incompatible with the legal and constitutional limits agreed upon by the combined opposition, enshrined in the round table agreements, and on the whole enforced by Hungary's active Constitutional Court.

THE RETURN OF RADICAL REVOLUTION?

There is a remarkable consensus in Hungary according to which the change of systems did not take a revolutionary path. My analysis confirms this consensus by demonstrating that only in some dimensions did the transformation correspond to the model of modern revolutions. At the same time I have shown that there is no agreement whether or not the avoidance of revolution has been desirable. The views of those minorities that lament the 'embezzlement' or 'betrayal' of revolution before it could occur would not in themselves add up to much unless they were parts of a general political programme to which they could contribute. There is such a programme in Hungary, one of revolutionary–restorationist *étatisme*.[2] In turn this programme would be less formidable if at least some of its components were not supported by individuals of very different political philosophies, left-wing and even liberal.

Let me identify four projects of the right that point to a radical revolutionary direction, or reinforce a revolutionary sensibility: (1) restoration, (2) purges leading to elite changes, (3) political justice, and (4) authoritarian state strengthening. Taken singly each of these is not exclusively a project of the right, but their combination is, and this combination is in fact embodied as such in the present governmental coalition. This coalition came to power on the basis of a clever combination of conservatism and systemic change. But in power, given popular dissatisfaction with the way things are and with its own performance, as well as the relatively modest appeal of its favourite themes of religion, nation and family, the coalition has been increasingly attracted by revolutionary themes. Many of its members thus compulsively talk as if not they, but someone else, were in power. This ploy, too, has been historically common in radical revolutions.

Restoration

Under the peculiar conditions of the Hungarian change of systems, revolution and restoration belong conceptually together. The rage to restore depends on diverse interests, the restorers differing greatly about what they wish to restore. The focal points have included the restoration of the 1947 post-land reform ownership of land (FKgP), the semi-compulsory religious education and church real estate of the same period – but in large part inherited from before the war (KDNP) – and the symbolism of the violation of Hungary by the Treaty of Trianon and even that of a just war against Soviet Communism (MDF). The first two of these parties in themselves restore elements of pre-communist political reality. More quietly the largely intact state apparatus would also like to restore something, specifically its own role and open dominance in both the pre-war and late-Kádárist epochs, willingly dressed up in the imagery of traditional pre-Second World War *étatisme* and paternalism. Finally veterans and partisans of 1956 wish to restore at least the symbols, and to some extent the programmes, of that revolution. Only the liberals have little wish to restore anything, given the backward and deformed nature of pre-communist liberal, democratic and capitalist institutions. (This is in contrast to the economic liberals of the Czech Republic with its very different history who are violent restorers with respect to property (reprivatization), and who in other respects, too, have jumped on the restorationist–revolutionary bandwagon (political justice, purges).)

As a pamphlet of the oppositional SzDSz rightly assumes, 1937, 1947 and 1987 do not represent symbols and arrangements supported by any general consensus, to say the least. Even 1956, as we have seen, does not inspire much enthusiasm. Equally important, the adherents of these dates, or rather of the four different targets of restoration, disagree among themselves, and often reject one another's dreams. Thus the idea of restoration could not make any more clear now than its previous incarnations what exactly should be restored and where to stop (Vogelin, 1975: 175ff.).

But if the restorationists need revolution, revolutionaries without a positive model of the future cannot do without restoration. Since the main revolutionary heritage of the West cannot be referred to, and the specific Hungarian traditions are clearly inapplicable in the present, only a highly selective use of these traditions and their semantic potentials is possible. In particular, omission of the philosophy of history of both revolutionary traditions – the progression of historical stages and the picture of the just society projected into the future, the very building blocks of revolutionary legitimacy – leaves these traditions impoverished. Without it the temporal relationship sustaining the difference between revolution and restoration, from the point of view of either, is gone. Forwards and backwards become meaningless terms. The road is open to try to replace the future by the past as the orientation point of a revolutionary–restorationist philosophy of history. The question then is whether an imagined past can become any more a focus for mobilization than an imagined future. If it cannot, the revival of other semantic aspects of the revolutionary tradition, in particular the whole vocabulary of enemies, conspiracy and betrayed revolution will remain rather shallow.

The problem with the restorationist revolution is not that it could in fact restore anything, Horthy's or Rakosi's, Bethlen's or Kádár's Hungary. Even reprivatization of land or church real estate might not achieve its goals in the face of determined opposition at all levels and the impracticality of the proposals once concretized. Hungarian society is simply too different from its predecessors for that. But, whatever the intentions of specific actors, this ideology could provide a legitimating cover for new authoritarian strategies.

Purges of elites

In Hungary as well as Poland, it is the right that wishes to *accelerate* the replacement of former office-holders by new individuals supposedly untainted by the past.[3] In both countries the Round Table agreements have been considered responsible for a type of transition that allowed members of the old elite to save or convert its power. The Polish right, excluded from the negotiations, cries out, ahistorically, against a red–pink alliance. The MDF's radicals, very much part of the negotiations in which the SzDSz was more intransigent than they, now pretend that there is a red–liberal alliance protecting the old elites. Indeed, the MDF has made the promise of 'spring cleaning' one of its most effective campaign slogans; it helped the party get rid of a certain collaborationist image acquired in 1989 at the conclusion of the National Round Table and during the referendum campaign that followed. It should be noted, however, that, contrary to the party's earlier promises 'spring cleaning' was directed against persons rather than institutions; in other words it removed job-holders but failed to confront the administrative structures of the existing paternalist–statist system (Szabó, 1992). After the election the resulting policy spared all officials who joined the parties of the ruling coalition, or who managed to establish links with government on a new basis. And while the number may not have been great so far, firings have been centrally located and sufficiently numerous to put officials, managers and expert employees on notice that lukewarm support for governmental programmes or joining or even slightly favouring opposition parties cannot be to their advantage.

Who is most exposed to the threat of removal? The crucial variable is conflict with the existing government, not collaboration in the past. Most exposed are those in a position to interfere with the political projects of the ruling coalition, especially members of the press and the electronic media, and office-holders in those areas where a network of second stringers who support the governmental parties and are willing to become its clients are available and ready (notably state and economic administration, and the realm of culture).

Political justice

Political justice is closely related to purges of personnel, but it is even more symbiotically linked with a revolutionary discourse. The close relation is evident of course in the 'lustration' bills passed in Czechoslovakia and Bulgaria, where retroactive justice would bar the road to public employment. Even in Hungary, where in the case of the retroactive Zétényi–Takács law aimed at the murderers, torturers and 'traitors' of the period between December 1944(!) and May 1990, the connection is more difficult to see technically, some proponents of the legislation see it as a way of breaking the surviving power of the communist 'new class'. Political justice very much helps to intensify the revolutionary stakes. Unlike purges, political justice in the context of a change of systems implies revolution in its own domain, a (revolutionary) break in legality. This is the case because, while the firing of present state employees after an election can be represented as only a question of policy, the punishing of individuals for their past acts under the old regime requires an answer to the delicate question: by what law should they be judged? Most relevant acts were not crimes or wrongs by the legal system of the time, and the laws of the present had not yet been written. The ban against retroactive legislation is fundamental for the rule of law, breaking that ban implies that there is no *Rechtsstaat*. Using the 'rubber paragraphs' of politically inspired and often changed communist statutes or governmental decrees, as in the case of the treason paragraph of the Hungarian criminal code which the Zétényi bill relied upon, means using the devices of a system permanently based on something inherited from revolutionary justice, the dominance of political prerogative over law. Such reliance can only weaken the respect for law in the present, because, far from being used, the legislation in question should be abolished as part of the move to a rule-of-law constitutional state.

There are pragmatic as well as normative difficulties in the face of political justice. In the ex-Soviet-type society a very large number of people could in principle be affected by the application of political justice in both criminal and civil cases. That could create legal chaos. But it's equally possible that courts would in the end condemn very few people, thus greatly diminishing popular support for the rule of law and independent courts. This surely would have been the case with the Zétényi–Takács law in Hungary which was resisted from the outset by the legal profession in general and judges in particular. For these reasons the government and the ministry of justice sought to escape responsibility for such a programme by hiding behind the coalition parties, especially the MDF. Nevertheless, the repeated intrusion of the issue in the public sphere, in and of itself promotes a revolutionary discourse that comes in handy for actors who feel constrained by the 'legal' character of the 'revolution'. The FKgP, for example, became interested in political justice only to help counter the court's decision on the question of land reprivatization, hoping to show the criminality of post- (but not pre-) 1947 expropriations which would supposedly make current expropriation of collectives and at least some of their originally landless members into acts of justice.

Authoritarian state structuring

Tocqueville's insight about the state-strengthening logic of revolutions has been amply confirmed by social historians for the great revolutions in the tradition of the French (Skocpol, 1979). Could systemic change directed against authoritarian states avoid this logic? If such was the aim of the Eastern European strategy of the self-limiting revolution, the actual changes in Eastern Europe during 1989 and 1990 have all raised the spectre of new forms of statism, responding to a variety of economic and political

problems. While most critics of authoritarianism feared in particular the institution of presidentialism, as the Hungarian case
shows, parliamentarianism too is not automatically incompatible
with statism, or indeed with forms of authoritarianism. It is well-
known, of course, that parliament in its classical form was meant
to be a mediation between civil society and state power, aggregating the wills of the former and controlling and limiting the latter
(Habermas, 1989). In spite of great changes in form, modern
parliaments, at least in Western Europe and North America,
continue to exercise these two interrelated functions. But, under
current Eastern European conditions, claims of a purely parliamentary sovereignty as well as the practice of majoritarian democracy interfere with both of them. They produce an aspiration
towards what would be a semi-permanent constituent assembly,
with implicitly revolutionary practice, in need of revolutionary
legitimation. In Hungary at least, such is the back door through
which revolutionary statism can re-enter during the transition.

In the celebration about the first free parliamentary elections,
many Eastern Europeans active in new political parties forgot
about all earlier demands for the devolution of power, and the
practice of democracy on the level of civil society. Increasingly,
leading political figures redefined democratic legitimacy in terms
of the results of national parliamentary elections. 'Who elected
unions to interfere in economic policy?' asked G.M. Tamás,
an economic liberal. 'Who elected the press to become an independent fourth branch of government?', asked I. Csurka. The
questioners did not realize, or in the second case did not care, that
the diminution of the power of the institutions of civil society
diminishes the source of parliament's own power. Parliament's
mediating role with respect to the state administration would itself
then be decisively weakened.

In Hungary, for example, actions have followed words – action
to the detriment of civil society. First, the governing parties have
attempted to impose a centralistic organization of local self-
government, in this respect continuing the heritage of both old
regimes, the Horthyist and Kádárist, along with some of the
symbolism of the former. If these attempts succeeded only in part,
this was due to the two-thirds rule, which the coalition tried
to bypass in vain and the liberal parties used to negotiate a
compromise. Local Hungary thanked the coalition for its efforts
by resoundingly defeating it in the local elections. Second, the

parliamentary parties not only eliminated as pseudo-democratic a constitutional provision requiring a period of public discussion before legislative enactment of a statute, but under the pressure of the coalition refused to replace it with required consultations with genuinely concerned organizations. Third, there has been an attempt to 'parliamentarize' the press and the electronic media by the MDF by distributing influence exclusively among the parliamentary parties as Csurka repeatedly proposed, and, with the failure of this attempt, to 'governmentalize' at least part of it by controlling the economic privatization process. It is astonishing how a press extremely respectful and initially only mildly critical of the government and the coalition has been over and over depicted as dominated by their 'enemies', with effects that have already harmed the freedom of the press, in spite of the eventual failure of government to control it. Next, the relative independence of television and radio, achieved in an agreement with the opposition, became the main target of attacks. For a year and a half the resistance of the president of the republic stopped the government and the coalition from appointing new vice-presidents and later firing the capable presidents of radio and television.

While the ruling parties had only mixed success in achieving their specific goals, they managed to greatly reduce the potential influence of civil society on parliament. This they did at a time when, as a result of the agreement of MDF and SzDSz, governmental power was greatly strengthened through the constitutional provisions of a constructive vote of no confidence, and the elimination of the responsibility of individual ministers. Hungary has in effect become a *Kanzlerdemokratie* where controlling or pressuring government through parliament has become exceedingly difficult. Without open channels of outside pressure, it was easy for government to turn the parties of the coalition into voting machines. Public opinion surveys and the results of local and by-elections have in the meantime documented the massive delegitimation of the originally victorious parties in particular, and, unfortunately, through low electoral turnout especially, the party system and parliament in general.

It is of course the state administration, still deeply penetrating the economy, which has tenaciously protected its operatives in the past and is most vulnerable to the charge of preserving or converting the power of old officials. From a structural point of view, this organization, benefiting from the intended and unintended statist policies of the government, has become the most important holdover from the old regime. Ultimately, the government's instrumentalization of parliament has refurbished the power of top bureaucratic officialdom. Thus they have reason to try to deflect popular anger from themselves. Such efforts could be well-described as the cynical Tocquevilleanism of the apparatus, which involves a recognition and manipulation of the administration strengthening power of radical revolutionary projects and mobilization.

Prime Minister Antall and his second Minister of the Interior, Peter Boross, are virtuosi of cynical Tocquevilleanism. They and their experts must always have known that the Constitutional Court would reject many of their schemes for reprivatization and political justice. It was in their power to submit better legislation or no legislation at all. Similarly, they have always understood that the parliamentary opposition and President Göncz can, for a long time, block their attempt at a full take-over of radio and television. It was in their power to make compromises highly beneficial to the government, as television under Hankiss had shown in the beginning at least. It would seem that the government wanted not so much the specific goal as the crisis attendant upon it, in order to deflect attention both from its own difficulties in policy-making and management of the economy, and from the growing, clientelistic administrative apparatus which would otherwise be the natural target of the critics of insufficient systemic change.

CONCLUSION

The various projects of restoration, purges of elites, political justice and state strengthening represent a curious yet coherent mixture. Taken together they seek to remedy the supposedly insufficiently revolutionary nature of the Hungarian exchange of systems. The project of restoration provides symbolic substitutes for the spent components of the revolutionary tradition. The project of elite purges hopes to make up for the slowness of systemic change in the different subsystems of society. The project of political justice seeks to chip away, that of parliamentary absolutism to eliminate entirely, the legal and constitutional dimension of the *rendszerváltás*. None of these, however, is able to produce a revolutionary experience of either liberation or public freedom for anything more than select, and even sectarian, constituencies. Even the determined use of selected elements of classical revolutionary semantics – the talk of betrayal and counter-revolution, the drummed up fear of enemies and conspiracies, and the timid call for a second (perhaps this time noisy and extra-legal) revolution – has done little to manipulate the relevant public sentiments. Inevitably the impression is left that the second revolution would have to be from above.

Revolutions from above, however, bring up only the worst memories in ex-Soviet-type societies. This is the Achilles heel of the whole radical revolutionary project. Each of its elements has its built-in contradiction: restoration is too ambiguous about what is to be restored and how far to go; mere purges of elites on the basis of political selection do not change the institutions and social mechanisms but do endanger economic functioning; political justice produces a climate of uncertainty and threat feared by almost everyone; and state strengthening via attempts at parliamentary absolutism weakens parliament and ultimately the government itself. This weakening of parliament does not make the government strong. On the contrary, it becomes more and more dependent on its apparatus, and is forced into repeated concessions which allow the rebuilding of the Kádárist administration in nationalist colours. Moreover, the reinforcement of the existing state apparatus only preserves and reproduces the clientelistic networks and elite bargaining processes that led to the economic failure of the Kádárist regime in the first place. In this sense, too, the strengthening of the state apparatus has not and cannot lead to a strong government. On the contrary, its weakness and inconsistency in the recent two years have been striking. When these become evident, the search for enemies in parliament, press and society as a whole in the name of national unity is resumed. This search has now become almost delirious in the writings of Csurka (1992a, 1992b). In the context of revolution from above, various fragments of traditional revolutionary semantics are used not only to legitimate projects, to establish symbolic links between their different adherents and to drum up support, but also to help manage the resulting conflicts. Especially the revival of revolutionary semantics organized around a friend–enemy complex is slated to play this role. The power of this language in its class form may be spent, but in its right-wing populist form it should not be underestimated.

NOTES

1 On this concept, invented by Jacek Kuroń, popularized by Jadwiga Staniszkis (who never understood its normative meaning), see Arato (1991).
2 Note how Csurka's aggressive and controversial August 1992 article in *Magyar Fórum* was motivated by recent by-election defeats and the low popularity of the MDF and the government (Csurka, 1992b). Evidently he believed that only a conscious and determined mobilization towards a right-wing second revolution could save his party. In preparation for this he went as far as to challenge the position of Antall as party leader. Nevertheless, little of substance in the long article is entirely new – neither its blatant anti-Semitism, nor its wild rewriting of history, and certainly not its idea of a global conspiracy of liberals, cosmopolitans, communists and Jews against Hungary.
3 In Bulgaria and the Czech Republic the character of this right is different – economic liberal rather than populist–authoritarian. Interestingly they have been more successful in passing relevant legislation, the so-called lustration laws. Poland was a close call in terms of anti-agent revelations; measures were narrowly defeated by Wałesa and the parliamentary opposition, and, after the event, the Constitutional Court.

REFERENCES

Arato, A. (1982) 'Critical Sociology and Authoritarian State Socialism', in D. Held and J. Thompson (eds) *Habermas: Critical Debates*, London: Macmillan.
—— (1991) 'Revolution, Civil Society and Democracy', in Z. Rau (ed.) *The Reemergence of Civil Society in Eastern Europe and the Soviet Union*, Boulder, Colo.: Westview.
Bozóki, A. *et al.* (eds) (1992) *Csendes? Forradalom? Volt?* (Quiet? Revolution? Did it happen?), Budapest: Twins kiadó.
Bruszt, L. (1990) '1989: The Negotiated Revolution in Hungary', *Social Research*, 1990, 57: 365–87.
Csurka, I. (1992a) 'Meg nem történt forradalom', in A. Bozóki *et al.* (eds) *Csendes? Forradalom? Volt?* (Quiet? Revolution? Did it happen?), Budapest: Twins kiadó.
—— (1992b) 'Néhány gondolat a rendszerváltozás két esztendeje és az MDF új progamja kapcsán', *Magyar Fórum*, 20 August.
Fekete, G. (1992) in *Magyar Fórum*, 1 January.
Habermas, J. (1989) *The Structural Transformation of the Public Sphere: An Inquiry into a Category of Bourgeois Society* (German edn 1962), Cambridge: Polity Press.
Hofer, T. (1992) 'Harc a rendszerváltásért szimbólikus mezöben. 1989. március 15-e Budapesten', *Politikatudományi Szemle*, no. 1.
Kis, J. (1989) 'The Restoration of 1956–1957 in a Thirty Year Perspective', in *Politics in Hungary: For a Democratic Alternative*, Boulder, Colo.: Social Science Monographs.

Petschnig, M.Z. (1992) *Jelentések az alagútból*, Budapest: Pénzügykutató Rts.

Pomogáts, B. (1992) 'Ezerkilencszázötvenhat halotti leple' (The Shroud of 1956), *Magyar Hirlap*, 16 June.

Skocpol, T. (1979) *States and Social Revolutions: A Comparative Analysis of France, Russia, and China*, Cambridge: CUP.

Sükósd, M. (1992) 'Ki beszél itt forradolomról? Az átmentés mint erkölcsi problёma' (Who is speaking here of revolutions? Conversion as a moral problem), in A. Bozóki *et al.* (eds) *Csendes? Forradalom? Volt?* (Quiet? Revolution? Did it happen?), Budapest: Twins kiadó.

Szabó, M. (1992) 'Akadozó rendszerváltás', in *A váltás rendszere*, Budapest: Politikai tanulmányok intézete.

SzDSz (1989) *A rendszerváltás programja*, Budapest: SzDSz.

Szilágyi, I. (1992) Discussion (pp. 61–63, 77–78, 81–83), in A. Bozóki *et al.* (eds) *Csendes? Forradalom? Volt?* (Quiet? Revolution? Did it happen?), Budapest: Twins kiadó.

Tamás, G.M. (1992) 'Gondolatok a rendszerváltásról' in A. Bozóki *et al.* (eds) *Csendes? Forradalom? Volt?* (Quiet? Revolution? Did it happen?) Budapest: Twins kiadó.

Teller, G. (1992) 'Az elit nem vész el, csak . . .', *Beszélö*, 2 February.

Vogelin, E. (1975) *From Enlightenment to Revolution*, Durham N.C.: Duke UP.

Zsille, Z. (1992) 'Békés ellenforradalom? Reklamáció az elmaradt rendszerváltozás ügyében' (Peaceful counter-revolution? Complaints about a system change that did not happen), in A. Bozóki *et al.* (eds) *Csendes? Forradalom? Volt?* (Quiet? Revolution? Did it happen?) Budapest: Twins kaidó.

Chapter 7

The power structure in Hungary after the political transition

Erzsébet Szalai

INTRODUCTION

The legacy of Hungarian state socialism – as compared to that of Czechoslovakia and Poland – can be characterized by two distinct features. First, the dissolution of state socialism was preceded by a destabilization process – within the structure of power itself – that lasted almost a decade. The political transition was initiated partly by groups who hoped to retain their positions in the new political regime, or at least to convert their political power into economic power. Second, from the beginning of the 1980s almost 70 per cent of the citizenry took part in the illegal second economy, thereby gradually loosening their dependence on the party-state and opening up to elements of an alternative political culture.

This chapter is divided into two parts. First, I shall give a short analysis of the power structure of state socialism in its post-Stalinist phase, and then discuss its evolution and destabilization. Second, I shall discuss power relations in the period following the political transition.

THE POWER STRUCTURE OF THE KÁDÁR REGIME AND ITS DESTABILIZATION

The power relations of the Kádár regime

In the post-Stalinist phase of state socialism, i.e. in the Kádár period, power was appropriated by the state and party bureaucracy and the corporate managers. The party and state bureaucracy consisted of two parts: the ruling estate (the upper party leadership) who set the goals, and the rest. Those in power in the Kádár period constituted an estate with class characteristics; I call them 'the power estate' for two reasons. First, they constituted an estate because of their inner-group relationships: those in power formed a sophisticated network of personal relationships, and came to share similar ways of life and sets of values. Their common ethos was essentially based on political self-righteousness. Second, they constituted an estate because their power was *originally* not economic. Those in power, however, came to display class characteristics in so far as their power was increasingly economic and manifested – though at a low level – in the market (Szalai, 1989, 1991).[1] This concentration of power also seems to have been decisive from the point of view of property relations: fundamental property rights were concentrated in the hands of the power estate[2] (in contrast to societies based on capitalist private property where property relations are not determined by power relations but rather the opposite).

It is very important to define the relationship of the intellectuals to the power estate in this system. A majority of the intellectuals – scientific workers in academic institutes, writers with state salaries, film directors, etc. – could be regarded as the intelligentsia of the power estate. They could enjoy their official status and get their salaries as long as they did not transcend the limits set by the ruling estate. A minority made up the democratic opposition – independent professionals who did not want to comply with the rules of the game set by the ruling estate and who thereby displayed a completely novel intellectual attitude. In addition to this consciously accepted role their chief aim at the beginning was to establish a 'second publicity' of non-official *samizdat* literature (cf. Szalai, 1990a).

The dissolution of Kádárism

From the late 1970s and early 1980s the crisis of the Kádárist economic structure became increasingly evident. The system devoured its own resources; this is why it inevitably led to over-distribution and external indebtedness. The power estate tried to prevent the extension of the crisis by 'reorganizing' its internal power balance in critical situations. The possibilities this solution afforded, however, were exhausted by the mid-1980s (Szalai, 1989).

Parallel with these processes new social actors appeared on

stage or got into formal – or at first informal – power positions. From the late 1970s and early 1980s onwards, a new more educated generation with a different socialization streamed into the lower, later into the middle, levels of the party and state bureaucracy (Gazsó, 1990). This was the famous beat generation, the 'big generation' as it was called in Hungary, with its characteristic liberal leanings and openly technocratic values – a generation now in its forties and fifties whose common socialization in adolescence included rock music with all that that implies culturally. Inclusion of the social in their thinking was quite alien to them. When they imposed the introduction of a market economy, however, they purported to remain value-free in their argumentation and language. Even so, they displayed elements of the socialized approach of their predecessors – notably a regard for force and power (some were strongly statist in their outlook) and a liking for back-room deals. I will call this group the *new technocrats*.

Similar generational changes took place within the intelligentsia of the power estate. A new generation was born and acquired more and more professional authority. The works of what I call the *new reform intelligentsia* implicitly or even explicitly propagated the thesis that the necessary economic reforms could not be carried through without accompanying political changes.

In the same period, by the early 1980s, the identity and strategy of the *democratic opposition* were also formed. The essence of the strategy seemed to be the conviction that by exerting pressure from *outside* the existing institutions it would be possible to force the adoption of political and economic reforms which would significantly erode the rigidity of the existing system (Kis, 1983).

Neither the new reformed intelligentsia nor the democratic opposition believed in the possibility of transcending the one-party system. Nevertheless, they contributed to it with their activity and ideas. Above all they were the social actors who prepared and carried through the political transition. The latent alliance between the new technocracy and the two groups of the intelligentsia was based on the fact that the new technocracy hoped to find its own ideologists in the new reform intellectuals and in the democratic opposition. This was very important to the new technocracy because it attempted to conquer the summits of power from the mid-1980s onwards (Szalai, 1991).

The period of the political transition

The most outstanding feature of the processes beginning in 1988 was the springing up of 'alternative organizations' and the appearance of the seeds of a new party. These processes were mainly initiated by the democratic opposition and the new reform intelligentsia. They had two focal points, The Alliance of Free Democrats (SzDSz) which was organized by the democratic opposition, and the Hungarian Democratic Forum (MDF), the main figures of which were new reform intellectuals and populist writers.

Roughly speaking, SzDSz consisted of two parts. The group of leading cadres operated illegally. It comprised people who, politically and professionally, were held in high regard, and who all promoted liberal ideas. The rest of the SzDSz was composed of people with varying value systems who had joined the Free Democrats for their unyielding anti-communism and not for their liberalism. The ranks of the MDF were more homogeneous; the bulk consisted of a middle-class group the roots of which were to be found in the Christian–national middle class of the interwar period. This party was first popular in the provinces.

The alliance of the new technocracy and the democratic opposition, including the aforementioned new reform intellectuals, became temporarily weaker in the period of the political transition. In the round table discussions which prepared the political changes, the representatives of the new technocracy in the ruling Hungarian Socialist Workers' Party (MSzMP) became increasingly predominant (Szalai, 1990b). The basic issue was whether the leading role in the new political system would be played by the new technocracy or the forces of the new parties-in-formation – i.e. the new reform intelligentsia and the democratic opposition. This was implicitly at issue during the referendum obtained by the Alliance of Free Democrats.[3] This referendum played a significant part in the division of the MSzMP that took place soon afterwards. The issue was only resolved by the general elections held in the spring of 1990, in which the Hungarian Socialist Party (MSzP), which represented the new technocracy after the division of the MSzMP, fared badly. (The rump MSzMP that remained loyal both to its original name and political outlook did not even get into parliament.)

The ruling estate of the Kádár system broke up during the political transition. The new technocracy that won a Pyrrhic victory in its traditional political role became weaker and more fragmented. At the same time, however, it gradually began to conquer both existing and new economic power positions, starting with the banking system. In the power vacuum left by spontaneous privatization, corporate managers considerably increased their property rights at the expense of the state bureaucracy, the economic environment becoming at the same time more unstable than ever before.

THE NEW POWER STRUCTURE AND ITS DYNAMICS

The starting point (Spring 1990 to the end of 1990)

The general elections of Spring 1990 brought six parties into the parliament. In the order of the votes: the Hungarian Democratic Forum (MDF), the Alliance of Free Democrats (SzDSz), the Independent Smallholders' Party (FKGP), the Hungarian Socialist Party (MSzP), the Alliance of Young Democrats (Fidesz) and the Christian-Democratic People's Party (KNDP). The government was formed by the MDF which chose as coalition partners the FKGP and the KNDP which had a similar outlook and programme. To make the functioning of the government easier they also agreed to reduce the number of laws requiring a qualified majority. Arpád Göncz, a former leader of the SzDSz, who enjoyed the support of both political forces, was elected president. Göncz is a politician of high authority; his presidential powers, however, are – as a consequence of the referendum held in 1989 – rather weak. Top power positions were conquered by leading forces of the Democratic Forum and the coalition partners. As a consequence of the fundamentally 'tribal' organization of these – and other – parties, *this conglomerate forms an estate*. It is characterized by a common ethos, derived from the mentality and attitudes of the Christian upper and middle class in the interwar period, and composed of the following: a Christian–national ideology, strong adherence to sub- and super-ordination, and tendencies towards intolerance, the distribution of power positions according to family and friendship connections, and the dominance of informal interest enforcement over explicit striving for power. The ideology may have changed, but practices associated with the ruling estate of the Kádár period have persisted.

The new ruling estate was mainly supported by the *state bureaucracy*. This was neither an accident nor a consequence of subjective errors. This dilemma is very well characterized by Agnes Heller:

Of necessity, this government proposes an economic (and social) project which has several justifications; among others the fact that the chief nominal proprietor of national wealth is the state itself. Without a programme of proposals concerning this wealth and, even more importantly, privatization, property relationships would continue to be wholly unclear. But preparation of a project for a reversed social and economic revolution at the same time obliges the new democratically elected government to do something very similar to the former totalitarian state; it obliges it to direct the economy in a predetermined direction by administrative means.

(Heller, 1990: 1405–6)

This inevitably increases the relative power of the state bureaucracy – although within this system it was not those who redistributed state resources (for there were ever-fewer resources to be distributed) who profited most, but rather those who redistributed property. Their task was, in principle, to dissolve what was state property in name and to 'create' a new bourgeoisie. This is why it was almost inevitable that the sharpest conflicts within the state bureaucracy concerned the control of state property and the related power positions.

Whom do we find in the middle and upper levels of the state bureaucracy? In the high positions there are the political commissars of the governing coalition who mainly represent the old guard of the intelligentsia of the previous power estate. This summit of power is partly occupied by those representatives of the new technocracy (the others holding somewhat lower positions) who did not even leave the state bureaucracy in the sinister atmosphere of the political transition.

The class of new technocrats who kept their bureaucratic positions consists of two clearly differentiated groups. First, there are members of the internationally accepted 'team' of the new technocracy who after temporary setbacks succeeded in stabilizing their positions and even in partly reconquering one part of the supreme economic power, thereby forming a sort of counter-power against the 'party commissars'. Their talents and authority made it more or less possible for them to remain politically neutral. Second, there are the 'former deputy heads of department'. They constituted the second level of the new technocracy; unlike the members of the 'team' their position was unstable –

which is why they were willing to conclude compromises with the 'commissars'.

A further important group of actors consisted of the state-controlled big commercial banks. Here power positions were held by those new technocrats who had left the destabilized state bureaucracy in the period of the political transition. Their power was primarily based on new interdependences which were created between the corporate sphere and the big commercial banks. Although in principle direct economic power was controlled by the big commercial banks, in practice the dependence was mutual; indeed, complicated forms of cross-ownership were by no means rare. The majority of corporate managers experienced their relationships to the banks more as official than market relationships; banks did favours in giving credit. At the same time, the banks were themselves dependent on the corporate sphere: they did not dare touch even those companies with hopeless indebtedness because a chain of bankruptcies would have menaced their own existence. New technocrats holding power positions in the big commercial banks tried to remain politically neutral. The parties of the governing coalition, however, felt a strong desire for the positions of the new technocracy almost from the outset.

The victory of the MDF meant the entry into government of a party with an ideology which was radically anti-monopolistic and directed against corporate managers and the corporate sphere in general. After the anti-corporatist steps of the first period (the most significant being the campaign for re-electing corporate managers), however, the structure of power stabilized (despite the replacement by the end of 1990 of 50 per cent of top managers following retirements, etc). Most of the new managers began their careers in the same company, moving gradually upwards in the hierarchy; they already held managerial positions before their election to the top (Szalai, 1992).

Several factors were responsible for the stabilization of the managers' positions. Among these the most important is that both economic ministers and experts in the governing coalition and the new technocracy felt a certain ambivalence towards corporate managers. Although they would have liked to claim at least part of the economic power of the corporate managers, in the short run they were dependent on their economic achievements. In short, there was a stalemate. The best expression of this was the establishment of the State Property Agency – a sign that spontaneous privatization could continue but only under state supervision.

Empirical investigations (e.g. Móra, 1990) show that during the process of spontaneous privatization only a very small part of nominally state property became private property in the classical sense. There was no real privatization. The cross-ownership with the banks was complemented by the cross-ownership of the nominally state-owned companies, i.e. each held equity in the other. Corporate managers were still free from real control by the owners.

With the establishment of the State Property Agency (whose outstanding new technocrat founder was soon replaced by a lesser technocrat loyal to the new ruling estate), the concentration of economic power intensified still further. The Agency soon came under government rather than parliamentary control, thereby becoming an integral part of the state bureaucracy. This signified an old–new chapter in the contradictory relationship of state bureaucracy and corporate managers. There are many indications that although the language in which the struggle for property and sharing is expressed is new, and the formal framework is set by modern legal norms, the whole process is still governed by the informal bargaining so characteristic of the late Kádár regime. A similar phenomenon can be observed in the relationship of the state bureaucracy, the big commercial banks and the corporate sphere.

The main agents of the new power structure born by the end of 1990 were the following: *the new ruling estate, the new technocracy and the corporate managers*. Dependent on each other, they were forced to make compromises. On the one hand, the group of new technocrats who joined the state bureaucracy was looking for legitimation in the new ruling estate and its ideology ('this is not a communist state any more, this is a Christian–national state'). On the other hand, the new ruling estate found support for its power strivings in the new state technocracy. But interdependency is only one factor in this contradictory relationship. Conflicting interests are also present, which is why the formula described proved to be a source of acute power struggles.

The governing parties, having promised a smooth transition in the general elections, soon lost their popularity. As a sign of this the local elections in Autumn 1990 were won by the SzDSz and Fidesz. Their representatives took over the local councils. It seemed that a sort of dual power was created in the country. In reality the situation of the local councils is extremely precarious, since they lack the most basic economic conditions for their functioning – partly because their political rivals at the top of the power hierarchy are not interested in their proper functioning.

The leading forces of the opposition parties (principally SzDSz and Fidesz) are partly inside, partly outside, the power structure – although this cannot be demonstrated empirically for there are no data on the extraparliamentary connections between governing and opposition parties. At any rate, the pact between MDF and SzDSz concluded after the general elections did not last long; indeed, the conflicts between the leading forces of the two parties are multiplying. Fidesz defines itself as pragmatic and shows more tolerance towards the governing parties on some issues, but it wants to remain a separate party and eventually secure power itself. The Hungarian Socialist Party finds it difficult to dissociate itself from its communist forebears. It finds itself in a trap – whenever the party openly intervenes on any issue, the reply is 'how dare they speak?' If they do not intervene the reaction is the same: 'they don't dare to speak, they have something to hide'.

I do not agree with those, such as Tamás Kolosi and Iván Szelényi, who claim that the political transition meant the coming to power of the intelligentsia. This argument is usually based on the fact that the majority of MPs originally belonged to the professional strata and some still retain their jobs. For a start, the primary seat of power is not parliament. Secondly, MPs are already politicians rather than intellectuals. Their legitimacy derives not from their professional knowledge, but from the votes they got – and this fact seems to be crucial even though their professional knowledge and distinctive values could have played an important role in getting those votes.

Nevertheless the remnants of the professional role-set are highly significant. Parliamentary politicians in Hungary are still thinking in terms of desirable social models rather than social forces and processes – a consequence of the artificial formation of the new parties. Many of them even insist on retaining their professional status both in an intellectual sense and in their professional activities. This, however, contradicts the norms and practices of modern society where there is a division between the role of the politician who seeks the exercise of power and that of the intellectual who seeks the self-reflection of society.

Conflicts within the power structure

During 1991 and 1992 the conflicts within the ruling elite got sharper. This meant on the one hand a conflict in the leadership of the Democratic Forum between Christian conservatives and right-wing radicals. This conflict remained partly an artificial one until the summer of 1992, for these groups mutually needed each other (Bozóki, 1991). In August 1992, however, vice-president István Csurka published an article with explicit Nazi overtones (Csurka, 1992), and this event made the conflicts within the MDF more visible and more sharp. As one part of the leadership and the membership of the party supports Csurka, there exists the possibility of crisis within the government itself. The secession of an extreme rightist group of about forty persons from the parliamentary party would be enough to bring the government – were it to repudiate Csurka – into minority. There are signs that the publication of this article and its consequences will further the dissolution and/or isolation of the governing party.

On the other hand there is an acute conflict between the core of the new ruling elite (the top leadership of the MDF) and the leadership of the Smallholders' Party. The conflict concerns first of all the so-called Reparation Act; the smallholders want a total compensation for the victims of nationalizations, the coalition partners only a partial one. This conflict – and others – led at the end of 1991 to the departure of the Smallholders' Party from the governing coalition and only thirty-five members of the parliamentary party (two-thirds of the original number) remained loyal to the government. In addition, in August 1992 the Christian Democratic People's Party declared itself an opposition *within* the governing coalition in the hope of ending its isolation. What this means is still unclear.

Another source of conflict is the fact that the new ruling elite and its political commissars in the state bureaucracy declared war against the power of the new technocracy, beginning with the 'team'. The war included, in 1991, attempts to capture top positions in the big commercial banks, personnel changes in the Ministry for Foreign Affairs, attacks against top judges, struggles around the National Bank Act and the attempt to subordinate the National Bank – culminating in the displacement of one of the most outstanding new technocrats, György Surányi, as National Bank President. This was a paradigmatic event since this was the first time that a top manager was dismissed explicitly and exclusively for political reasons.

Nevertheless, the nomination for minister of finance of Mihály Kupa, himself a new technocrat, showed that the offensive against the new technocracy was not indiscriminate; it was directed only at those people who were not willing to identify themselves with the politics and aims of the new ruling elite. The power position of Kupa, however, did not remain stable for long. The ideas of the prime minister were not concordant with those of his principal economic minister. According to Antall, the prime minister is expected to be the first authority in the country and in the government; in addition he is expected to control some so-called national institutions. According to Kupa, the country has two political heads – the president and the prime minister – and one person, the minister of finance, has to control economic affairs; government has to be led by the prime minister and the minister of finance. Prime Minister Antall succeeded in overcoming this division by changing the responsibilities of his minister of finance and organizing his own information network independently of his minister. In any case, as soon as he became an MP with the support of the MDF, Kupa was drawn into the leading circles of the governing party.

In the first half of 1992 the attacks against the new technocracy and the 'team' became stronger than ever. Independent or oppositional new technocrats and experts were dismissed or forced to resign from the upper leadership of the State Property Agency (Voszka, 1992). In several ministries impartial administrative secretaries of state and independent experts were replaced by appointees loyal to the governing coalition. Within the new technocracy, too, new conflicts were born – although they were already familiar from the sphere of state bureaucracy. With the appearance of Mihály Kupa, the internal cohesion of the already unstable economic government became even weaker. In his struggle for economic supremacy, Kupa began in early 1991 to elaborate his own programme with the help of his own apparatus. This provoked continuous counter-attacks by other top offices, especially by branch ministries supported by the corporate sphere whose attitude was still determined by an earlier model of economic policy. Not only the political leadership but also the minister of finance wanted to extend the minister's influence over the State Property Agency – which caused many conflicts. Last but not least, the debate on economic policy continued in ever more acute forms within the new technocracy: should we go on with monetary restriction or is it time to begin economic regeneration?

The consquences of insecurity

One of the main sources of conflicts within the power structure was a sort of power vacuum that was actually created at the end of 1990 (as a consequence of the taxi-drivers' blockade[4]). All public opinion polls showed the rapidly decreasing popularity of the leaders of the governing parties and the members of the government – the only exception being Mihály Kupa. In addition, members of the state bureaucracy were, and are, afraid of losing influence over social and economic processes with the formation of a real market economy, the emergence of a propertied middle class and the emergence of effective pressure groups. Their loss of influence was compounded by their failure to attract younger professionals into bureaucratic positions, following the departure of the majority of professionals with a liberal outlook, and multiple expertise into banks and the private economy, because working for the state administration had been devalued and the pay was too low (the only exception being the National Bank with its high prestige and solid position in the power structure). This determined the personal composition of the state bureaucracy: dominant positions were held by professionals who espoused liberal principles whilst still favouring state intervention. They were drawn from the 'deputy department heads' mentioned before.

The characteristic insecurity of the members of the state bureaucracy and the conflicts it generates explained many known and unknown phenomena: support for centralization and publicly owned firms, the enforcement of the Reparation Act in order to extend their social base, the 'radicalization' of the MDF top leadership (the Kónya paper), then its 'calming down' (the national conference in December), the offensive of Csurka (and the right-wing radicals within the MDF), the search for scapegoats (the Zétényi–Takács draft bill on retroactive jurisdiction for the crimes committed under state socialism), and the success propaganda of the second half of 1991.

Among the centralizing moves the following are worth mentioning: the centralization of the privatizing process and its institutional background; the partly instinctual, partly conscious, slowing down of real privatization (limitation of the growth of the propertied middle class);[5] the narrowing down of the competences of the president of the republic who wished to control governmental actions, the subordination of the National Bank; and the curbing of budgetary reform aimed at the reduction of state bureaucracy (Szántó, 1992). In the beginning of 1992 the top managers of the big commercial banks were obliged to finance budgetary deficits that far exceeded the planned level (only a prominent member of the 'team', Lajos Bokros, president of Budapest Bank dared to refuse). This was not only a financial step, but also a demonstration of who was in charge. In 1991, for instance, big commercial banks were obliged to finance a new government daily paper, *New Hungary*. In 1992 the governing coalition also exerted strong pressure on President Göncz to dismiss the heads of radio and television because they adopted a politically independent programme policy. Following a decision of the Constitutional Court, this attack failed – but the 'media war' is far from over.

In the political vacuum surrounding the government, and in the context of conflicts within government about economic policy, both the minister of finance and the representatives of institutions in the orbit of the state bureaucracy tried to find allies in the corporate sphere. With the dissolution of the party-state, corporate managers, too, felt themselves politically and economically isolated and showed interest in restoring links loosened during the political transition (Bossányi, 1991; Szalai, 1992). In spite of this a full restoration of the old relationships between the state and corporations is out of the question – one reason being that the central resources needed to reactivate the old system are no longer available. In any case, the overtures to the corporate sphere weaken and divide the government and the state bureaucracy whilst strengthening corporate pressure (Szalai, 1992).

Since the beginning of 1992, partly as a consequence of the new Bankruptcy Act, a large reorganization has taken place within the corporate sphere which has diminished the bargaining power of corporate managers. Several factors indicate, however, that this power has not disappeared altogether; corporate managers are still able to exert a considerable influence on the internal relationships of the state bureaucracy and the political sphere (Kozma, 1992). To counter this strength and to discipline corporate managers, a new government measure was taken in the beginning of 1992, obliging all nominally state-owned enterprises to effect their transformation by the end of the year; as a consequence of this around 400,000 or 500,000 managerial positions have become insecure.

There is a dangerous centralizing spiral here. Closer links with the corporate sphere lead to increased internal division within the government and the state bureaucracy; centralization to restore hierarchical order and discipline then seems a necessary counter to this disintegration. But centralization aimed at reinforcing the government and the state bureaucracy only seems to reproduce at a higher level the same disintegrating tendencies and the same inherent tensions in the economic processes, for which the remedy then appears to be yet more centralization. The behaviour of top economic management becomes increasingly hesitant and fraught. At the same time the particularistic, informal character of economic management (including the bargaining relationships with the big commercial banks) does not disappear; quite the contrary it sometimes becomes even stronger (Szalai, 1992).

Fearful that they could lose political power in the next general election, the governing parties are motivated to capture and retain as much economic power as possible. Just like the communists of old, they try hard to convert political into economic power. The sense of insecurity of those in power prompts the search for scapegoats. This endeavour found its expression in the Zétényi–Takács Draft Bill. One aim of the bill was to direct social emotions towards well-defined social actors and to divert attention from more fundamental issues. Another – not always conscious – function of the same draft was to satisfy the need for self-legitimation on the part of the new ruling elite.

In the hope of restoring social trust, the government emphasized in the second half of 1991 that Hungary was the only peaceful country in the whole region. It also engaged in economic success propaganda, the quintessence of which was the claim that with 1991 the most difficult year was already over, the rate of inflation was decreasing, and an economic boom would begin in 1992. In practice, things have worked out differently. Although inflation has slowed, the crisis in industry has deepened and unemployment has become a mass phenomenon.

The capacity of the president to counter-balance the government is limited. His powers are few, but he has charisma and he uses it to exercise a personal authority. This was the fundamental reason for the acute conflicts between him and the prime minister. More significant still are the powers of the Constitutional Court.

The power structure we have outlined seems to be extremely plastic; its internal processes are very unstable. Generally we can state that the position of the ruling estate within the power structure has become unstable and the 'team' has lost its dominant role in the state bureaucracy. The new technocracy as a whole – in spite of heavy losses and the rise of former deputy heads of ministries – has retained its position (partly by controlling the commercial banks whose close links with the state bureaucracy have not changed). This tendency was further reinforced by the fact that the new ruling estate had no 'reserve' guard of experts which could have staffed the state bureaucracy and the banks following the dismissal of the new technocracy. The power positions of the corporate managers have become weaker but they have still to be reckoned with.

New actors

As expected, the self-organization of the propertied middle class has accelerated since 1991. They had had their own pressure groups before, and now they have made their first attempts at conquering the political sphere. According to Kocsis and Széles

> the native bourgeoisie has no real political party. As an organized force it is not present in the Hungarian Parliament . . . A conciliation is needed! A conciliation not among the political parties in the first instance, but a conciliation between the new power elite and the native bourgeoisie.
>
> (Kocsis and Széles, 1991: 7)

Native businessmen not only wish to take part in economic and political power, they want to make the whole 'political elite' serve them. This has a special significance since, with the exception of corporate managers, there are hardly any social groups capable of self-organization and of influencing the 'political elite'. In the long run they might even be able to expropriate or at least strongly influence political power.

The slowing down of privatization by the government and the state bureaucracy restricted the growth of a significant rival – the propertied bourgeoisie. At the same time would-be venture capitalists who were not able to secure enough capital to buy the bigger state enterprises also favoured a slow-down in privatization; they were to be found among the supporters of almost all parliamentary parties. A possible resolution of the manifold conflicts between governing parties, state bureaucracy and the venturer 'class' could be the formation of a client bourgeoisie closely linked to the state bureaucracy. This client bourgeoisie would probably resemble the corporate manager lobbyists of the Kádár regime, who, from the economic reform of 1968 onwards, sought to enjoy the comforts of the market and of liberalization while charging its discomforts to the state.

POWER – OPPOSITION – SOCIETY

The consequences of the MDF–SzDSz pact were already being strongly felt in 1991 and 1992. Although parliamentary opposition became more radical, it could not defeat the governing coalition. The predominantly oppositional local self-governments continued to be helpless for want of material resources. The air of general helplessness seems to be one reason for the internal tensions of the opposition parties and the crisis of the SzDSz. There would seem to be only one way out of this situation: the mobilization of the citizenry. However, with the successful exception of the socialists, who wanted to break out of their ghetto, the liberal parties hesitated to take this step.

Another reason for the internal tensions of the parties goes back to their formation at a time when an alignment between party divisions and social divisions was not possible. This was partly because different parties were formed by different coteries of intellectuals, and partly because the peaceful transition obscured the need to articulate differences of social interest politically. As a consequence decisions which differentially affect different social groups always divide their leaders and members alike. This applies to the parties of the governing coalition as well as to the opposition. The opposition parties, although they sometimes vote together, do not form open alliances; they are still searching for their own identities.

The self-organizing attempts of employees have proved to be weak, and the trade union movement has been torn by conflicts of interest. These conflicts have partly concerned the top function-aries of the different trade unions. We can mention as paradigmatic the conflict between the successor of the state-socialist unions, the National Alliance of Hungarian Trade Unions (MSzOSz), and the Democratic League of Independent Trade Unions. In the state–management–employees triad, the relationship of the actors to each other had been contradictory and fluid even in the Kádár period; there had always been an alliance of two against one but its composition constantly changed. This plasticity and incalculability has survived the political transition for a number of reasons. First, as a consequence of the slowing down of the privatization process and the small number of 'real' owners, the position and economic role of the state bureaucracy and the corporate management remains ambiguous and uncertain. In these unstable circumstances the MSzOSz (according to its traditions) is primarily interested in the opposition state employees and promotes large-scale 'macro bargains', whereas the League wants to take part in the handling of local conflicts between management and employees. The interest conflicts among the different trade unions were made more acute by the parliamentary resolution in the summer of 1991 which obliged the MSzOSz to account for its wealth and make public the size of its membership within a month – which proved to exceed one million. Conflicts among the trade unions became more acute in 1992, the prime issue being the division of assets (the suspicion arose that the MSzOSz put the common property of the unions into economic societies). A national vote of all citizens was suggested for the autumn with the assets of the unions divided according to the results. The government's ambition to divide the trade union movement also plays a considerable part in the acute conflicts among the unions (Bossányi, 1992).

There is a deeper reason for the weakness of attempts at self-organizing. The social structure is changing in these decisive years in ways which will probably determine for a long time who will be able to rise or climb and who will probably lag lastingly behind. This situation recalls characteristics of the Kádár era: the prosecution of interests on an individualized basis, and loyalty towards one's superiors whomever they be. In a word, instead of solidarity, competition prevails. This also colours attitudes towards large-scale politics. The pre-bourgeois tries to hide himself from political power rather than wanting to control or influence it democratically (Schlett, 1991: 17).

After the shock of the taxi-drivers' blockade in October 1990 several personalities and political organizations foresaw a 'hot autumn' for 1991. These expectations did not come to pass. Large social disturbances have not occurred, since radical forces have not been – and probably will not be – capable of mobilizing society generally. This reflects the positive elements of the Kádár legacy: sobriety, the rejection of political radicalism and radical personalities, the sense of pragmatism. These are the qualities that ensure the survival of the Hungarian economy in spite of all the shocks. They are also one reason why Arpád Göncz is the most popular politician in this country.

The second reason flows from his role and personality. His functions are mainly integrative, and his is truly an integrative personality. He calls for social solidarity and support for the poor and the weak, and his popularity reveals that sympathy and community are still hidden values of Hungarian society. This is also shown by the influence of the Democratic Charter. The Charter was drafted in September 1991 by liberal and left-wing intellectuals – underpinning those forces in the SzDSz and the MSzP which were ready to approach each other. The document specifies seventeen criteria of democracy ('there will be democracy, if . . .'). So far 26,000 people have signed it. The Democratic Charter movement recognizes that democracy requires not just a parliament and a multi-party system but also the self-organization of civil society. It does not want to become a party itself. This first sign of the alliance between liberal and left-wing forces poses a severe challenge to those in power who know that the Charter's democratic principles are directed against them.[6] Given that the Charter is on the one hand a forum for those elements in two opposition parties who are ready to co-operate, and on the other an initiative of civil society, the possibilities of internal conflicts are present from the outset. These conflicts became public in the summer of 1992 (the immediate reason being the alienation of the SzDSz from the MSzP). The future of the Charter depends on whether it will be able to contain them constructively.

CONCLUSIONS

The prospects for the stabilization of democratic institutions and the formation of a market economy in Hungary are menaced for the foreseeable future by dangers coming from the extreme right – the ideologies of a radical right are formulated within the governing party itself. The Nazi ideas of MDF vice-president

Csurka and his companions are directed at the Christian–national middle class but have elicited no response for the moment as this stratum is practically non-existent in the wider society. As indicated above, the middle stratum that still exists in Hungary (after the radical division that took place during the political transition) is neither Christian nor nationalistic and it is not inclined to embrace extremist ideologies. In the short run, therefore, the main danger is not a widespread social crisis but the beginning of an international isolation of the country with all the consequences that such a process implies.

If, however, the formation of a by nature pragmatic, private property oriented, economic power were to fail to counterbalance the fundamentally ideologically minded political power, or if economic power were to be concentrated in the hands of a narrow propertied group that, with the help of foreign capital, formed islands of modernity whilst other sectors of the economy and society sank or found themselves forced to the periphery with mass unemployment and poverty, then extremist ideas could find a larger echo. Were this to happen, it would seriously endanger the functioning of both the economy and the institutions of democracy. Under such circumstances the West might be interested in the formation of a fundamentally authoritarian structure with all the formal trappings of democracy, for this might seem the only way of controlling and localizing social unrest. Such a system would continue the trends of the Kádár regime both politically and economically.

This is why the formation of a wide propertied 'class' must be regarded as highly significant – the most important precondition for which is rapid privatization. We may add that in the short run the political system and the trade union movement must undergo a transformation in order to be able to reach a wide social consensus as to which social groups are expected to bear the economic and social burdens of the transition and to what degree.

POSTSCRIPT: FEBRUARY 1993

A characteristic political feature in the autumn and winter of 1992 was that, despite major and minor internal struggles and conflicts (Mézes, 1992), both the presidium of the MDF and the government (including Prime Minister Antall) were unwilling to make explicit their relationship to the extreme right. Disciplinary proceedings were initiated against the television president, Elemér Hankiss, one of the main advocates of independent television, and two of his colleagues. This was consistent with one of the former aims of István Csurka who had insisted on government control of television and radio programmes. At the beginning of January 1993 the presidents of both Hungarian television and radio resigned. The position of Csurka strengthened; he became even more aggressive and events at the two national meetings of the populist-national wing of the MDF confirmed his growing influence. At the beginning of 1993, Prime Minister Antall even stressed the necessity for the MDF to remain in power for another electoral period in order to be able to carry through the transition in its entirety, which caused a significant upheaval among the opposition and the freelancers. The conflicts between the moderate politics of Antall and the extremist politics of Csurka intensified in the run-up to the national meeting of the MDF at the end of January 1993, but diminished during the meeting itself. More precisely they were swept under the carpet. Both parties could feel that their position was more stable afterwards than before. Antall was reinforced in his position of party president while the number of Csurka's friends in the presidium increased.

From the second part of 1992 onwards we have also witnessed the formation of a new social and power group which I call the *new clientele*. I am speaking of people with economic power who are committed to the parties of the governing coalition which are the sources of their power. Around the three governing parties a threefold client system has formed which is also characterized by internal struggle. The new clients have been recruited from the former second and third echelons of the new technocracy which have more and more openly changed their views and thereby displayed their loyalty to those in power, from certain groups of intellectuals in the countryside and from certain MPs.

The new clients have already occupied some key positions in the state bureaucracy; they are sitting on the boards of state enterprises – among them large banks. Some corporate managers who were appointed after a certain elimination process also belong to this group. To all these we may add – although not as a direct part of the power system – certain entrepreneurial groups who benefited from privatization.

The core of the new technocracy – the 'team' as I called it above – has now completely disappeared from the state bureaucracy.

Some have taken managerial positions in the big commercial banks. Most, however, have become managers of international private banks or private entrepreneurs.

The emergence of the new clientele, however vague its outlines, reinforced the economic foundation of the new ruling estate and its commissars. The main rival of the clients proved to be the new technocracy; the outstanding feature of the struggle for power became the fight between the two groups. It was against the power background of the beginning, and later the sharpening, of this conflict, that Csurka's essay was published in August 1992. The technocratic economic experts of the MDF, who increasingly felt the day-to-day troubles of managing the economy, and some MDF near-business circles were ready as early as mid-1992 to make compromises with certain groups in the new technocracy. On the other hand, some of the entrepreneurial groups which had previously supported the MDF were beginning to distance themselves from the largest governing party. These movements and rearrangements made the representatives of the actual and the would-be members of the new clientele (who were, incidentally, followers of Csurka) frightened and more active. The struggle between the technocracy and the new clients appeared at the highest levels of MDF politics as well. This is one explanation why those who warned about left-wing dangers targeted not communists in the traditional sense but new technocrats (Antall, 1992).

In the autumn and winter of 1992 the new entrepreneurial groups and managers tried to make their conversion of influence into economic power more effective. Through their representatives they suggested modes of privatization that not only would place them in a more favourable position, but would also make it possible for them to win influence over the management of state wealth not yet privatized (Emöd, 1992).

In this same period social tensions became more acute. To mention only the most important: there were the protest actions of the miners and railwaymen, the forty-one-day hunger strike organized by the Society of Persons Living Below the Minimum Subsistence Level against unfavourable changes in the taxation system, and subsequently the collection of petitions by the same society for the dissolution of the Parliament – although this action was deemed unconstitutional by the Constitutional Court in January 1993. Partly as a consequence of these actions and the weaknesses of the government, there was a considerable reduction in the conflicts between the trade unions and they succeeded in forcing concessions from Parliament and government.

In spite of growing social tensions, Csurka and his colleagues have not been able to win broad social support for their ideas. Moreover, seeing the danger coming from the extreme right, the managing body of the Democratic Charter organized a mass demonstration on 24 September 1992 for the defence of democracy. More than 80,000 people took part in the biggest and most effective demonstration since the political changes began.

NOTES

1 I use the concepts 'class' and 'estate' in the sense Max Weber used them. Weber (1967) used the concept 'class' exclusively for the description of market economies, whereas for non-market economies he used the notion 'estate'. The power relationships of the Kádár regime cannot be described with the unambiguous notions of Max Weber, for its economy was a sort of transition between centrally planned economies and a market economy which was also expressed by the fact that the political values and prospects of the possessors of economic power were to some extent influenced by their achievements in the market.

2 As the internal division of ownership rights was not explicit and unambiguous, these property relationships permanently induced a diffuse and temporary struggle, the chief aim of which was to conquer ever more rights and to divert ever more duties. These property relationships have been analysed in detail in Szalai, 1991.

3 During the round table discussions on the position of the president of the republic, the MSzMP wanted a strong president elected by referendum. The party thought that this position would be filled by the then very popular leading personality of the new technocracy, Imre Pozsgai. Fearful of this outcome, the opposition parties supported a weak, parliamentarily elected, presidential position. There was no agreement on this issue during the discussions and it was the most important of the four questions in the referendum. A small majority of the voters supported the line of the opposition parties.

4 At the end of October the government unexpectedly increased the price of petrol despite denying that it would only the day before. As a reaction taxi drivers and other transportation employees blockaded the most important traffic junctions of the country for three days. Two-thirds of the population sympathized with the protest which was also considered legitimate by several oppositional parties. The blockade was regarded as a civil rights movement by András Bozóki (1992), who attributed a considerable role to moral indignation.

5 This was expressed among others by the formation of the State Property Holdings: the government wanted to determine the group of those

enterprises and money institutions that must remain exclusively – or majority – state-owned. The purpose of this measure, apart from slowing down privatization, was to enable the government and the state bureaucracy to influence the whole economy through state-owned economic units by means of the agreed prices, wages, customs and capital strength formed in this sphere.

6 Concerning the Charter, Bozóki reformulated the question raised by György Konrád and Ivan Szelényi: is the intelligentsia of a 'politocracy' capable of preserving the power it acquired in an exceptional historical moment? His answer was a clear 'no', for:

> The critical intelligentsia in Hungary has had no success to date in power-oriented, technocratic and bureaucratic policy-making. The formation of the Democratic Charter shows the critical intelligentsia returning to the role it played before 1989: it is a 'mediacracy' in forming educated public opinion, at the same time it is 'meritocracy' at the universities and research institutes. Having made its excursion into professional politics, the intelligentsia returns to the sites of the politics of 'movements' but its voice will not be decisive any more: it will be lost in the noise of the social interest conflicts of the new democracy.
>
> (Bozóki, 1992: 23–4)

REFERENCES

Antall, J. (1992) 'Az MDF igazi ereje középen van' (The Real Force of the MDF Lies in the Middle), *Magyar Hirlap*, 16 November: 3.

Bossányi, K. (1991) 'A vágy titokzatos tárgya' (The Mysterious Object of Desire), *Beszélö*, 19 October: 17–19.

—— (1992) 'Szociális partnerek – pórázon' (Social Partners – On Leash), *Mozgó Vilag*, January: 51–61.

Bozóki, A. (1991) 'Az MDF alakváltozásai' (The Metamorphosis of the MDF), *Magyar Narancs*, 18 December: 1–2.

—— (1992) 'Democrats against Democracy? Civil Protest in Hungary Since 1990', Paper presented to the Annual Conference of the British Sociological Association, University of Kent, Canterbury, 6–9 April.

Csurka, I. (1992) 'Néhány gondolat a rendszerváltozás két esztendeje és a MDF új programja kapcsán' (Thoughts Concerning the First Two Years of the Transformation and the New Programme of the MDF), *Magyar Fórum*, 20 August: 9–16.

Emöd, P. (1992) 'Széles: 50–60 milliárdot elmenedzselnénk' (We Would Manage 50–60 Billions), *Magyar Hirlap*, 11 December.

Gazsó, F. (1990) 'A káderbürokrácia és az értelmiség' (The Cadre Bureacracy and the Intelligentsia), *Társadalmi Szemle*, November: 3–13.

Heller, A. (1990) 'Kelet-Európa dicsöséges forradalmai' (The Glorious Revolutions of Eastern Europe), *Holmi*, December: 1399–414.

Jelentések az alagútból. Az Antall Kormany elsö éve (Reports from the

Tunnel: The First Year of the Antall Government), Pénzügykutató Részvénytársaság, May 1991.

Jelentések az alagútból. *Jelentés gazdaságunk 1991, évi helyzetéről* (Reports from the Tunnel: A Report on the Situation of Our Economy in 1991), Pénzügykutató Részvénytársaság, May 1992.

Kis, J. (1983) 'Gondolatok a közeljövöröl' (Thoughts on the Near Future), *Beszélö*, 3, *Beszélö összkiadás*, 1981–84: 115–22.

Kocsis, A. and Széles, G. (1991) 'Második kiegyezés' (A Second Reconciliation), *Magyar Hirlap*, 3 August: 7.

Konrád, G. and Szelényi, I. (1989) *Az értelmiség útja az osztályhatatalomhoz* (The Road of the Intelligentsia to Class Power), Gondolat Könyvkiadó.

Kozma, J. (1992) 'A kiemelés még nem támogatás. Szalai Erzsébet szociológus a nagyvállalatokról' (Differential Treatment Does Not Mean Subvention. Sociologist Erzsébet Szalai on Large Companies), *Népszabadság*, 29 July: 13.

Mézes, F. (1992) 'MDF viták I. A párt kedvence' (MDF Debates I. The Favourite of the Party), *Heti Világgazdaság*, 5 December, 78–80; 'MDF viták II. A legek ura' (MDF Debates II. The Master of 'Most'), *Heti Világgazdaság*, 12 December: 80.

Móra, M. (1990) 'Az állami vállalatok (ál)privatizációja' (The Pseudo-Privatization of State Enterprises), *Gazdaságkutató Intézet Tanulmányai*, December.

Schlett, I. (1991) 'A magyar csoda' (The Hungarian Miracle), *Népszabadság*, 24 December: 17.

Szalai, E. (1989) *Gazdasági mechanizmus, reformtörekvések és nagyvállalati érdekek* (Economic Mechanism, Reform Endeavours and Corporate Interest), Közgazdasági és Jogi Könyvkiadó.

—— (1990a) 'Utelágazás' (At the Crossroads), *Valóság*, August: 44–53.

—— (1990b) 'Szereppróba' (Dress Rehearsal), *Valóság*, December: 14–29.

—— (1991) 'A hatalom metamorfózisa?' (A Metamorphosis of Power), *Valóság*, June: 1–26.

—— (1992) 'Perpetuum mobile' (Perpetual Motion), *Valóság*, April: 1–25.

Szántó, A. (1992) 'Allamháztartás a dirigizmus jegyében' (State Budget in the Sign of Dirigism), *Társadalmi Szemle*, January: 1–11.

Vértes, A. (1992) 'A rózsaszin bumeráng (Helyettesithetö-e a gazdaságpolitika gazdaságpszichológiával?' (The Pink Boomerang. Can One Replace Economic Policy with the Psychology of Economics?), *Társadalmi Szemle*, February: 1–12.

Voszka, É. (1990) 'A katarzis nélküli átmenet elviselhetetlen könnyüsége' (The Unbearable Lightness of a Transition Without Catharsis), *Közgazdasági Szemle*, June: 687–701.

—— (1992) 'Az ellenkezöje sem igaz: a központositás és a decentralizáció szineváltozása' (Not Even the Contrary is True: The Changing Face of Centralization and Decentralization), *Külgazdaság*, June: 1–14.

Weber, M. (1967) *Gazdaság és társadalom* (Economy and Society), Közgazdasági es Jogi Könyvkiadó.

Chapter 8

Privatization in East-Central Europe
Similarities and contrasts in its application

Vic Duke and Keith Grime

This chapter examines the different policies and varied progress of privatization in East-Central Europe, with particular emphasis on case studies of Hungary, Poland and Czechoslovakia. The first section discusses the alternative definitions and contexts of privatization in Western and Eastern Europe. The second summarizes in general terms the main issues, debates and choices involved in the privatization of East-Central Europe. Thereafter, in the following three sections, each of the countries are considered in turn. Hungary is dealt with first in that economic reform began there prior to the fall of communism. Political reform developed earliest in Poland, which is analysed next. Last of all is Czechoslovakia which experienced neither economic nor political reform prior to 1989. Finally, the conclusion identifies similarities and contrasts in the application of privatization in the three countries.

ECONOMIC PRIVATIZATION IN CONTEXT: WESTERN AND EASTERN EUROPE

Privatization has emerged as one of the key concepts in European politico-economic debate over the last decade. Few European citizens in both West and East can be unaware of privatization as an instrument of government policy. In the 1980s most Western European countries experienced some degree of privatization inspired by a revival in New Right thinking and the practical example set by the Thatcher administrations in Britain. In the 1990s, following the democratic 'revolutions' of 1989 and the fall of communist regimes, Eastern European countries have adopted privatization as a central element in their transformation from socialist, centrally planned economies to capitalist, market economies.

For sociologists the term 'privatization' has an earlier usage and a rather different meaning in the literature. The affluent worker study in the 1960s documented the increased privatization (home centredness) of family lifestyle (Goldthorpe *et al.*, 1969). In order to distinguish between the two usages, the government policy to expand the private/market sector and contract the public/state sector should be referred to as *economic privatization* in contrast to the *social privatization* of affluent workers identified by Goldthorpe. This chapter is concerned solely with the former process in Eastern Europe, and all references hereafter are to economic privatization.

The various privatization programmes underway in Eastern Europe are different in both scale and kind from those undertaken in the earlier period of privatization in Western Europe. For instance, in Britain during the 1980s, 5 per cent of business assets were privatized in 10 years. By contrast, all three countries of East-Central Europe (ECE) – namely, Czechoslovakia, Hungary and Poland – proposed initially to privatize 50–60 per cent of enterprises within 3–5 years. In practice, reality has not yet matched the rhetoric of the plans as privatization has been slower than expected, but the distinctive magnitude of the process is readily apparent.

Beyond the mere disparity in scale lies an important difference in context. Western Europe has undergone a process of *marginal privatization* in a mixed economy, which was already overwhelmingly private. On the other hand, Eastern Europe is experiencing a process of *total privatization* as part of the transformation from a state-dominated economy to a predominantly private market economy. Privatization in Eastern Europe is not taking place in an established functioning market economy. On the contrary, the privatization process is itself a major contribution to the creation of a market environment.

The literature on Western (marginal) privatization encompasses many different forms and exhibits a variety of definitions (for a fuller discussion than occurs below see Edgell and Duke, 1991: ch. 7). Some authors adopt a narrow definition of privatization as the transfer of ownership from the state/public sector to the market/private sector. Others employ a broader definition incorporating a diversity of measures which reduce the state's role in economic activity. Heald (1983: 298) proposed a broad view of privatization as 'strengthening the market at the expense of the state' and outlined four separate components: (1) *denationalization*, the transfer of assets/activities from the state sector to the private sector; (2) *liberalization*, the removal of obstacles which inhibit private sector competition against the state sector; (3) *contracting out*, the privatization of the production of a service financed by the state sector; (4) *increasing charges*, the reduction of subsidies for services provided by the state sector.

One of the authors has argued in an earlier work on Britain for a broad definition of privatization, because this encompasses all the processes involved in the Thatcherite project of rolling back the state (Edgell and Duke, 1991: ch. 7). Writing on ECE, Stark (1990) and Grosfeld and Hare (1991) maintain that privatization is not just the transformation of state enterprises into private enterprises, but also the independent growth of a private sector alongside the state sector. Certainly, a broad view of privatization provides a better fit with the Eastern European context of total privatization. However, the measures emphasized in the latter context are unlikely to be the same as those advocated in a situation of marginal privatization. It is important to stress that in the circumstances of total privatization, analysis should not be confined to the transfer of enterprises from the state sector to the private sector, but should also include the switch from state provision of services to greater private provision of these services (see Duke and Grime, 1991).

In fact, the (English Language) literature on privatization in Eastern Europe has tended to concentrate on the transfer of large state enterprises into the private sector (e.g. Stark, 1990 and 1992; Grosfeld, 1991; Reynolds and Young, 1992). Some authors have adopted a broader framework, which matches discussions in the Eastern European media of three main privatization components: (1) the *small-scale privatization* of shops, restaurants, etc.; (2) the *large-scale privatization* of state enterprises; and (3) the *reprivatization* of property to former owners (e.g. Bartlett, 1992; Kowalski, 1992). This framework will be applied below in the sections on the three countries of East-Central Europe.

The decision to compare and contrast the three ECE countries is partly geopolitical in that they are all located on the boundary with capitalist Western Europe and are the most likely of the Eastern European countries to be integrated first into the European Community, ahead of countries like Bulgaria, Romania or the republics of the former Soviet Union. Furthermore, the privatization process is more advanced in these countries than in the rest of Eastern Europe.

THE MAIN ISSUES RELATING TO PRIVATIZATION IN EAST-CENTRAL EUROPE

The pace of privatization

The most fundamental choice concerns the pace of the privatization process. On the one hand, there are advocates of the *shock therapy* approach. The aim here is to privatize as quickly as possible, despite the risk of adverse socio-economic (and possibly political) consequences in the short term. Proponents of rapid privatization argue that speed increases the irreversibility of the whole reform process but dwindling popular support may well cause the brake to be applied abruptly. Not surprisingly, the Adam Smith Institute is in favour of speeding up microeconomic reform and privatization. They argue that, at the current rate of progress, it will take an average of 28 years for Czechoslovakia, Hungary and Poland to privatize 50 per cent of their enterprises (Reynolds and Young, 1992: 131). Carlin and Mayer (1992) suggest that the ultimate constraint on the speed of transition is the extent to which the West is willing to provide managerial and financial resources at prices that the East can afford.

On the other hand, there is some support for a more *gradualist* approach. This proposes a slower rate of privatization, which builds on existing institutions and the stock of existing personal knowledge. Murrell (1992) proclaims the superiority of gradualism (which he calls piecemeal social engineering) in terms of the greater productivity of small changes, and also proffers a timely reminder of Eastern Europeans' historical experience and suspicion of utopian blueprints (see also Hare and Révész, 1992). Arguments for gradualism may be located in the evolutionary theory of economic change (Nelson and Winter, 1982; Hannan and Freeman, 1989).

Methods of privatization

The most common technique for the small-scale privatization of shops and restaurants is straightforward *sale by auction*. This strategy is less feasible for the large-scale privatization of enterprises because of a lack of domestic buyers with sufficient financial resources (the question of foreign purchasers is discussed below on pp. 150–1). Much of the literature is concerned with alternative methods or techniques of privatization for large state enterprises.

A more appropriate method for large state enterprises is to transform them into joint-stock companies, prior to the *sale of shares* in the company. The debate then revolves around who is allowed to participate in the purchase of shares and under what conditions. Strict allocation according to economic principles would open the shares to all economic actors, but various attempts have been made to control the participants in the share issue. One of the major problems with the sale of large enterprises is the absence of adequate criteria for the valuation of assets. Centrally planned economies were not accustomed to Western market economy methods of valuation. In the final analysis an asset is worth what somebody is willing to pay for it.

Privatization schemes involving the sale of shares may be usefully classified according to the level of participation among three key categories – employees, management and citizens. *Employee participation* in share issues is often advocated as a means of binding the workers to the future of the enterprise. One proposal has been that a proportion of shares, usually in the region of 10–20 per cent, be allocated as a gift to the employees of an enterprise. The trade unions are the strongest supporters of workers' participation, but critics cite the danger of employees in the uncertain ECE situation preferring immediate consumption to investment. This can be overcome by placing time restrictions on the sale of employees' shares. Employee ownership is more conceivable in cases of liquidation of large enterprises, where the assets are divided up to be sold off. In the latter case employees are capitalizing on their positional resources in relation to the assets (Stark, 1992).

Another group with even more opportunity to convert their positional resources into property or share ownership are the management. *Management participation* is enhanced by their insider status within the enterprise, which places them in an advantageous position in relation to share issues. Managers are more likely to possess the financial means to buy shares (and/or assets), they have the expertise to appraise the viability of the enterprise and the power to influence the valuation of assets. Such is the position of managers during the phase of transition to a market economy that many are able to consolidate their status. This process has been described as '*nomenklatura* capitalism', whereby political capital under the old system is converted into economic capital under the new system. There have been many examples in ECE of managers setting up subsidiary companies to which all the assets are transferred, thus leaving the parent as a shell company. The managers ensure that they control shares in the subsidiary. Critics of *nomenklatura* capitalism point to the potential abuses of power, but the lack of experienced replacements means that the managers are still required in the new system.

Unique to Eastern Europe is the attempt to employ *citizen participation* in the sale of shares. Nowhere else in the world has this form of *mass privatization* been attempted. Participation in this process is based on civic rather than economic principles (Stark, 1992). All citizens are awarded vouchers, which they can exchange into bids for shares of selected enterprises. A supplementary issue relates to whether or not a registration fee should be charged for participation in the bidding. Opponents of an inclusion threshold point to the positive political impact of the free distribution of vouchers. Defenders of a registration fee argue that the resultant accelerated differentiation of wealth will create a property-owning middle class, which is seen by some as an essential ingredient of a successful transition.

The main advantage of such a mass privatization scheme is that it is potentially the fastest way of transferring a large number of state enterprises into the private sector. But given the untried nature of this process, the outcome (as yet) remains uncertain. An additional advantage to those of speed and building political support is that mass privatization provides an element of learning by doing, which makes it an institutional vehicle for creating a market environment (Murrell, 1992). Disadvantages of such a scheme of mass participation are that the citizens lack adequate information about the enterprises, the high administration costs of this process and the problem of oversubscribed and undersubscribed share offers.

A lack of fit between bids and shares can be addressed by a series of iterative rounds, where the price of oversubscribed shares is increased and the price of undersubscribed shares is decreased. However, a residual pool of undersubscribed shares in unprofitable enterprises is liable to remain unsold. In order to address this problem, Reynolds and Young (1992) propose the use of unconventional privatization techniques such as *market access privatization* (offering a state contract or licence as an inducement) and *negative value privatization* (paying investors to take over). They argue that it is impossible even to give away an unprofitable enterprise.

The role of the state

Another important issue is the degree of state intervention in the privatization process. To what extent should the government adopt an active or passive role? Arguments for *controlled privatization* rest on the government maintaining control over the transition to a market economy and preventing excessive profiteering. Critics highlight the need for a market environment to evolve rather than attempt to create capitalism by design.

The opposite extreme to controlled is *spontaneous privatization*, sometimes referred to as uncontrolled or wild privatization. It occurs spontaneously as a result of market forces without state assistance. Removal of bureaucratic involvement has the effect of speeding up the transition process. However, critics associate spontaneous privatization with *nomenklatura* or political capitalism. Even those favouring spontaneous privatization require some action from government in the form of establishing the ground rules by a combination of liberalization (removing market restrictions) and regulation (preventing anti-competitive behaviour).

The degree of foreign investment

A further choice relates to the adoption of a restrictive or liberal policy towards foreign involvement in the privatization programme. ECE is politically sensitive to the prospect of high levels of foreign investment in their enterprises. There are fears that foreign investors will undervalue assets and that the country will be sold too cheaply with a possible loss of national economic sovereignty. In reality political and popular overvaluation of assets may be the greater problem. Often only foreign investors have the requisite financial resources to restructure large state enterprises, and the vehicle for this may be *joint ventures* between a foreign company and either a domestic company or the state. An important advantage associated with foreign ownership is the introduction of advanced Western technology into the enterprises, but a probable side effect of this will be labour shedding and increased unemployment.

The involvement of financial intermediaries

For the mass privatization schemes to operate successfully, an institutional structure of financial intermediaries is likely to be necessary. Organizations such as investment funds/trusts act as intermediaries between the citizens and the enterprises. The investment funds act as asset managers and may be operated by foreign investment companies. This kind of foreign involvement has the political advantage of combining direct access to Western expertise without conceding direct ownership. Debate centres on whether these intermediary institutions can be relied upon to develop organically in the market environment or whether the government should actively create them. A related point extends the argument to cover the need for an effective framework of functioning banks and stock exchanges.

Dispersed versus concentrated ownership

Proponents of a more dispersed ownership of enterprises cite moral justification in terms of greater equality and the associated political advantage of increased popular support for privatization. The proposals for mass privatization are likely to produce the greatest dispersion, in the initial phase at least. Thereafter the willingness and the speed with which individual shareholders sell out to wealthier individuals or institutions will determine the degree of concentration of ownership. The dangers of too many small shareholders are highlighted by those favouring more concentrated ownership. A divergence between formal ownership and effective control is likely to increase the power of the enterprise managers or the foreign investor in the case of joint ventures.

Restitution to former owners

A crucial question facing Eastern European governments is that of *reprivatization*. Should the government return property to the former owners (or their descendants) prior to the communist regime's appropriation of private land and property? Restitution to the former owners may take the form either of physical restitution or suitable financial compensation. Already there are amusing tales from ECE of individuals in small urban flats being awarded a herd of cattle in restitution.

Certainly the case for restitution occupies the moral high ground and receives the political support of those likely to benefit from it. Others see in it the advantage of enlarging the property-owning middle class. Restitution is, however, not without difficulties. There are often genuine problems of identification and verification of claims, and the administrative burden of a restitution programme is very high. The prospect of reprivatization of their homes may also politicize tenants' groups into taking collective action to defend their interests.

Restrictions on new owners

Resentment against those who in various ways benefited under the communist regime has led to calls for their ownership rights to be restricted in the new system. Clearly, a moral case for such a policy can be made, but in economic terms the financial resources possessed by these individuals are needed in order to ensure that privatization is successful. A large proportion of the savings available for investment are held by former party officials, *nomenklatura*, and black marketeers under the central planned economy.

Social costs and political acceptability

The total privatization of ECE societies will inevitably result in adverse socio-economic consequences for sizeable social groups. The high level of social costs will inevitably test the political tolerance of the populations and the overall stability of the political system. Political pressure not to close down unprofitable enterprises will increase as the unemployment rate rises. It is likely that ECE privatization programmes will respond to political pressure by reducing the pace of privatization. A resurgence of former communists/social democrats standing on a platform of slowing down privatization and increasing subsidies to state enterprises is evident already in parts of Eastern Europe.

The residual state sector

It follows from the previous item that ECE governments must endeavour to improve the efficiency of the residual state sector. Some large state enterprises are likely to continue for at least 10 years. The proportion of unprofitable state enterprises will increase over time as the more viable ones are privatized. All of these residual state enterprises will require restructuring prior to any attempt at privatization. In other words, commercialization is an essential first step, which will further assist the creation of a market environment.

POLICIES AND PROGRESS OF PRIVATIZATION IN HUNGARY

Economic reform began in Hungary in 1968 but Czechoslovakia was, figuratively speaking, plunged into darkness because of the Soviet-inspired invasion. Although Hungary, Czechoslovakia and Poland were communist countries and had command economies, then, as now, they approached the management of their economies in different ways. Hungary reformed itself from within; there was no need for civil unrest, as in Poland, or an abrupt ending of communism as in Czechoslovakia. The Hungarian communist government paved the way for its own demise.

The path to the creation of a market environment has certainly not been trouble free. The 1970s investment boom was funded by foreign capital which led to Hungary accumulating the largest per capita external debt in the world. Hare and Révész (1992) argue that the best solution to the debt problem is for Hungary to maintain its existing resolve to service the debt and for Western governments and banks unilaterally to offer generous debt relief. They suggest, further, that this – together with free access to EC markets – would be the most beneficial form of aid. They feel that a success story for Hungary could act as a role model more effectively than any number of official reports.

If Hungary is now to be cast in the role of an exemplar it would not be for the first time. The reforms of the 1970s and 1980s can be viewed in much the same light. Hungary, throughout the period, was a 'test bed' for the concept of 'market socialism'. The really significant issue which distinguishes Hungary from Poland and Czechoslovakia is that by 1989 the reforms had led to the establishment of many of the institutions and practices of a market economy. From the early 1980s legal, small-scale businesses developed rapidly and Hungary has therefore been able to adopt a gradualist approach rather than the shock therapy treatment initially applied in Poland and likely to be implemented in Yeltsin's Russia.

It has been pointed out by Bartlett (1992) that rapid progress in large-scale privatization has been combined with agonizingly slow progress in small-scale privatization. In considering the reasons why progress has been slow it must not be forgotten that during the 1980s many new private businesses were created, especially in the service sector, most of which continue to flourish (Bolton and Roland, 1992).

The current problem concerns existing state-owned small businesses, the privatization of which has been seriously delayed by the ambiguous structure of property rights caused by the government's decision to reprivatize both land and church property nationalized after 1948. This decision was forced on the leading party in the coalition government, the Hungarian Democratic Forum, by its junior partners the Independent Smallholders' Party and the Christian Democratic People's Party. Bartlett (1992) considers that this politicization has had two serious effects: it has confused an already highly complex and uncertain system of property rights in the small enterprise sector, and it has exacerbated the general political and socio-economic tensions which threaten to compromise the broader privatization campaign. Quite apart from the problems arising from the restitution issue which concern land and buildings, there are further constraints caused by the fact that large state enterprises control the retail chains, and local authorities usually own the actual buildings which have been built since 1948. Clearly these important questions have to be solved before progress can be made.

The first large-scale privatization deal took place in December 1989 when the majority stake in the Tungsram light bulb enterprise was sold to General Electric of the United States for $150 million. This was an example of a Western company 'cherry picking' a Hungarian enterprise in order to give itself immediate access to the Hungarian market. However, unease with the process of Western corporations buying Hungarian firms was expressed during the run-up to the first free elections held in Hungary in the spring of 1990. Accordingly, in March 1990, three months before the coalition government headed by the Hungarian

Democratic Forum took office, the State Property Agency (SPA) was created to supervise not only the selling of companies to Western interests but also to oversee the *spontaneous* privatization of enterprises (in whole or part) which appeared to give existing communist managers unfair opportunities to safeguard their existing positions. Paradoxically the state appeared to some observers to be taking control of the privatization process and led to calls from opposition parties to 'privatise the privatisation' (Stark, 1992). As a result, after the election, the SPA put up for tender the rights to manage the restructuring of the twenty state-owned enterprises which were identified in the first round. Many Western consulting firms and investment banks were quick to respond, submitting tenders for a number of enterprises. In the event the twenty enterprises were distributed to twenty consulting firms and investment banks and these organizations have become, in effect, partners in the privatization process.

Although the SPA has the legal authority to supervise privatization, the current form of transformation is described by Stark (1992) as the decentralized reorganization of property. By this he means that the directors of many large public enterprises are quite legally (under the guidelines of the 1989 Law on Transformation) breaking up the organization along divisional, factory or departmental lines into numerous autonomous units each being registered separately with their own boards of directors but with the shares held overwhelmingly by the state enterprises themselves. It is not suggested that this type of privatization is going on behind the back of the SPA. Rather, it is being done with its approval because, while it is possible to deal with a small number of large privatizations, it cannot closely supervise a large number of smaller sell-offs. In effect, it appears that the practice which was criticized back in 1990 continues to exist.

Hungarian large-scale privatization has quite clearly been strongly influenced by Western institutions, and most of the big sell-offs have placed Hungarian firms under the control and ownership of Western investors. The transition to a market economy has been more painful than expected. In 1991 GDP fell by 10.2 per cent and was not expected to grow in 1992. Industrial production did not recover; it fell by 18.9 per cent in the first four months of 1992 compared to 19.1 per cent in the whole of 1991. According to European Economy (1992) the official statistics did not fully take into account the expanding private sector and tended to overestimate the falls in production. In 1991, the industrial companies employing less than 50 employees, where most of the private sector is concentrated, increased their production by 50.1 per cent compared to a fall of 21.5 per cent for companies with more than 50 employees. In 1992 the contribution of the private sector to GDP was expected to increase from 25 per cent to 33 per cent.

The restructuring process has caused (or coincided with?) large increases in unemployment. In June 1992 547,000 people were officially unemployed – around 10.1 per cent of the workforce. It is no surprise that the coalition government is unpopular and it has tried to respond by assisting domestic investors to involve themselves in the privatization process. What seems to have happened is that, after early 'successes', the sale of state assets to Western enterprises and investors is becoming more difficult because the best items in the portfolio have gone. It probably is not too cynical to claim that the West took the best, the Hungarians take the rest.

To placate criticism, measures have been announced in which domestic investors will be preferred to foreign companies where bids are similar, and also help will be given to domestic investors through concessional leasing and payments by instalments will be allowed. The government is to make an effort to divide up state companies before sale, partly to stimulate competition and partly to give locals a better chance in the market-place. Denton (1992) reports that Hungary has recently taken a leaf out of the Czechoslovakian book by distributing rather than selling state property, although there appears to be no intention to use a voucher system. Hence there is to be no attempt at mass privatization.

Hungary, where the privatization process overall has proceeded furthest, illustrates how complicated the whole issue has become. The highly visible early take-overs of some large enterprises by Western institutions perhaps led to the belief that the transformation could be undertaken quickly. Much has been accomplished but there is still a long way to go.

POLICIES AND PROGRESS OF PRIVATIZATION IN POLAND

In Poland a substantial private sector persisted throughout the communist era. Outside towns most land and property was not appropriated permanently by the state and so the problem of rural land restitution hardly exists (unlike in Czechoslovakia and Hungary). In urban areas it was a different story; most land and buildings were taken into public ownership. Extractive, manufacturing and service industry was nationalized down to the last shop.

Not only did a large proportion of agriculture remain in private hands but privatization in urban areas began before the ruling Polish United Workers Party was overthrown in 1989. The rise of Solidarity in 1980 began 10 years of political struggle which of course included the martial law imposed by Jaruzelski, but the 1980s also saw the formation of private firms capitalized with money raised in the West. These firms were allowed to manufacture consumer products which were in short supply, such as cosmetics and shoes. They were given the generic name 'Polonia'. The setting up of these firms was insignificant when set against the background of the control which the state exercised over all sectors of the economy. Tinkering with the system proved ineffective when it was clearly the macroeconomic framework and the political structure which needed to be changed.

Clearly, if command economies were to be restructured then a market environment had to be created. According to Grosfeld (1991) it was realized at an early stage that markets cannot function efficiently in the absence of private ownership of capital assets, and the debate has been centred on the way of transferring these assets from the public to the private sector. Even before the formation of the Solidarity-led government of 1989 a wide range of solutions to the problem of the reassignment of property rights had been discussed. They included the transformation of state enterprises into joint-stock companies, transferring the property rights to the employees and introducing privatization of state assets by issuing shares and selling them on a stock exchange which, it was assumed, would be created.

Until September 1989 the debate was purely academic, but suddenly what had been an intellectual exercise became a matter of urgent economic and political necessity. The Polish people appeared in 1990 to support the moves towards privatization. Some 61 per cent of a random sample thought that the creation of a free market economy was right for the country's future (Eurobarometer 1990) but they were very undecided on the question of the economic reform programme: 32 per cent thought it was succeeding, 35 per cent thought it was not and 33 per cent did not know! Later, in 1991, only 43.2 per cent of the electorate bothered to vote in a general election, indicating disillusion with politicians, democracy and the economic reforms.

There is a strong feeling, especially among the working-class element which forms the bedrock of support for Solidarity, that the workers should have the right to control enterprises and many see it as an alternative to the appropriation of state assets by the *nomenklatura* elite. Initially *nomenklatura* companies were defended even by economists from the opposition because they were sup- posed to help overcome the resistance of the old power elite to market-oriented changes. Undoubtedly this was a big mistake because most Poles view *nomenklatura* capitalists as privileged people taking advantage of their position to advance themselves in the new conditions. It has proved to be economically inefficient as well as politically and socially dangerous.

In July 1990 the Polish Parliament passed the Act of Privatiza- tion which represented a compromise between those who had been advocating the transformation of all state enterprises into joint-stock companies and those proposing self-management. The Act allows for different methods of privatization and different forms of ownership: free distribution through vouchers and the sale of shares, individual and commercial property, employee ownership, and the possibility for the employees to elect one-third of the numbers of the Board of Directors.

European Economy (1992) suggested that the declining trends which were evident in the Polish economy during 1989 were exacerbated by the radical stabilization measures introduced on 1 January 1990. This stabilization provided for price liberalization and an end to most subsidies, a devaluation of the złoty and the introduction of convertibility for current transactions, strict control of wage rises and a reduction in the state budget deficit to 1 per cent of GDP. This monetarist policy was considered to be necessary by external forces such as the World Bank and accepted by the Polish government which had as a main objective a desire to join the 'free market' as soon as possible.

The stabilization programme helped to reduce hyper-inflation from 640 per cent in 1989 to 149 per cent in 1990 and 60.4 per cent in 1991. In the first six months of 1992 prices increased by only 22.3 per cent The reduction in inflation allowed the National Bank to lower the key interest rates from 40 per cent to 38 per cent in June 1992. The stabilization programme has plunged the economy into recession. GDP declined by 12 per cent in 1990 and by a further 7 per cent in 1991. The small private sector actually grew by 25 per cent in 1991 but this could only partially compensate for the slump in state-owned enterprises; overall industrial production in 1991 was 14.2 per cent lower than in 1990 and 35 per cent lower than in 1989. Unemployment, which is obviously a key indicator of the effect of such a policy, rose from virtually zero in 1989 to 2.3 million in June 1992 which represented 12.6 per cent of the workforce (All the above statistics are taken from *European Economy*, 1992: 12–13.)

The Polish government made an agreement with the International Monetary Fund that the state deficit would not exceed 5 per cent of the state budget, and the 1992 forecast suggested that the deficit at \$4.8 billion would just be on the right side of this target. Planned changes included the introduction of charges for some health services, the limitation of public sector wage and pension increases, and the gradual removal of subsidies on transport and energy. European Economy reported that although parliament approved the budget, the Constitutional Court ruled against the cuts in public sector pay and pensions, which cast doubt on the ability of the government to stay within the IMF guidelines.

Some of Poland's problems relate back to the Gierek regime of the 1970s, when borrowing from Western banks on a large scale was used to increase investment in projects intended to improve the standard of living. In the first half of the 1970s such a strategy appeared to be working but, largely because little progress was made in exporting for hard currency, the accumulated debt could not be serviced. Indeed, Poland has been unable to service its external debt fully since 1982, and by February 1991 it stood at around \$48.5 billion. The IMF suspended all remaining credits in September 1991.

It is hardly surprising that popular support for the stabilization programme has continued to weaken, but further structural adjustments still need to be implemented. Personal income tax was introduced from the beginning of 1992 and applied to all people except those working in agriculture, and value added tax is scheduled to be introduced in 1993.

A large number of medium-sized enterprises have already been privatized, either by auction or through liquidation. Significant transfers of ownership have occurred in retailing with more than 80 per cent of shops (100,000 businesses) privatized by 1992

(Bobiński, 1992). Thus the small-scale privatization has proceeded rapidly.

Liquidation is a process which appears to be unique to Poland and had resulted in some 540 'liquidations' by the middle of 1992, employing around 180,000 people. Essentially the process involves incumbent managers and workers creating a private firm to lease assets from the state with the original state-owned enterprise being wound up. In effect the process is a 'buy-out' in which the value of the enterprise is determined by a consultant hired by management and workers and approved by the Ministry of Privatization. Around 20 per cent of the 540 liquidated firms employed over 500 people but were mainly non-industrial. Hardly any state enterprises have been sold by auction.

Large-scale privatization in Poland has proceeded very slowly. As Carlin and Mayer (1992) point out, privatization transfers ownership, restructuring redeploys labour and physical assets, while the monolithic state enterprises have to be dismantled to create viable private enterprises. All these processes are very time-consuming and their implementation has been held up by fears about the social consequences.

Plans for the Polish mass privatization scheme have been reformulated several times in response to the shifting balance of political forces. Areas of contention have been the number of state enterprises to be included in the first round, and the percentage of shares to be set aside for employees in the enterprise. Under the scheme, citizens will place their vouchers with investment funds, which will act as intermediaries. The proposal is for the investment funds to be operated by Western financial managers, thereby providing access to Western expertise without conceding ownership. Mass privatization may well be further delayed by political factors. The 1992 split in Democratic Union meant that the Democratic Left Alliance became the largest parliamentary grouping. The Alliance wanted to slow down the privatization process.

In contrast to the difficulties experienced at both the micro and macro levels in privatizing state enterprises, the emergence of new private firms has been very impressive. Grosfeld (1991) reported that private activity (including agriculture) accounted for some 40 per cent of GDP and 45 per cent of employment in 1991. Even setting aside agriculture, private firms accounted for 22.1 per cent of industrial output, 43.9 per cent of construction and 16.3 per cent of transport in March 1991. She also suggested that in September 1991 there were 3,512 joint ventures and that foreign investments were worth around $700 million.

Foreign investment is inhibited by domestic political and economic uncertainty on the one hand, and the recession which has overtaken many West European economies on the other. Bobiński (1992) reported that privatization through foreign investment in 1992 has been meagre. ABB, the Swedish power plant producer, bought 51 per cent of the equity in the Elta transformer factory in Łódź for $10.4 million, and CPC, the US company which produces Knorr and Marmite, bought Amino, a dehydrated foods processor in Poznań, for $8.8 million. The biggest deal to date has been Fiat's $2 billion stake in the FSO car plant in Nowy Tychy not far from Katowice. Fiat have long-standing links with the Polish car industry and in Nowy Tychy the firm produces the new Cinquecento model. It was hoped that further foreign investment would be made by Fiat's own suppliers keen to locate near the main plant and take advantage of lower production costs.

There are some successes but the whole process has proceeded much more slowly than originally envisaged; worse still, in a survey conducted in June 1992 by the government's own policy unit, only 18 per cent said privatization would serve the interests of the economy.

POLICIES AND PROGRESS OF PRIVATIZATION IN CZECHOSLOVAKIA

Discussion of the Czechoslovak case is complicated by the recent split into independent Czech and Slovak republics on 1 January 1993. The occurrence of the 'velvet divorce' so soon after the 'velvet revolution' of 1989 was partly the result of a rising tide of nationalist fervour in Slovakia, but also reflected the outcome of the June 1992 election, which produced radically different mandates in the two republics. Both the leaderships and the electorates had conflicting views over the need to speed up or slow down the economic reform process. Whereas the Czech electorate supported the shock therapy approach of Klaus, the Slovaks voted for Mečiar who advocated a gradualist strategy with more state subsidies of enterprises in order to preserve jobs (unemployment in Slovakia was four times that in the Czech Republic by August 1992). The two republics retained a customs union immediately after independence, and began to develop separate privatization policies. A further comment on the probable consequences for privatization will be made after describing the pre-existing federal situation below.

Of all the countries of Eastern Europe, Czechoslovakia was the most prosperous during the inter-war period as a successful market economy (Begg, 1991). Even during the era of state socialism its standard of living remained the best in Eastern Europe. In the early phase of transition back to the market, Czechoslovakia's macroeconomic situation was more stable than that of Hungary and Poland. It was the only country in ECE without a large external debt and has not undergone an equivalent level of rampant inflation.

The new Czechoslovak regime proceeded quickly with respect to *small-scale privatization*, which covers small shops, pubs and restaurants. A simple method of sales by auction for cash was employed with the organization of the auctions decentralized to local area committees. The initial auction took place in Prague in January 1991; a greengrocer's shop was the first item to be privatized. More than 120,000 small businesses were earmarked for privatization over a three-year period.

In the first auction of a small business bidding was restricted to Czechoslovak citizens, but if a second auction was required because items did not reach their reserve price, foreign investors were welcome to participate. A condition for taking part was that individuals had to deposit either 10,000 crowns (about £200 at the beginning of the small privatization programme) or 10 per cent of the initial price in a bank as a declaration of serious intent. In addition, there was a fee of 1,000 crowns (about £20) for entry to each auction. In the first 15 months of the scheme small-scale privatization progressed relatively smoothly with over 20,000 small businesses privatized.

The Transformation Act of February 1991 forms the corner-stone of the *large-scale privatization* in Czechoslovakia. Each enterprise has been obliged to formulate a privatization plan. They have two options, either direct sale (probably via a joint venture with a foreign investor) or participation in the mass privatization scheme. The latter provided each citizen with vouchers equivalent to 1,000 investment points in large state enterprises. In order to take part in the auction of shares, citizens had to pay a registration fee of 1,000 crowns (about £20).

There are to be two waves of *mass privatization* of which the first began in May 1992. Between 20 and 97 per cent of a firm's capital was available for bidding in the voucher scheme (a minimum 3 per cent was retained towards a restitution fund). Relevant ministries determined the initial asking price in terms of investment points. In subsequent rounds of bidding (up to five) the price was adjusted upwards or downwards according to whether the shares in the enterprise were oversubscribed or undersubscribed. The final (market) price was determined by the supply and demand for shares at successive auctions.

Early results from the mass privatization scheme were encouraging. Participation was high as 80 per cent of the electorate took up the option of buying vouchers (making for a total of 8.5 million participants). The first wave of privatization involved shares in 1,491 large state enterprises. After the first round of bidding, 48 enterprises (3 per cent) were fully privatized with all their shares sold. Of the remaining enterprises around a third were oversubscribed (more bids than shares) and two-thirds undersubscribed (more shares than bids). Following two rounds of bidding in the first wave, 122 enterprises (8 per cent) were fully privatized and 56 per cent of the total shares had been bought. Predictably, several very large unprofitable engineering conglomerates failed to spark any early interest.

An interesting development has been the growth of intermediate organizations designed to assist the citizens in placing their bids and at the same time taking their share of any profit. Fully 72 per cent of voucher holders entrusted their vouchers to one of 436 private investment funds. In order to prevent overconcentration of ownership in key companies, the investment funds are limited to a maximum of 20 per cent of the shares in any one enterprise.

At the time of writing it is too early to pass considered judgement, but mass privatization seems to be working. Completion of the first phase should create millions of new citizen shareholders. Uncertainty remains over what will happen afterwards – will the newly privatized companies be profitable? And will the initially dispersed pattern of ownership soon alter to one of concentrated control by the largest private investment funds? The Czechoslovak method of mass privatization contains the paradox of strong state control, which at the same time is intended to nurture a market environment. For the citizens there is an element of learning by doing as they cope with the simulated capital market established by the state's voucher scheme. The state hopes to achieve a functioning equity market at the end of the process.

One of the earliest developments after the change of regime was a rapid increase in *joint ventures* with foreign investors from 27 in 1989 to 135 in 1990. By the end of 1992 there were over 4,000 joint ventures but most of them were small in scale. The only example of mega foreign investment was that of Volkswagen with Skoda, the manufacturer of Czech cars. Only a fraction of the joint ventures were operational already and these were overwhelmingly German and Austrian. Historical circumstances dictate that this progress has been accompanied by fears of German economic domination. The other major problem with joint ventures concerns their location. There was a marked concentration in the capitals of the two republics (Prague and Bratislava), which reflected the relatively better infrastructure and closer proximity to the administrative centre. More alarmingly, for the newly independent Slovak Republic only 10 per cent of joint ventures were located in Slovakia.

Post-communist Czechoslovakia also moved quickly in relation to the *reprivatization* of property confiscated or nationalized by the communist regime. There have been three restitution acts which cover property taken on or after 25 February 1948, the date of communist seizure of power (Cepl, 1992). The legislation sought to ensure natural restitution to former owners (or their heirs) wherever possible, although there was also provision for financial compensation. Only the return of immovable property (residential and commercial buildings) was included and the thorny issues of land and church property were excluded (unlike in Hungary). Restitution was restricted to Czechoslovak citizens, but expatriates (there are over 500,000 Czechs living abroad) who returned permanently and reclaimed citizenship were eligible to apply for restitution. A 6-month time limit was placed on restitution claims so as not to impede the privatization process (especially the small-scale privatization). In other words, reprivatization had to take precedence over other forms of privatization. Indeed the speed of action on reprivatization also facilitated relatively rapid progress on the small privatization.

If Czechoslovakia has opted for the high moral ground with respect to restitution, this stance has been less evident in the case of retribution for beneficiaries of the former communist regime.

Czechoslovak society has undergone a process of *lustration* (or purification) with the removal of previous secret police informers from positions of authority. Estimates indicate the existence of around 140,000 such informers (Cepl, 1992). The October 1991 law on lustration provided a framework for the dismissal of informers from certain posts and positions within the state sector hierarchy. Notably, lustration had no similar effect in the private sector.

A related question concerns the presence of 'dirty money', which is held by those persons advantaged in one way or another under the old system, and which is now available for use in the privatization sales. Tomas Ježek, the Czech Minister for Privatization, has suggested that the best method for cleaning the money is precisely to let them invest it. Not everyone shares this benevolent view of economic advantages bestowed on the *nomenklatura* and black marketeers.

Finally, returning to the question of the division into Czech and Slovak republics, there are remaining problems with regard to privatization policy. The division of property was easier to agree on items covered by the small-scale privatization than it was on the large. At the time of writing, the division of federal property and assets has not yet been finalized. Interestingly, 10 per cent of Slovaks have given their vouchers to Czech investment funds as compared with only 1 per cent the other way round. Similarly, only 10 per cent of foreign investment has gone to Slovakia. Independence is likely to result in the pursuance of privatization with renewed vigour in the Czech Republic. By contrast, it is expected that the pace of privatization will be slowed down in Slovakia. The Slovak Minister for Privatization favours direct sales rather than the voucher scheme and, moreover, advocates a greater role for employee ownership. It looks as if the second wave of mass privatization will take place only in the Czech Republic.

CONCLUSION

A useful starting point in reviewing the progress of privatization in ECE is to contrast the three countries on the three components of privatization – small-scale, large-scale and reprivatization. Table 8.1 summarizes the progress on all three fronts in general terms. The summary expands and updates the conclusions of Bartlett (1992).

When comparing progress in the small and the large privatization policies, a clear difference emerges between Hungary and the other two. Hungary has proceeded more rapidly with large-scale privatization, due largely to the existence of prior legislation under the communist regime which facilitated the transformation of large state enterprises into private companies. Hungary's small privatization programme was delayed by uncertainties over the question of reprivatization of property, which added to the already complex legal framework in relation to small enterprise property rights. Czechoslovakia and Poland both moved quickly and successfully on small-scale privatization, but were slower in devising a legislative structure for large-scale privatization. Since the countries have established a legislative framework, Czechoslovakia has been much faster in executing the plan than Poland. This is despite (or perhaps because of) Czechoslovakia having by far the smallest private sector under the communist regime (less than 0.5 per cent of non-agricultural output in 1988).

Table 8.1 The progress of privatization in Czechoslovakia, Hungary and Poland

Component of privatization	Czechoslovakia	Hungary	Poland
Small-scale	Early legislation and rapid execution	Substantial pre-existing private sector but slow progress since	Early legislation and rapid execution
Large-scale	Slow legislation but rapid execution	Prior legislation, therefore rapid progress	Slow legislation and slow execution
Reprivatization	Early legislation and rapid execution	Politicization delayed legislation	Less of an issue due to rural private sector

The situation with respect to reprivatization reflects the different contexts in the three countries. Rapid progress has been made in Czechoslovakia in resolving the question of restitution in a consensual manner. After initially opting not to reprivatize land and property, the Hungarian government experienced a political rift among the coalition partners on precisely this issue. The resultant compromise legislation has failed to eradicate all the uncertainties undermining the small privatization. Reprivatization has not been such a salient issue in Poland, largely because of the persistence of private property in rural areas during the communist period.

An examination of the main aspects covered on pp. 147–53 reveals the continued presence on most issues of a dichotomy between Hungary and the other two ECE countries. On the pace of privatization, Hungary has consistently followed a gradualist approach, in contrast to varying degrees of shock therapy in Czechoslovakia and Poland. Both Stark (1992) and Bruszt (1992) stress the importance of different structural and institutional legacies in Hungary. The presence of a thriving second economy and a legal framework for privatization gave Hungary a built-in advantage with respect to large-scale privatization, and made the adoption of a gradualist strategy both possible and appropriate. Slovakia's switch to a more gradualist approach after independence was based more on political considerations than on a pre-existing economic and legal framework.

The methods employed to achieve small-scale privatization are similar throughout ECE. However, there is much greater variation regarding techniques of large-scale privatization, and the distinctiveness of Hungary emerges yet again. Whilst Czechoslovakia and Poland have made citizen participation in a mass privatization scheme the centrepiece of their policies, the Hungarian policy has relied more heavily on managerial initiatives. The end product is a system of what Stark (1992) calls institutional cross-ownership. Poland is intent on combining mass privatization with a limited degree of employee participation, which reflects the residual strength of Solidarity. Stark argues that the voucher scheme in Poland is being used as a means of legitimizing the market, whereas the Czechoslovak scheme is seen as a way of creating the market environment.

Further confirmation of the main split in policy orientation between Hungary and the other two may be observed on some of the other main issues relating to privatization. Hungary exhibits a higher degree of spontaneous privatization (with Czechoslovakia the most controlled), the most liberal attitude to foreign investment (with Czechoslovakia the most restrictive) and the most concentrated ownership of shares (unlike the more dispersed nature of the mass privatization schemes).

Bolton and Roland (1992) stress the important role of the parallel creation of new firms in the private sector (often in new industrial or service sectors) alongside the more conventional process of privatization, which transfers an existing enterprise from state to private ownership. When the independent growth of the private sector is taken into account, they estimate that privatization need involve only about half the number of state assets originally envisaged. Many of the other unprofitable state enterprises can, according to them, be closed down.

There are signs that the high social costs of economic reform and privatization are encouraging the growth of a political backlash with the re-emergence of former communists and social democrats, who want to slow down the reform process and privatization. This trend is clearly evident in (and contributed to the independence of) Slovakia and is visible also in the development of the Democratic Left Alliance in the Polish Parliament. Following on from this is the debate of whether or not privatization (especially the shock therapy variant) is essential to reform in ECE. There have been recent suggestions that it is competition rather than private ownership *per se* which is the crucial factor. An alternative solution often cited is that of the Chinese microeconomic reforms, which emphasize the introdution of competition into the state sector.

Privatization is progressing at varying degrees of speed and success between and within ECE. The whole reform process is now approaching a particularly difficult period of increasing unemployment and other social hardships such that the potential for a political backlash is at its highest. The unfortunate coincidence of economic reform in ECE (and the rest of Eastern Europe) with the world recession may yet have grave consequences. There is a dearth of data on the effects of privatization on households and social groups in ECE. Given the widely divergent interpretations of whether or not privatization is succeeding, there is an urgent need to review progress regularly. The authors hope to contribute to this research agenda.

ACKNOWLEDGEMENTS

We are grateful for the detailed information provided by the Czechoslovak, Hungarian and Polish Embassies in London. Also we have benefited from discussions with colleagues and friends, especially Jan Kára in Prague, Zoltán Kovács and János Ladányi in Budapest and Grzegorz Węcławowicz in Warsaw.

REFERENCES

Bartlett, D. (1992) 'The Political Economy of Privatisation: Property Reform and Democracy in Hungary', *East European Politics and Societies*, 6: 73–118.

Begg, D. (1991) 'Economic Reform in Czechoslovakia: Should we Believe in Santa Klaus?', *Economic Policy*, 13: 243–86.

Bobiński, C. (1992) 'Much Lost Time has to be Made Up', *Financial Times*, 3 July.

Bolton, P. and Roland, G. (1992) 'Privatisation Policies in Central and Eastern Europe', *Economic Policy*, 15: 276–309.

Bruszt, L. (1992) 'Transformative Politics: Social Costs and Social Peace in East Central Europe', *East European Politics and Societies*, 6: 55–92.

Carlin, W. and Mayer, C. (1992) 'Enterprise Restructuring', *Economic Policy*, 15: 312–52.

Cepl, V. (1992) 'Retribution and Restitution in Czechoslovakia', *European Journal of Sociology*, 33: 202–14.

Denton, N. (1992) 'From Infancy to Mid-life Crisis', *Financial Times*, 3 July.

Duke, V. and Grime, E.K. (1991) 'Urban Cleavages in the Emerging Democracies of Eastern Europe', Paper presented at the IPSA World Congress, Buenos Aires, July, 1991.

Edgell, S. and Duke, V. (1991) *A Measure of Thatcherism*, London: Harper Collins.

Eurobarometer (1990) *Results of Polls in Czechoslovakia, Hungary and Poland*, Released in November 1990 by the European Community, Directorate-General for Information, Communication and Culture (Surveys, Research and Analysis Section).

European Economy (1992) *Economic Situation and Economic Reform in Eastern Europe*, Supplement A, No. 8–9, Commission of the European Communities, Directorate-General for Economic and Financial Affairs, August/September 1992.

Goldthorpe, J.H., Lockwood, D., Bechhofer, F. and Platt, J. (1969) *The Affluent Worker in the Class Structure*, Cambridge: Cambridge University Press.

Grosfeld, I. (1991) 'Privatisation of State Enterprises in Eastern Europe', *East European Politics and Societies*, 5: 142–61.

—— and Hare, P. (1991) 'Privatisation in Hungary, Poland and Czechoslovakia', *European Economy*, Special edn no. 2, 129–55.

Hannan, M. and Freeman, J. (1989) *Organisational Ecology*, Cambridge, Mass.: Harvard University Press.

Hare, P. and Révész, T. (1992) 'Hungary's Transition to the Market: The Case Against a Big Bang', *Economic Policy*, 14: 227–64, April 1992.

Heald, D. (1983) *Public Expenditure: Its Defence and Reform*, Oxford: Martin Robertson.

Kowalski, J. (1992) 'Transformation from the Centrally-planned to the Market Economy System', Mimeo, University of Karlsruhe.

Murrell, P. (1992) 'Conservative Political Philosophy and the Strategy of Economic Transition', *East European Politics and Societies*, 6: 3–16.

Nelson, R. and Winter, S. (1982) *An Evolutionary Theory of Economic Change*, Cambridge, Mass.: Belknap Press.

Reynolds, P. and Young, P. (1992) *Eastern Promise: Privatisation Strategy for Postcommunist Countries*, London: Adam Smith Institute.

Stark, D. (1990) 'Privatisation in Hungary: From Plan to Market or from Plan to Clan?', *East European Politics and Societies*, 4: 351–92.

—— (1992) 'Path Dependence and Privatisation Strategies in East Central Europe', *East European Politics and Societies*, 6: 17–54.

Chapter 9

The great transformation and privatization
Three years of Polish experience

Tadeusz Kowalik

FROM LABOUR MARKET SOCIALISM TO THE NEO-LIBERAL OPTION

Given that the very term 'the great transformation' was coined to stress that the transition from a non-market to market economy lasted centuries, three years' experience in transforming a socio-economic system may be regarded as too short a period for making convincing generalizations. It should be remembered, however, that the 'Balcerowicz Programme' introduced in Poland on 1 January 1990 promised to bring about fundamental systemic changes within two years. We are fully justified, then, in asking how fundamental the systemic changes actually implemented have been.

Let us recall how the neo-liberal option was chosen. August 1980 saw the famous agreement between the communist government and the Gdańsk strikers on trade union pluralism. The trade unions obtained not just independence from both the ruling party and the state apparatus, and not just the right to strike, but also 'a genuine opportunity to express their opinion in public' on major economic decisions such as the allocation of social funds, the basic principles of wage determination, long-term planning, the direction of investment and even price changes. Needless to say, 'expressed opinion' was backed by the power to strike; it was thus more than simply a right of consultation.

The recognition of trade union pluralism was the first fundamental change in the communist system. However the strikers' demands did not go beyond the system (sometimes called 'monoarchy' as opposed to 'polyarchy'). Indeed, their assurance that they would not contest the leading role of the Communist Party and the principle of social ownership could be seen as legitimization of the communist system by representatives of society. Even the programme of 'A Self-Governing Republic', a document ratified by the first congress of Solidarity in October 1981, remained within the same general framework in so far as it challenged neither state property nor – at least directly – the domination of the Communist Party. The demands for workers' self-management and the democratization of planning could also be regarded as demands for the fulfilment of earlier communist promises.

The debates on economic reforms at the time of martial law, and subsequently, did not fundamentally alter the situation. It is also worth noting that, in spite of all the social and political differences between the blueprint drawn up by the Communist Party on the one hand, and that of Solidarity on the other which demanded the restitution of trade union pluralism and limits on *nomenklatura* power in the economy, economic issues were dealt with in a similar way. Both sides demanded (or promised) extension of market mechanisms, equal opportunity for various forms of property, and 'industrial democracy'. Illegal Solidarity did not accuse the government of proposing the wrong economic reforms, but of failing to recognize the importance both of democratizing political institutions and of winning the social support for economic reforms without which they cannot succeed..

The Round Table Agreement (the last contract between the communist government and Solidarity, signed in early 1989) brought substantial changes in the political system (a contractual share of opposition parliamentarians in the Sejm and free elections to the Senate). Economic matters, however, remained on the traditional track of reforming 'really existing socialism'. The Round Table Agreement on economic reforms outlined a sort of market socialist model which went further than the Gdańsk Agreement (*Stanowisko*, 1989). It was a clear product of the evolution of views in the Communist Party. In line with the thinking of old socialists and right-wing communists, the negotiators agreed to introduce self-management at the factory level, pluralism and equal treatment of different forms of ownership, a far-reaching liberalization of prices, and abandonment of administrative planning in favour of steering the economy with mainly economic levers. In addition, the two most important parties to the talks each postulated the expansion of the private sector. Private firms had been mushrooming since 1981. The Round Table

Agreement increased the likelihood of state firms being transformed into joint-stock companies, something legally allowed since 1987.

The unexpected victory of Solidarity in the June 1989 election catapulted its leaders into government. This constituted a turning point in the authorities' approach to systemic changes. Immediately, the new prime minister, Tadeusz Mazowiecki, announced that his government's main goal was the creation of a private market economy, a system which had proved itself in the developed Western countries. This aim was elaborated in the government's economic programme (Council of Ministers, 1989). In addition to some obvious anti-inflationary measures (which will be considered below), it proposed:

- ownership changes to make the property structure in Poland similar to that in industrially developed countries,
- the application of a full market mechanism (free pricing),
- the opening of the Polish economy to the world market by introducing the full convertibility of the zloty,
- the introduction of a capital market and a labour market.

The programme explicitly stated that the most fundamental changes would be introduced in the years 1990–91. The transition process was understood as a sudden 'great leap forward' into a market economy with predominantly private ownership.

It is not an easy task to explain the reasons for this overly optimistic blueprint. Several factors, however, do seem clear. Probably the most important internal factor was the sudden, unexpected, and yet peaceful and easy, collapse of the communist regime, which tempted the new elite to try to repeat a similar overnight success in the economic sphere. Jeffrey Sachs, a key American economic adviser to the new government, wrote at the beginning of 1990 that 'Poland's goal is to establish the economic, legal, and institutional basis for a private-sector economy in just one year'. He added that 'Other countries should pursue programs of similarly rapid transformation, tailored to national circumstances; as one Polish economist has put it, "You don't try to cross a chasm in two jumps"' (Sachs, 1990: 236). (What is more surprising is that he repeated these words a year later when the failure of the great leap forward was already glaringly obvious (Sachs, 1991: 236).) No doubt linking the short-run stabilization measures with the more ambitious tools and targets, and presenting all of them as a necessary and consistent package of 'shock therapy', looked like a great opportunity. Then, as now, hardships could be presented as the unavoidable costs of taming (hyper) inflation. Haste also precluded public debate on the transition proposals, which were presented as the product of professional expertise which left no room for lay opinion. According to official government propaganda, there was no alternative.

The government rightly expected the initial enthusiasm created by a peaceful revolution to be short-lived. Thus, the more the fundamental and difficult changes were made in the initially favourable climate, the better. Some political leaders may well have feared that the great majority of Poles, Solidarity's rank and file in particular, would generally become hostile to a programme of capitalist restoration involving mass unemployment, growing income disparities, etc. Such a fear would explain Wałęsa's claim that strengthening the trade unions and striving for radical economic changes were obviously contradictory (Lawinski, 1989), which in turn would explain his hasty acceptance of the Balcerowicz Programme, in his capacity as the then chairman of Solidarity, without any prior negotiation or even internal debate.

For all the above reasons, the new authorities probably regarded radical change as a race against time. There were also, however, external factors obliging them to hurry. In 1989 the belief was widespread that Poland could not escape from deep economic crisis without substantial foreign assistance. But Poland, like many countries in the Third World, was caught in a debt-trap with all that that implies. In order to secure more credits, the Polish government had to accept IMF and World Bank conditionality – and those two international financial institutions wanted rapid economic reform.

Immediately after their unexpected victory in June 1989, Wałęsa and his close allies had launched their dramatic appeal to the West for assistance.

Poland is pioneering the transformation of totalitarian communism into democracy. It is also initiating the transformation of a centrally planned economy into a market economy. The changes in Poland may serve as an example for other countries. If successful, these peaceful reforms will alter the existing situation within the socialist bloc and will furthermore have a decisive impact on the future shape of East and Central

Europe . . . If these reforms are not carried out, the result will be a deepening economic crisis with ensuing political destabilisation and a return to dictatorship.

(Wałęsa and Merkel, 1989: 1)

Asking for a credit of US$10 billion, the appeal acknowledged that foreign assistance would be linked with IMF and World Bank endorsement and monitorng of the stabilization programme and the programme of systemic changes. Even so, it is difficult to say what the role of conditionality was in shaping fundamental systemic changes. Many official declarations suggest that the views of the new Polish rulers closely resembled those of both IMF and World Bank experts and American neo-liberal advocates of the free market. One of the latter, Jeffrey Sachs, is widely regarded as the co-author of the Balcerowicz Programme. We can thus say that the main systemic choice was made the moment Mazowiecki selected an economic team headed by Leszek Balcerowicz and assisted by several of his colleagues. We can also say that the US government has had great influence on Polish economic policy, not through crude interference, but rather through the IMF, the World Bank, and its own strong ideological and political impact on the economic thinking and policy of the Polish ruling elite.

THE AMBIGUOUS RESULTS OF THE 'BIG BANG'

The stabilization programme implemented from 1 January 1990 has brought highly ambiguous results. The stabilizing effects have been rather modest and the negative consequences have been painful and long-lasting and have drastically exceeded the government's expectations.

Perhaps the most spectacular success of the 'shock therapy' has been the transition from a shortage economy to a demand constrained economy. Many markets, especially food, suffer now not shortages but a lack of effective demand. Internal convertibility has been introduced, and the rate of exchange has been relatively stable and fully controlled by the government. The rate of inflation has been tamed, though it still remains one of the highest in Europe (over 600 per cent in 1990, 71 per cent in 1991 and 42 per cent in 1992) (Głowny, 1993). The cost of these achievements has, however, been very high. Over the first year alone (1990), GDP declined not by the forecast 3 per cent but by 12 per cent, and industrial production fell not by the forecast 5 per cent but by 23 per cent. Real wages were lower by about one third. Personal consumption declined by 15 per cent (mainly in the demand for industrial products and services). Economic performance in 1991 was only slightly better. Even now, at the beginning of 1993, signs of recovery are very erratic. Thus a severe recession has turned into a protracted depression, or – if high inflation is taken into account – 'slumpflation'. The sharp fall in production led to a budget deficit by autumn 1991 as deep as in the last days of the communist regime. Even the most basic expenditures in health, education, science and culture have been cut. The situation is so dramatic that the World Bank has proposed for Poland 'The Budget of National Salvation'. To some extent this is all a consequence of the collapse of trade with the former USSR, but the main reason is the orthodox, and very rigid, austerity policy. It is well known that the IMF recipe usually results in recession, but in a non-market economy the negative consequences are apparently still more painful.

The authorities expected the recession to bring about a typical Schumpeterian 'creative destruction' leading to a modernization of industry. Liberalization of prices, tight money and free foreign trade policy, and a high demand barrier created chiefly by almost frozen wages, would all force enterprises to strive for greater efficiency. Enterprises which failed to meet efficiency requirements were supposed to go bankrupt. Unemployment was to improve work disicipline, raise the quality of products, etc. Open unemployment was to reduce the 'unemployment on the job' or disguised unemployment.

The results are far removed from government expectations. The exceptionally austere state parameters hit not only efficient firms with obsolete equipment, but also recently modernized plants. Overburdened by taxation (in 1991 the state took from state firms almost 100 per cent of gross profits) and high interest rates, firms have not had the money for modernization. Some researchers are alarmed that there are clear disincentives to modernize in that the more technologically modern the enterprise the more tax per capita it pays (Strzelecki, 1992). Since employment is declining more slowly than production, disguised unemployment is relatively higher than before. Workers now care about their jobs and absenteeism has fallen, but managers are either uninterested in taking advantage of increased labour commitment (because of their monopoly position) or unable to do so (because they lack the investment funds for a reorganization of work). In addition there is the almost insurmountable barrier to the more rational use of labour posed by the housing shortage.

In sum, the market mechanism did not, and does not, work as expected, despite a very high demand barrier. We may say that recession brought about much destruction but very little creativity.

THE PRIVATIZATION STALEMATE

'Slumpflation' has generated a very unfavourable environment for privatization. The problem lies in the drastic impoverishment of the population and thus in the decimation of private savings. During a recession people defend first the standard of living they have previously enjoyed. Perhaps more important still, slumpflation generates a pervasive anxiety in society, and pessimistic expectations among potential investors. Society's confidence in Poland's economy depends immensely on confidence in the government and its policies. Since 'shock therapy' has brought results radically different from its promises, people have become very sceptical, often suspicious, about any programmes launched by more or less the same government. The feeling is widespread that recession and unemployment are the deliberate product of a government intent on building a new socio-economic system on the ruins of the old. Thus, in contrast to the stabilization programme, which at least at its inception enjoyed tacit societal approval, the privatization programme meets with growing opposition.

The diagnoses given by authors differ greatly, but the terms used are quite similar: vicious circle, blind alley, stalemate, the end of good weather for reforms, fear of privatization. Even a gift from the state in the form of (free) vouchers entitling citizens to obtain shares is being disavowed (Robinson, 1992). Opinion poll respondents say they prefer buying shares to receiving vouchers, though only 2 per cent intend to take part in buying publicly owned shares. Many people think that privatization simply means growing unemployment for 'us', further enrichment for the already privileged 'them'. The negative attitude of Poles towards privatization can lead to political hypocrisy. Some journalists have praised political parties for forgetting their electoral promises immediately after the election (Gadomski, 1991).

ON THE ROAD TO DESPERATE PRIVATIZATION

The privatization law enacted in July 1990 gives the government the relevant powers without specifying the timing of privatization, the procedures for the valuation of assets or the implementation programme. The Act makes it clear that privatization is obligatory and that almost all decisions pertaining to it are the prerogative of the government and its agencies. The government has the right to transform any state firm, even prospering ones, into a one-person (i.e. Treasury-owned) joint-stock company, as well as the right to liquidate any enterprise or to sell it off as a whole or in parts. The number of firms to be privatized is also largely a decision for government. Parliament's discretion is minimal and there is next to no role for public opinion, trade unions or the self-management movement.

The authorities planned two stages in the privatization of state firms. The initial stage was supposed to be 'commercialization', i.e. the transformation of state firms operating according to the old communist legislation into joint-stock companies owned by the Treasury. Within two years shares owned by the latter were then to be sold in the market – privatization proper. In practice, commercialization has brought no changes in the functioning of enterprises. The same people, by and large, remain in management, and the organization of work has not altered. The only visible change has been the abolition of employees' councils and the subordination of state firms to the central bureaucracy. This is why 'commercialization' has often been labelled 'renationalization', 'recentralization' or 'bureaucratization' of the state sector. In this respect our neo-liberals turn out to be *étatistes*.

The blanket character of the privatization clears a way for what has been called 'desperate privatization'. So far, however, the results of the privatization drive have been quite modest. Table 9.1 includes data for 1990–91. At the time of writing complete data for 1992 are not yet available, but by the end of June 1992 36 enterprises had been privatized by selling equity and 271 by means of liquidation (Głowny, 1992). Official reports include 'commercialized' firms in the one quarter of state firms indicated for transformation by September 1992, but only a few per cent had actually been privatized. So far the only true success is the so-called 'small privatization' of shops, restaurants, retail pharmacies, etc. By mid-1992, employees in private firms amounted to

Table 9.1 Data on the privatization since the day on which the Act took effect

	Overall	Aug.–Dec. 1990	Jan.–June 1991	July–Dec. 1991
State enterprises indicated for privatization by the Ministry of Privatization	1,258	130	375	753
of which: indicated for privatization by sale of equity	308	58	104	146
of which: completed privatizations	26	6	7	13
indicated for privatization by liquidation	950	72	271	607
of which: pursuant to the State Enterprises Act (Art. 19)	543	28	145	361
of which: pursuant to the Privatization Act (Art. 37)	416	44	126	246
of which completed privatizations*	198	–	100	98
pursuant to the State Enterprises Act (Art. 19)	44	–	21	23
pursuant to the Privatization Act (Art. 37)	154	–	79	75

Source: Statystyka Polski, no. 1, 6 February 1992, Supplement to Rzeczpospolita as translated by Economic Review, Polish News Bulletin of the British and American Embassies.
Note: * State enterprises crossed out of the REGON registry.

nearly 90 per cent of the total in this sector, but privatization had begun in it much earlier.

One of the most bizarre conclusions drawn from the experience of 'shock therapy' is that privatization should be speeded up. Rapid privatization is presented in official propaganda as a cure for slumpflation. Wałęsa has called for privatization 'at lightning speed even if compulsory' (Wałęsa, 1992). At the same time he promises to cope with unemployment. How he expects to be able to do both is not clear. There should be no doubt, however, that rapid privatization would bring, at least initially, further worsening of the budget deficit and most probably another drop in production output.

THE REJECTED ALTERNATIVE

The Round Table Agreement of spring 1989 considered the 'new economic order', acknowledged the merits of the participatory movement (in Poland inadequately called 'self-management') and declared that the role of self-management councils would be strengthened. This statement fuelled great hopes among self-management activists for what was called a 'socialization' of state property – especially after the Solidarity-led government came to power.

In Poland there were at least 15, perhaps even 20, per cent of state firms which had conscientious self-management bodies and which obtained better than average economic results. The self-management movement had gained great prestige since 1981 thanks to the struggle it fought for freedom and workers' rights and because of that it was widely regarded as the legal arm of illegal Solidarity. After the victory of Soldarity in 1989, many activists started to work with renewed energy on proposals for changes in property relations. Before long several alternatives for participatory enterprises were published. The most popular was the employee-owned company. Unlike the American employee stock-ownership plans (ESOPs), however, but in accordance with Polish tradition, the Polish projects envisaged some rights of participation in decision-making and control, not only for share-holders but also for employees. For example, one proposal allowed the state to own the bulk of the shares but gave the employees privileged shares entitling them to run the company collectively. Alberto Chilosi (1991) called it 'the privatisation of management'.

The main difficulty in creating ESOPs is that employees do not usually have enough money to buy the enterprise they work in. Even in a country as rich as the United States, employees creating an ESOP usually gain a controlling fraction of the shares, and still more buy the whole firm, over a period of years and with the help of tax privileges and loans (Blasi, 1988). In Poland, this process would have had to have taken longer, and state support would have had to have been greater, because of the general impoverishment of state sector employees.

The very idea of employee companies is deeply rooted in the doctrine of Pope John Paul II (it is one of the messages of *Laborem Exercens*) as well as in the non-communist socialist or social democratic tradition. But as a practical proposition it came to Poland from America. Lipton and Sachs (1990) found it ironic that many supporters of American ESOPs had travelled to Eastern Europe to organize support for worker ownership and were convinced that the effect was pernicious. Both Solidarity cabinets accepted Sachs's advice that ESOPs were not a solution and initially rejected the very idea of employee ownership, later creating only a very narrow path for their establishment. Even the Privatization Act of July 1990, which was the outcome of a long struggle between government officials and participatory movement activists, and which is commonly regarded as a compromise, set up financial barriers which could be surmounted by the workforces of only a few enterprises.

PARTICIPATION

Let us look more closely at the behaviour and performance of state enterprises challenged by the 'big bang' policy. I shall present some results from one investigation into the operations, internal social structure and performance of state firms during the first year (1990) of shock therapy. Dąbrowski, a Polish economist, Federowicz, a Polish sociologist, and Levitas, an American political scientist who studied under Kornai at Harvard, are a uniquely qualified team. They researched fifty small, medium and large state enterprises in nine different branches of industry, including a number of firms producing textiles and shoes, electronics and machines. Their work is interesting from many points of view but we shall confine our attention to the causes of the stalemate in the privatization process and the prospects for overcoming it.

First, the authors argue that:

contrary to the extremely pessimistic assessment of state firms by reformers, many firms, especially small and medium-sized ones, have adjusted fairly dynamically. Moreover, much of the blame being placed on firms for their failure to adapt had little to do with their worker-run character and instead lay in the failure of the state to undertake other institutional reforms.

(Dąbrowski *et al.*, 1991: 413)

Since 1989 workers' councils have been constantly blamed, by top government officials as well as by managers, for blindly striking out at factory managers and for a 'distributivist' attitude to their factory. The researchers did not find evidence to support this. In twenty out of twenty-three cases of fired managing directors, the change was positive; 'new managers were able to implement painful reforms more often than incumbents. Deep organization of reform was always associated with the appointment of new managing directors' (ibid.: 414). They also argue, contrary to the conventional wisdom, that at least in small and medium-sized firms, rivalry between the employee councils and the trade unions more often than not 'facilitated adjustment by inclining one or another group toward taking a long-term perspective on firm survival. It insured that management had some allies in the reform process' (ibid.: 415).

The authors also reject the accusation that unions and self-management bodies lack realism in demanding wage increases. They found 'surprisingly few' cases of industrial conflicts over wages in the first dramatic months of shock therapy. The situation was different in the second half of 1990, but there were usually particular reasons for this including attempts at reform of the internal wage structure. In general the behaviour of workers' councils did not confirm Lipton and Sachs's (1990) belief that workers usually vote blindly for increased wages irrespective of their firm's situation. Similarly, the behaviour of state firms at a time of shock therapy did not confirm the widely held opinion that they are an insurmountable barrier to market reform. On the contrary, they have taken 'sufficient responsibility for themselves to allow markets to approach equilibrium, and at a minimum have not dismembered the state's attempt to impose financial discipline on the economy as a whole' (ibid.: 426).

The three authors rightly point out that workers' participatory 'property rights' are the product of a long process and cannot easily be dismissed by the state. We may add that this is not only an outcome of forty years of communist rule and the struggle against it, but has a much longer history. Indeed this is one of the paradoxes of Polish history. It is well documented, for example, that skilled workers' wages in relatively underdeveloped Poland in the interwar period were higher than in France and almost as high as in Germany even though per capita national income was only one-third that of those countries (Herer and Sadowski, 1990). Despite her backwardness, Poland was already a pioneer in such workers' rights as the eight-hour day, and in some welfare privileges. Poland had also a developed co-operative movement and municipal self-government. All this happened not because of some benevolence on the part of businesses and the state, but because of the militancy of Polish workers, and of society following the long struggle for national independence. These are facts of Polish traditions which can be deplored, or labelled as 'the unbearable burden of history', but they cannot be ignored with impunity.

Already real life has proved stronger than the government's attempt to implement neo-liberal economic principles. It has had to step back and at least tacitly accept the strength of participatory tendencies. Classical British-style privatization – case-by-case transformation into joint-stock companies – appears too slow and costly. Neither Polish nor foreign capital has showed much interest in it. Hence the desire of government to speed things up by adopting 'privatisation by liquidation'. Initially it was thought this would allow rapid sale by open auction. Few outsiders, however, have been prepared to buy state firms. The unintended consequence of privatization by liquidation has thus been worker–management buy-outs in 90 per cent of cases (Wolf, 1991). Even Sachs has recently stopped criticizing employee companies, simply accepting that in Hungary and Poland at least 'workers and managers are granted clear ownership rights, usually through some form of leveraged buy-out of the firms on highly concessional terms' (Sachs, 1992: 320). He now apparently believes such privatization to be better than none.

THE PACT ON STATE ENTERPRISE AND ITS PRIVATIZATION

After the summer 1982 wave of strikes, and clearly as a reaction to it, the minister of labour, Jacek Kuroń, launched a proposal for a 'pact on state enterprise and its privatization'. In the course of many weeks of negotiations, the government, representatives of employees and the trade unions have provisionally accepted the agreement, which must now be ratified by national committees of employers and trade unions, and given legislative effect by parliament. The agreement provides first for centralized negotiations on wage ceilings, and second for worker and trade union participation in the privatization process. Some changes in financial arrangements facilitate the transformation of state enterprises into employees' companies, an option favoured by many workforce circles.

The final agreement, suspended for several months following the miners' strike in the winter of 1992, was signed in February 1993. And yet even now it is difficult to predict its final fate. Even the pact's architect, Jacek Kuroń, has publicly regretted that the idea of the pact is one-and-a-half or two years too late to be easily accepted. There are also pitfalls in the pact which risk failure. The most significant is arguably the time allowed for the privatization decision in each firm. The right given to the workforce and trade unions to choose the mode of property transformation is in force for only six months. If employees and their representatives fail to make their minds up in that period, the decision reverts to the government. It is extremely difficult for workforces to make such quick decisions given such factors as the deep recession, the still high inflation which threatens long-term strategies, the small number of legal experts, and limited access to bank credits. The right to co-determination may prove more apparent than real. Indeed it may be that the main goal of the pact is to quicken privatization by winning over the unions and public opinion for a desperate programme of transformation. Yet for all the pitfalls, it is also possible to interpret the pact as an unorthodox attempt to break out of the vicious circle, to overcome 'the balance of the powerless', by implicitly recognizing that the 'revolution from above' has exhausted its potential. Even if they fail this time, the talks point to a new road which may yet lead to a 'consensual transformation'.

THE CONSENSUAL TRANSFORMATION

There is a close connection between the fate of the pact and a more general social contract. To succeed a pact needs a general consensus. Both the more favourable government attitude to employee companies and the pact on state enterprises have occurred in conditions of sharp social polarization and resentment, if not open hostility, between government and trade unions and the remnants of the self-management movement. It is hard to imagine how a continued austerity policy can be reconciled with the pact provisions on centralized wage negotiations and privatization. Even if union leaders wanted to respect signed agreements, they would be under constant pressure from members not to. Therefore a radical change in the general lines of economic and social policy, a change in the very concept of systemic transformation, seems to be an indispensable precondition for any social pact. This change of policy must be recognized not only by the political elites but also by ordinary citizens. That is why we need a general social agreement.

There are, of course, major obstacles in the path of a general accord, but its achievement is not beyond the bounds of possibility, not more difficult than the famous Gdańsk Accord of summer 1980. If it were achieved, there would be a danger that it would degenerate into a Peronist-type populism, but this is not the only outcome historical experience suggests. There are successful and durable systems based on institutionalized consensus. If we think the examples of Austrian partnership and (West) German co-determination are difficult to emulate because of the greater economic and social maturity in those countries, the Swedish model, which was shaped in the harsh times of the Great Depression, may be instructive. The Swedish economy then was on approximately the same level as the Polish economy now, and Poland has, after all, a much better educated society than the Sweden of seventy years ago.

For a new social contract between the state authorities and representatives of the main social groups in society to be possible, very fundamental questions about the 'great transformation' would have to be reconsidered. For this the shortcomings of the 'big bang' may be a convenient point of departure. At stake are the pace of systemic changes, the system model we are to choose, and identification of social vehicles for, and supporters of, systemic changes. Let us touch upon the first two issues.

Recently, many politicians, foreign experts and representatives of international financial organizations have begun to realize that the process of transformation will last much longer that previously expected. Reconsideration of the Polish experience is incomplete, however, in so far as it invokes only the communist legacy to explain the slowing down in the implementation of reform. Accusations are very commonly directed either at society as a whole or at the managerial stratum. In particular, failure to restructure firms is attributed to the deplorable behaviour of state managers, a hangover from the communist past. Similarly, the defeat of the Mazowiecki cabinet was presented as evidence of the persistence of *homo sovieticus* in Polish society. Almost nobody, however, is addressing the question whether the emergence of a new social order is not by its very nature a drawn-out process which, even with better policy, would take a long time to complete. It needs to be remembered that much more modest systemic changes elsewhere have taken more than a couple of years. Let us recall two well-known examples: post-fascist Spain and West Germany. Spain, a country similar to Poland in many respects, required at least three decades for the transition from a state corporatist to private market economy and integration within the European Community. Even West Germany, a developed market economy greatly helped by the Marshall Plan, needed more than ten years to get rid of its war economy (Feinstein, 1990).

These two examples should indicate more credible time requirements for systemic transformation in Central and Eastern European countries which are in any case compelled to solve their problems in radically less favourable environments than Spain and West Germany enjoyed. The latecomers do have a chance to accelerate not only the process of technological modernization but also institutional changes. But this means only that changes which in former times took centuries may nowadays be accomplished in decades. The Polish authorities wanted to cut these processes down to a couple of years, thereby wrongly treating the whole problem as a technocratic task, as a question of implementing from above a blueprint of the new society designed by a small group of professionals. The social and historical character of the process of transformation has been forgotten.

Unlike economists and top politicians, historians, ethnographers and sociologists have understood very well the dangers connected with such a constructivist approach. As the distinguished sociologist Jan Szczepański put it:

It is easy to change legal acts, ideological declarations, institutional statutes, but it must be remembered at the same time that society can be said to have changed only when each and every one of its members has changed his way of thinking and doing things, his habits and his work patterns, his sense of duty, his values as well as his sensibilities and perceptions on what is natural and what is not in a given community.

(Szczepański, 1989: 135)

Among economists, Karl Polanyi, with his famous saying that 'the market economy can only develop in a market society', was a notable exception. If this was widely understood, there would be no constructivist attempts to implement a new socio-economic order in a purely technocratic manner.

This leads to an equally important question about the range of choice with respect to a future new system. The Polish authorities constantly repeat that they want to create in Poland 'the market economy institutions [which have] proven themselves in developed Western countries' (Council of Ministers, 1989: 20), and that there was not, is not, and cannot be, any alternative programme. If they have to refer to other blueprints, they do so in the manner of true believers for whom other religions can only be inferior.

One of the co-authors of the shock therapy programme, Marek Dąbrowski, presents the crux of the present dilemma as 'the choice between the model of contemporary capitalist economy and the differently understood "third ways"' (Dąbrowski, 1991: 3). Dąbrowski fears that all proposals for state interventionism are part of a hidden drive to return to a centrally planned economy. What matters to us, however, is the remarkable juxtaposition of multiple third ways and a single model of a capitalist economy. In which Western country has this single model of a capitalist economy been proved? In Austria with its substantial state sector and developed institutions of partnership? In West Germany with its co-determination? In Sweden whose system has transformed a poor country at the time of the Great Depression into one of the richest? There is a variety of models of a private market economy and each of them has succeeded in some respects and failed in others. Contemporary Western economies represent various combinations of private and public organization, of markets and administrative regulations. New models of modernization have been revealed by Japan as well as by the newly industrialized countries.

Speaking of the problems of transformation, Ralf Dahrendorf rightly pointed out that:

The road to freedom is not a road from one system to another, but one that leads into the open spaces of infinite possible futures, some of which compete with each other . . . To drive the point home with utmost force: if capitalism is a system, then it needs to be fought as hard as communism had to be fought. All systems mean serfdom, including the 'natural' system of a total 'market order' in which no one tries to do anything other than guard certain rules of the game discovered by a mysterious sect of economic advisers.

(Dahrendorf, 1990: 37)

History is stronger than the will of rulers and the sociological imagination of a society. Thus we can be sure that the Central and East European countries starting their march towards new socio-economic systems with their particular burdens of history, their different institutional structures, and their much higher educational standards and social security nets than were the case in the pre-industrial West, will arrive not at a simple replication of existing models but at hitherto unknown variations.

We have mentioned above three developed Western countries whose socio-economic policies have been based on partnership or social consensus. All three reached their social agreements not by starting with one (written) Act but by a process of trial and error. Despite these precedents, I would argue that a new social contract for Poland should take the form of single document clearly opening the new era of transformation. Many arguments could be raised in favour of such a general agreement. Three seem particularly important. The first is connected with shock therapy and its economic, political, social and psychological results – often termed vicious circles. Without spectacular change in socio-economic policy, negotiated with representatives of the most important social groups, it will be difficult to regain society's support for necessary reforms. Second, and perhaps still more important, is an argument connected with the rapidly growing nostalgia for the communist past. This is the most dangerous aspect of the official formula of a programme for which there is no alternative. If people are deprived of alternatives to a project in which they lack confidence, they will turn to the familiar past. Note how post-communist parties have come in the top four in each of the last two elections. And their constituency seems to be much more conservative than these parties themselves. At least a part of it expects them to restore the past.

The third and most important argument in favour of a general agreement is that participatory institutions, like infant industries, require a period of protection. This goes beyond access to loans, fiscal concessions, etc. As the American researchers Levine and Tyson (1989) have emphasized, market systems may be systematically biased for or against participatory enterprises. Such enterprises are better sustained in an environment created by a policy of full employment, taxes which restrain income disparities, and a Keynesian policy maintaining high and steady aggregate demand, than in a free market economy based mainly on rivalry.

ACKNOWLEDGEMENT

An earlier version of this chapter was presented at a seminar at the Stockholm Institute of East European Economics on 1 April 1992. I am grateful for comments made on that occasion.

REFERENCES

Act on the Privatization of State-Owned Enterprise, Warsaw, 13 July 1990.
Blasi, J.R. (1988) *Employee Ownership: Revolution or Ripoff*, Cambridge, Mass.: Ballinger.
Chilosi, A. (1991) 'The Case for Immediate Privatization of Management and Slow Privatization of the Property of State Enterprise', Mimeo.
Council of Ministers (1989) 'Outline of an Economic Programme for Poland', Warsaw, Mimeo.
Dąbrowski, J., Federowicz, M. and Levitas, A. (1991) 'Polish Enterprises and the Properties of Performance: Stabilization, Marketization, Privatization', *Politics and Society*, 19: 403–37.
Dąbrowski, M. (1991) 'The Course and Stages of Passing from the Centralized Economy to Free Market', in J. Hausner and T. Jeziorański (eds), *The Polish Economy in Transition*, Kraków and Warsaw: Towarzystwo Pracowników i Autorów Zycia Gospodarczego.
Dahrendorf, R. (1990) *Reflections on the Revolution in Europe*, London: Chatto & Windus.
Feinstein, C. (1990) *Historical Precedents of Economic Change in the Soviet Union and Central Europe*, Oxford: Oxford Analytica Ltd.
Gadomski, W. (1991) 'Wąski Margines' (Narrow Margin), *Gazeta Bankowa*, no. 50, 15–21 December.
Główny Urząd Statystyczny (1993) *Rocznik Statystyczny* (Statistical Yearbook), Warsaw.
Herer, W. and Sadowski, W. (1990) 'The Incompatibility of System and Culture and the Polish Crisis', in S. Gomułka and A. Polonsky (eds) *Polish Paradoxes*, London and New York: Routledge.

Lawinski, P. (1989) 'Ile wytrzymacie?' (How Much Can You Stand?), *Tygodnik Solidarnośc*, 29 September.

Levine, D.I. and D'Andrea Tyson, L. (1989) 'Participation, Productivity and the Firm's Environment', in A. Blinder (ed.) *Paying for Productivity: A Look at the Evidence*, Washington, DC: Brookings Institution.

Lipton, D. and Sachs, J. (1990) 'Privatization in Eastern Europe: The Case of Poland', *Brookings Papers on Economic Activity*, no. 2: 293–341.

Robinson, A. (1992) 'Poles Reject Idea of Shares Gift from State', *Financial Times*, 28 February.

Sachs, J. (1990, 1991) 'Eastern European Economies: What Is To Be Done?', *The Economist*, 13 January 1990; reprinted in A. Koves and P. Marer, *Foreign Economic Liberalization: Transformations in Socialist and Market Economies*, Boulder, Colo.: Westview, pp. 235–46.

—— (1992) 'Spontaneous Privatization: A Comment', *Soviet Economy*, no. 4: 317–21.

Stanowisko w sprawio polityki społecznej i gospodarczejoraz reform systemowych (Statement on Social and Economic Policy and on Sytemic Reforms) (1989) in *Porozumienia Okrągłego Stołu*, Warsaw: NSZZ 'Solidarność' Region Warminsko-Mazurski.

Strzelecki, M. (1992) 'Przemysł Lekki i Polityka Fiskalna: Żywiołowość Mało Skuteczna' (Light Industry and Fiscal Policy: Spontaneity Not Very Successful), *Rzeczpospolita*, 10 March.

Szczepański, J. (1989) *Poland: Facing the Future*, Warsaw: University of Warsaw.

Wałęsa, L. (1992) 'Jestem spokojny, kapital musi tu przyjsc' (Don't Worry: Investment is Sure to Come Here), Interview in *Rzeczpospolita*, 26 October.

—— and Merkel, J. (1989) 'International Assistance Program for Poland', Brussels, Mimeo.

Wolf, M. (1991) 'The Giant Leap to a Capitalist System', *Financial Times*, Supplement on Poland, 3 May.

Chapter 10

The great deformation
Polanyi, Poland and the terrors of planned spontaneity

Maurice Glasman

> Labour is only another name for a human activity that goes with life itself . . . To allow the market mechanism to be the sole director of the fate of human beings and their natural environment, indeed, even of the amount and use of their purchasing power, would result in the demolition of society. For the alleged commodity 'labour power' cannot be shoved about, used indiscriminately, or even unused, without affecting the human individuals who happen to be the bearer of this particular commodity. In disposing of man's labour power the system would, incidentally, dispose of the physical, psychological, and moral entity 'man' attached to that tag. Robbed of the protective cover of cultural institutions, human beings would perish from the effects of social exposure; they would die as the victims of acute social dislocation through vice, perversion, crime and starvation.
>
> Karl Polanyi, *The Great Transformation* (1944: 72–3)

INTRODUCTION

The central problem addressed in this chapter is why the most successful model of economic and social transformation in world history has been ignored in the debate in Eastern Europe. The West German post-war settlement combined the creation of a sustainable and efficient market economy, liberal-democratic institutions and parties, and the development of a welfare state structure based on ideas of solidarity and justice and the institutionalization of trade union responsibilities. Why has the social-market model in general, and co-determination in particular, been ignored as a necessary part of the transition from a closed to an open society? The question is all the more puzzling in so far as the four conscious goals of transition in Poland – (1) the construction of a market economy with recognized property rights and incentive structures; (2) the establishment of legitimate and popular democratic political institutions and parties functioning within a framework of rights enforced by law; (3) the creation of social stability through the establishment of minimal standards of justice and fair public procedures; and (4) the integration of the country into Western Europe – were all achieved by the Federal Republic of Germany after the Second World War. Thus the model for transition exists in the most politically powerful and economically successful state in Europe, which is also a directly neighbouring country. The question is particularly pressing as the principal agent of communist rejection, the Solidarity movement, was based precisely upon the values of the West German consensus, of which the most fundamental was the idea that the precondition of economic reconstruction was effective societal restoration. It will be argued that Polanyi's concept of the market utopia and his appreciation of both its appeal and its pathologies is the best available starting point for trying to explain this weird state of affairs.

THE SUBSTANCE OF SOCIETY, THE SHAPE OF HUMAN ASSOCIATIONS AND THE IDEA OF ORGANIC RATIONALITY

This section has three purposes. The first is to analytically define the basic elements of Polanyi's system, most particularly the role of labour in the reproduction of a culture. The second is to develop his analysis of Speenhamland and the consequent introduction of a free market in labour in Britain and to show that it is of comparative relevance in understanding the transition from Bolshevism to a market society in Poland. Paternalist authoritarianism, it will be argued, is a precondition of societal commodification. It will be further argued that the Solidarity programme of 1981 embodied Polanyi's idea of organic rationality, and that an internal consensus existed in Poland for the type of regime that was established in West Germany after the war. The third is to emphasize the importance of reason in the framing of agendas, and the fundamental role that feasibility plays as a force in mobilizing political support. Polanyi's work provides resources for

an explanation of how it came to happen that a workers' movement became the guarantor of a reform programme that removed
unions, solidarity and justice from Polish politics through the
acceptance of market utopianism. Polanyi's two general laws of
transformation will be developed and then applied in the second
section.

Tradition and transition: Polanyi's first law of transformation

> To separate labour from the activities of life and to subject it
> to the laws of the market was to annihilate all organic forms of
> existence and to replace them by a different type of organisation,
> an atomistic and individualistic one.
>
> (Polanyi, 1944: 163)

Polanyi's work is framed by a notion best summarized as 'organic
rationality'. This is the philosophy that human transformation
begins not *ex novo* but rather with existing structures and patterns
of co-operation, and, further, that human thought and action can
comprehend and control these changes. It is an industrial philosophy
in which solidarity and freedom are both created and sustained by
human labour; thus work and its democratic organization become
its distinctive central concern. Work is the means by which reason
and community are reconciled in freedom. Through this Polanyi
tries to explain the paradox of modernity which can be summarized
as follows: as it develops in size, technological power and complexity,
society tends to self-liquidate as the centralized state grows on one
side and the decentralized economy on the other. Amorphously
squeezed between the collective aggregator and the individual
maximizer, society as a functional moral entity disappears.

The emergence of the modern state with its national currency
and uniformity of tariffs destroys the existing institutions of social
organization such as municipalities, corporations, unions, parishes
and estates. The legal constitution replaces the ethical ties generated by shared vocational institutions. The central bureaucracy
and national police replace more immediate forms of discipline
and organization. The market, in its turn, undermines racketeering
and rigging. Confronted by stable patterns of production with
strict barriers to entry, quality control and labour restrictions, the
market solution is to abolish co-operation, not to democratize
rackets. The state creates the conditions, the market makes the

moves, and the result is the amputation of the body politic and the destruction of society.

The nationalization of politics and markets produces a further paradox. The new state becomes embedded in a structure of international economic competition but retreats from internal regulation and moral authority, surrendering the ordering of social relations and the distribution of resources to the market. Simultaneously the state becomes increasingly hostile to the intervention of other states in its national market. War between states becomes the parallel political order to that of international trade. (This conflict can take the form of imperial rivalry and issue in attempts to expand the size of the internal market, border disputes, or ethnic conflicts.)

Polanyi's first general law of transformation is that atomism and nationalism are logically and structurally linked through their mutual contempt for societal institutions and traditions. The atomism of classical economic theory is transformed into the nationalism of state conflict through the process of collectivism which disintegrates and then aggregates without mediation. An individualistic internal order is complemented by an anarchistic global order with sovereignty doing the transitional work; for both the sovereign agent of rational choice and the sovereign state of politics see dependency as a weakness, a denial of autonomy, and are constantly resisting the demands of social and economic co-operation brought about by the increasing division of labour, international markets and the complex skills and knowledge required to function in the modern world. As a consequence of the state's attempts to maintain international recognition of its currency, which remains its last surviving economic responsibility, society is further subordinated to the demands of the market in the name of protecting its purchasing power. Labour and land, the substance of society, are commodified to this end, and the particular forms of ownership, association and tradition through which they are combined have no rational or productive function left.[1] The lack of intermediate institutions then leads to the construction of an abstract community enforced by the state apparatus in order to restore order and the values of community. Nationalism is the most abstract of ideologies; it is an attempt to bureaucratically revive an emaciated corpse. It is also a necessity, for the state is the only institution left to which people can turn for relief from the market.

Polanyi's explanation for the savagery characteristic of the first half of the twentieth century is primarily conceptual and boils down to the thesis that once economic rationality and 'reasons of state' became severed from an organized social base both democracy and stable co-operation become irrational. Disembedded rationality and disembodied polities lead to the institutionalization of two extremely powerful abstractions – the state and the market – which monopolize societal organization. The state lacks the power to influence the economy directly, and thus can only act against outsiders. The self-regulating market refuses to accept the logic of co-operation, seeing all intervention as ultimately ruinous. Polanyi's question, which is ethical as well as empirical, is this: how can enough of society's traditional functions and shape be retained to resist the claims of both state and market subordination while modernizing production and renewing institutions? Polanyi was neither a nostalgic nor a utopian; his work is splattered with disdain for both modes of thought. Ultimately he was a social democrat who struggled to reconcile commitment to freedom, with the energy and possibilities it unleashes, and the need for solidaristic stability, without which the meaning of life disintegrates into brutish desolation.

Polanyi's idea of organic rationality, which he proposes as an alternative to the domination of states and markets, is derived from that moral tradition which seeks to reconcile the claims of reason with the demands of historical association. This philosophy has distinctive roots, the most important of which are the Catholic and socialist responses to liberalism defined in terms of competitive labour and labour markets in the newly created self-regulated economic sphere and the centralization of political power in the state through the idea of citizenship.[2] Both citizenship and economic self-regulation break the power of intermediate institutions and solidarities while severing politics from economics through the elevation of private property claims to the level of a human right. The constitutional separation of powers effectively means the separation of people from power over their economic lives. The domination of economic rationality in the organization of society is predicated upon an impoverished conception of the importance of economic institutions in the substantive reproduction of society (Polanyi, 1968).

It will be argued that the twin components of socialist syndicalism based on the idea of self-organized democratic power, and Catholic social doctrine with its stress on solidarity and co-operation, were the distinctive features of the Polish form of opposition to communism and that they found positive articulation in an alternative mode of societal organization developed most coherently in the Solidarity document of 1981 (pp. 326–90). The tradition of organic rationality can thus shed light on the Solidarity movement and the chance Poland had to reconstruct authentically its own traditions and ethical inheritance within the demands made by the global economy and the new international consensus.

Labour and the body politic

The most general category that Polanyi uses to frame his conception of society is culture. Three elements form its 'substance' – 'human beings, their natural surroundings and productive organizations' (Polanyi, 1944: 162). They are the units around which societal resistance clusters when the culture is in danger, and they are all threatened by the demands of a market society.

A necessary feature of organic association is that it does not allow the first element, the individual human being, to starve. 'It is the absence of a threat of individual starvation which makes primitive society, in a sense, more human than a market economy' (ibid.: 164). People, Polanyi insists, are not produced by the market or for it, neither are they produced by the state and its laws and institutions. Human beings are humanized by the plurality of institutions – work, church, family, etc. – that recognize them as bearers of an identity based on the possession of responsibility, skills and conscience.

The second element, land, is 'inextricably interwoven with man's institutions' (ibid.: 178). The commodification of land led to the breakdown of many of the characteristic institutions and practices of society, its distinctive way of life and meanings.

It is the third element, labour, however, which Polanyi regards as the most fundamental to social organization. This is what gives society its 'human shape' (ibid.: 83), and failure to recognize this leads to 'degeneration'. As labour is one of the primary activities of any culture, the institutions of its reproduction are constitutive of society itself; 'the organisation of labour is only another term for the forms of life of the common people' (ibid.: 75). The development of a market in labour means the subordination of society to the economic system, and the foisting of a market economy upon a differently organized community is 'only a short formula for the liquidation of every and any cultural institution in an organic society' (ibid.: 159). As every society must produce and transform, labour organizations prove the most vital and durable feature of its continuation, and it is these that must, above all, be removed if a transformation is to be successful, or renewed if society is to survive.

The key factor in any transformation, the rate of change, is the outcome of the conflict between tradition and change. Change is slowed by the delaying tactics and resistances which allow a community to preserve its meanings, institutions, freedoms and practices in the face of challenges and changes which *may* be necessary but which are also extremely painful. At issue is the renewal of existing institutions and practices through effective functional redefinition. Each change that society confronts is further distinguished for Polanyi by its 'degenerative' and 'reconstructive' possibilities. The former are characterized by a combination of social dislocation compounded by a removal of freedoms, the latter by a clear recognition of dependency and a broadening of the possibilities for freedom implicit in that recognition. Each significant change is marked by a 'storm' during which the 'substance' of society is imperilled. The three storms Polanyi analyses are the enclosure movement of sixteenth- and early seventeenth-century England; the Industrial Revolution of the late eighteenth and the nineteenth centuries; and the breakdown of the gold standard and the balance of power, the Great Depression and the rise of autarchy that characterized the 1920s and 1930s and which culminated in fascism and the Second World War.

Polanyi's most original development of the idea of organic rationality lies in his analysis of the Speenhamland scale that dominated British welfare policy from 1795–1834.

> The justices of Berkshire, meeting at the Pelikan Inn, in Speenhamland, near Newbury, on May 6, 1795, in a time of great distress, decided that subsidies in aid of wages should be granted in accordance with a scale dependent upon the price of bread, so that a minimum income should be assured to the poor irrespective of their earnings.
>
> (Polanyi, 1944: 78)

This practice was quickly copied through most of the countryside, and later even in some manufacturing areas. Superficially,

Speenhamland appears to be a classic device by which society resists the claims of the market through the introduction of a basic income or 'right to live' – the eighteenth-century equivalent of the citizen's wage. It obstructed the commodification of labour following the privatization of landholdings during the century of enclosures. It also undermined, or ignored, the fundamental role that human labour plays in the maintenance and transformation of society and culture. It destroyed standards of work by severing the link with quality maintained by apprenticeships and wages, it outlawed the guilds as organizations that taught and reproduced skills, and it ended up by transforming self-sufficient farmers into paupers dependent for their existence on the local parish bureaucracy.

> Speenhamland was an unfailing instrument of popular demoralisation. If a human society is a self-acting machine for sustaining standards on which it is built, Speenhamland was an automaton for demolishing the standards on which any kind of society could be based.
>
> (Polanyi, 1944: 99)

Speenhamland had an effect on English culture similar to that of Bolshevik rule in Poland. It not only led to the pauperization of the self-sufficient, the erosion of personal morality and the destruction of work skills vital to the health of the body politic, but it also deprived labour of its market value. In consequence, no self-organized class of employees was in place to resist the demands of the new commodified economy. On the contrary, a pacified, disorganized, demoralized society was helpless before the demands of the self-regulating market. The effects of paternalism on the 'substance' of the common culture were so devastating that anything seemed better in comparison. In time the victims of the new regime either passively acquiesced in, or actively supported, market utopianism as a way of rescuing their freedom and dignity.

The tragedy of industrializing Britain (cf. contemporary Poland) was that the people were faced only with degenerative choices: either the degradation of paternalist stagnation without political liberty through the decommodification of labour as in Speenhamland (cf. Bolshevism), or the annihilation of solidarity in the name of freedom associated with the unregulated commodification of labour and land (cf. the Balcerowicz Plan in Poland).

Polanyi links the wrecking of labour value in the reproduction of culture with the attempt to find refuge in the values of idealized community and belonging, which are usually plundered by paternalists as an alternative to confronting the demands of modernity through the institutionalization of justice. The rhetoric of reaction is just as dangerous to society as the bestialization of man proposed by the political economists. The coerced community of communism is even more injurious than the decommodified chaos of unregulated commodification. The tragic choice is that of either rotting in subsidized decay in a crumbling home or being left exposed and unprotected in that most inhospitable of terrains, a cultureless desert ruled by the law of the jungle. The alternative to communitarian oppression and stagnation, however, is not isolation. Polanyi cites Aristotle approvingly for stressing the self-sufficiency of domestic units (the *oikos*) as the non-contractual foundation of society and for treating the person outside reciprocity as either a beast or a god. The two poles of the idiot dialectic that recur in Polanyi's work are stagnant holism and methodological individualism. The former cannot explain change; the latter ignores society. Both misunderstand people.

Polanyi's second general law: communitarian authoritarianism as a precondition of market utopianism

The experiences of Speenhamland and Bolshevism illustrate Polanyi's second general law that the prior desolation of society in the name of its protection is a necessary precondition for the creation of a market society. Authoritarian protectionism leads to pathologies so enormous that anything seems better in comparison. In both cases there is a discrediting of intervention, and democratic resistance, as 'paternalism', which is considered injurious to civilization through its ignorance of the basic laws of nature, and immoral through its denial of freedom and responsibility. Paternalism was imposed at the price of the self-organization of labour, as was also the case in communist Poland. The anti-combination laws of 1799–1800 made worker association a criminal offence. The Bolshevik welfare system was similarly based on the denial of independent trade unions. The abolition of Speenhamland was welcomed as an act of freedom just as the Solidarity movement has embraced market utopianism as a means of achieving liberation from communism. In industrializing England, the dual process of legislative paternalism, with its exclusion of legal trade unions, and of subsidized wages institutionalized through Speenhamland, destroyed employment, quality of work, incentive, cohesion and discipline.

In the late eighteenth century the new order was justified by a turn in the new discipline of political economy exemplified by Townsend's *Dissertation on the Poor Laws* (1776). Political economy, as it was then known, discarded the inheritance of humanism and put the animal in its place. By approaching the law and order of human societies through the equilibrium achieved by dogs and goats on a fictitious island, it avoided the need for political and moral argument. While Hobbes argued that men behaved like beasts, Townsend believed that they really were beasts. Townsend, Ricardo, Malthus, Bentham and others supposed a biological foundation for the political order; the demands of the body itself displaced the body politic and gave a society its order and distribution. The naturalistic fallacy became the real foundation of societal discipline.

The appeal of this new science was based on its ability to link freedom with competition and survival. It resolved the opposition between nature and freedom by establishing global competition as the test of survival, it so happening that the freest societies were also the strongest. Humanist sympathies for the poor robbed society of vitality and self-respect and distorted the natural laws of supply and demand, as Speenhamland proved. The role of politics, understood in terms of state-enforced regulation in the name of the common good, was to protect the freedom of the market through the free exchange of private property holdings. Greed was 'elevated to a moral principle' (Polyani, 1944: 84). When all societies had been subordinated to the market, there would come into existence the optimal relation of freedom and scarcity in the form of one functionally integrated global society of unrestricted human exchange and productive distribution. The entire world would be based on 'market relations' as defined by Friedman and Friedman (1980: 14), i.e. 'co-operation without coercion'.

Polanyi underestimates the moral attractiveness of the market as a foundation for freedom and prosperity – a crucial part of its appeal in Eastern Europe at present. Apologists for the market present it as the system that guarantees the greatest possible freedom given constraints on sustainable production in a world characterized by scarcity (cf. the discussion of Hayek and the New

Right in Glasman, forthcoming, ch. 7). They also point to the empirical fact that alternatives to the market as an allocation principle have not only been unsustainable, but have also undermined morality by generating a culture of mass dependence characterized by a lack of responsibility, a proliferation of scroungers and skivers, and the breakdown of the family, self-respect and ethical relations generally. There is no doubt that the West is a better, freer, healthier and richer society than the East. Authoritarian protectionism in the East has done the work of Speenhamland on a grand scale.

Reflection on the general law of paternalist pacification as a precondition of competitive disintegration leads Polanyi to the defining position which structures his work and underpins his philosophical scheme. It consists of opposition to both paternalism and atomization and it includes an explanation of their shared structure. Polanyi's point is not that people need protection, but that they need each other. That is what it means to be human. They do so in conditions of freedom by mutually recognizing labour as the dynamic tie of their dependency. Society is not reducible to the state, which can be coercive and reactionary. Neither is it reducible to the individual or the family unit. It is rather something human beings recognize as their own creation, something constructed out of the raw materials of nature by means of their combined energy and governed by their combined reason – a product of their freedom to think and co-operate. Rephrased, human society is the transformation of external nature through human nature, which in turn is the realization of freedom through the moral relations afforded by productive association. The institutions of work – the firm, the union, the trade association and the municipality – are thus the organizations which protect and renew both fredom and community. This, it will be argued in the next section, was precisely the argument of Solidarity in its opposition to communism.

In post-war Germany as well as in France, Scandinavia, the Benelux countries and others, the market was subordinated to the needs of society through a myriad of regulations, restrictions, accommodations and mediations. The challenge for all those who believe that freedom is a relation that holds *between* people and is amenable to their reason and action is to tease out the core elements of post-war success and to strengthen them. The present domination of the political agenda by either organic irrationalists, in the form of nationalists and ecologists, or inorganic rationalists, represented by the neo-classical commissars of the World Bank, is a result of the ideological breakdown of a Western European left which seems to have lost faith in both its inheritance and its achievements.

FROM SOLIDARITY TO DISINTEGRATION: POLANYI'S SECOND LAW APPLIED

The result of the move from protectionist authoritarianism to atomism is the same in contemporary Poland as it was in nineteenth-century Britain: coercive community gives way to the commodification of human labour. In the shift from Marxist to market Leninism, civil assocations and co-operation – society in short – have still been ignored. The Balcerowicz Plan was not worked out with representatives of society, but was imposed by the state in the name of the market. State and market were the only two institutions that mattered. This ran counter to the traditions of Solidarity.

Solidarity was well named in that the atomization of Polish life through the abolition of self-organized social activity had been the goal of Bolshevik rule. It is worth examining its 1981 programme in detail, for this document expressed the political, economic and ethical aspirations of a movement which enjoyed broad popular support. It was the only public, democratically decided and practically relevant statement of political and social philosophy produced by the opposition movement in Eastern Europe.

The inheritors of the Chartists: the principles of the Solidarity document of 1981

There are three distinct but complementary commitments outlined in the document:

(1) Worker democracy within a decentralised competitive economy.
(2) 'The self-governing republic' in which inter-party competition would take place at elections, but in which there would also be democratic control of the bureaucracy and the workplace.
(3) Justice as fairness in which the principles of liberty, equality

and solidarity were defined as equal basic liberties for all within a context of fair opportunity, characterised by a 'maximin' based equilibrium in which social and economic inequalities work for the greatest benefit of the least advantaged [cf. Rawls, 1970: 152–3 on the idea of 'maximin']. This 'difference principle' is clearly articulated in thesis four of the document: 'The union recognises the need for restoring market equilibrium within the framework of a reliable anti-crisis programme, which would be in line with principle of protecting the weakest groups of the population'.
(Solidarity, 1981: 334)

In short, Solidarity combined the different strands of Polanyi's philosophy of organic rationality, or freedom within an industrial society, and proposed them as a practical programme for the restoration of the body politic.

Worker democracy

Solidarity analysed three related pathologies in the communist command economy: (1) centralization, (2) monopoly and (3) bureaucratic management.

Centralization meant that calculations and forecasts were made on the basis of evidence that was unreliable due to the sheer volume of data, setting aside the veracity of the information received. Command from centre to periphery destroyed the signals given by prices and led to dysfunctional distribution, arbitrary allocation and sub-optimal networks of exchange. Initiative was subordinated to directives within the context of a career structure which rewarded loyalty not merit. For these reasons state-based centralization was seen as an inappropriate, inefficient and unjust method of economic regulation.

Monopoly ensured that there was no competition and therefore no means of innovation in the development of productive techniques. There could be no appeal outside the state apparatus in trying to institute new procedures, and no labour bargaining power due to a state monopoly of employment and the abolition of unions.

Bureaucratic management referred to methods of microeconomic discipline in which power was distributed according to political correctness, and the dignity and efficiency of work were degraded and impeded by a 'military' command structure established within the economic system.

Monopoly and centralization were to be removed through a process of decartelization and redefined property titles. The new owner of the decentralized firms would be the enterprise as run by a management team appointed through the democratically elected works councils. This goal of competitive self-management was the means both of creating stable property relations and of establishing a system within which responsibility for decision-making, and knowledge of the complexities and demands made by market competition, were facilitated by access to all records and information. Democracy was a form of wage substitution during recession within the framework of restoring incentive structures, quality of work and firm loyalty. It was a means of establishing a pattern of embedded market relations in which workers participated constructively in the transition from a closed to an open society.

The decentralization and decartelization of Polish industry, and the mode of worker democracy institutionalized in the new competitive enterprises was central to the 1980 plan. The self-managed enterprise was to be the 'basic organisational unit of the economy' (Solidarity, 1981: 330). The plan for a self-governing republic, in which the self-management of enterprises was to play a fundamental role, permeates the whole document. Its implementation was also the central demand made in the declaration of 8 September 1981 in which the workers' councils were to have the 'right to nominate and dismiss managers' (ibid.: 394).

Work was part of the 'common human values' that Solidarity claimed gave them legitimacy as the 'force willing to build a just Poland for everyone'. In what reads like a summary of Polanyi's central thesis, they wrote:

> Work is for man, and what determines its sense is its closeness to man, to his real needs. Our national and social rebirth must be based on the restored hierarchy of those goals. While defining its aims, *Solidarność* draws from the values of Christian ethics, from our national traditions and from the workers' and democratic traditions of the labour world.
>
> (Solidarity, 1981: 327)

Solidarity retained a distinctive commitment to the theory of labour value. Worker democracy was the means of restoring society on the foundation of associational liberty and this lay at the heart of their programme: 'Genuine self-management of employees will be the basis of the self-governing republic' (ibid.: 347).

The Solidarity programme was the post-war West German industrial relations system of co-determination in embryo in its combination of worker democracy, state regulation and the social market system. The works councils would have control over the appointment of managers and a shareholder function as the final court of appeal in the decision-making process; the appointed managers would run the enterprise on a day-to-day basis. The owner, or capital side, however, could not be filled as there was no capital, the only owner being the state. This problem was compounded in so far as the state's claim to ownership was challenged by the ministries, the ministries were challenged by the industrial branch associations to which each enterprise belonged, the industrial branch associations were challenged by the party in the name of the people, whilst the people, in as much as they could express themselves, supported Solidarity. The disorganized irrationality of Bolshevism had led to the creation of institutions which represented no self-organized group within society but which employed huge numbers of people and controlled societal resources. These institutions blocked the development of organizations which could represent the different classes and interests of society and then frame a consensus within which each could find a productive place.

Worker self-management was the issue over which the government and Solidarity broke off negotiations. The 'expert' economists chosen to arbitrate in the dispute criticized the authorities for not providing 'authentic participation of Trade Unions and workers' self-government in mangement and control' (ibid.: 392). The union pursued self-management as their top priority, were not prepared to make all other goals subordinate to it and threatened a general strike if it was not implemented (ibid.: 395). The government–Solidarity talks were resumed on this specific issue as Warsaw Pact forces began extensive manoeuvres on the Polish border and martial law was imposed. There was no opportunity to organize publicly for a decade after that, by which time the population had been demobilized, the experts had changed their minds, the economy was in further ruins and freedom had changed its meaning.

The philosophy of the IMF/Sachs plan of 1990 is completely opposed to that of the economic reform programme of 1981. The decision by the Solidarity-led government to abandon its previous commitments in favour of the enthusiastic enforcement of the IMF/ Sachs plan excluded Solidarity, as a union, from playing a constructive role. As Wałęsa recently said, 'If I build a strong union, I will be building an obstacle to reform' (Surdej, 1992: 7). This has enabled the old/new capitalist managerial class to remove Solidarity from any institutional power leading to it destruction as a union, a movement and a national party. It had no role beyond facilitating imposition of the 'stabilization' plan on a disillusioned and demobilized society.

The self-governing republic

The reform of the state institutions in Poland had to obey two potentially conflicting principles: liberalism and democracy. A liberal democracy is a potentially incoherent amalgam because the priority of rights limits democratic authority, and majoritarian domination can limit freedom. The reform programme confronted this problem by trying to reconcile the autonomous logic of different sub-systems in society (the economy, law, politics, religion, science) without surrendering democratic aspirations to the control and supervision of bureaucracies. It did so by introducing a plan for a 'system democracy' in which the legal system, the medical bureaucracy and the scientific and educational apparatuses would each run their own affairs without direct state interference (Solidarity, 1981: 350, 345, 355, 354). (In effect, they tried to give substantive meaning to Polanyi's idea of freedom in a complex society (Polanyi, 1944: 21).) In those areas where the state had a legitimate function such as in the appointment of judges, the selection of a national syllabus, or the choice of medical technology, there would be an institutionalized democratic balance in favour of representatives of the sub-system in question on each committee. These measures were justified according to the principle that experts know best, and that their expertise was best judged by their colleagues. In those cases where the experts were divided, political considerations would be decisive.

Justice as fairness

John Rawls's *A Theory of Justice* (1970) rests on the premise that fairness is the fundamental value of modern political societies, and that reason must subordinate markets in the name of society. It is Rawls who articulated the philosophical system closest to the ethics that characterized the rejection of communism (cf. Glasman, forthcoming, ch. 1). A commitment to fairness leads to a hierarchy of three principles which serve as ground rules for the regulation of societal institions. The first states that each person has an equal right to a full schedule of equal liberties, compatible with an identical right for all. The second is that of equal opportunity, and the third is the 'difference principle'. This is the idea that in a society characterized by market relations and private property, inequality is justified in so far as, but only in so far as, improvements in efficiency and wealth do not diminish the welfare of the least advantaged.

Rawls's first principle is expressed in thesis 23 of the Solidarity document:

> The system must guarantee basic civil freedoms and respect the principles of equality before the law as far as all citizens and all public institutions are concerned . . . regardless of their convictions, political views and organisational affiliations.
>
> (Solidarity, 1981: 349)

The fundamental principle of reform was an assertion of basic human and civil rights which were not open to political negotiation, violation or surrender. They constituted the inviolable first premise of Polish reconstruction – the lexical priority of liberty (cf. Rawls, 1982b), which recalls the 'spheres of arbitrary freedom, protected by unbreakable rights' that Polanyi argues were the necessary condition of a free society (Polanyi, 1944: 255).

The second principle – that of equal opportunity – was expressed in the critique of institutionalized privilege based on party membership and generalized subservience. The creation of democratically controlled workplaces was an attempt to break the institutionalized domination of the party in the economic sphere; democratic control of bureaucracies was a means of controlling the party's domination of the institutions of state. Taken together, they would remove the party from their domineering position in societal organization. The argument for equality of opportunity was based on a commitment to the development of talents in a system of fair competition on the grounds that active attainment was a superior principle of selection to inheritance or reward based on obedience. They also argued that equality of opportunity is in the collective interest as it aids efficiency, maximizes talent allocation, and increases the ability of all to enhance their self-respect by gaining recognized positions of power and prestige in society on the basis of their work. This equality is not only formal – as in equality before the law, fair procedures of justice and equality of job opportunity – but also has a substantive content in terms of the collective provision of what Rawls calls 'primary goods', defined as the precondition of effective agency (Rawls, 1970: 90–95; 1982b). In this lies the morality of welfare provisions concerning health, education, housing and labour organization. If the goal of Solidarity was to 'create decent economic and political conditions in an independent Poland – that is, conditions of a life free of poverty, exploitation, fear and deception in a society that is democratically and lawfully organized (Solidarity, 1981: 326) – then the role of the 'difference principle' can be clearly understood. If changes in society take place which secure the rule of law but ignore fundamental inequalities in life chances, a large number of citizens will be excluded from the benefits of societal activity. The principle means of exclusion is unemployment, which severs people from both recognition as productive partners and material resources. Rawls's solution to the existence of formal equality and substantive inequality is to justify redistribution of primary goods in order to facilitate equality of opportunity. Both the right to work and the priority of primary goods turn each citizen from being an individual *part* of a political community into an active *participant* in the life of society.

Why have workers remained unrecognized in the new regime that Solidarity has created? After their struggle for human recognition (Laba, 1991), they are the active agents in imposing the law of the jungle on their own society. Why is it that this Catholic syndicalist movement has adopted the market utopia as its central commitment with its bestial notion of starvation-based incentives and its contempt for the traditions of values of Polish society?

From Marxism to the market without mediation

If the conditions facing Poland in 1989 are seen in comparison with West Germany in 1945, then the similarities and divergences can be clearly apprehended. In Germany, as in Poland, political parties were banned. The state bureaucratic class was implicated in the old regime in both cases and had lost any claim to impartiality. While all unions were illegal under Nazism, Poland had both an illegal union in the form of Solidarity and a legal state-sponsored union in the form of OPZZ. The split union movement has been a communist legacy with debilitating consequences for Polish reconstruction, and is a clear difference from Germany. Property rights in Poland were as ill-defined as they had been in Germany. The leading forces in Poland with capital were the ex-*nomenklatura* whose legitimacy had been undermined under communist rule and who were seen as the principal defenders and enforcers of the old system. Productive power resided, as it had in Germany in 1945, where there was minimal damage to industrial machinery, but the definition and future organization of the material context remained uncertain.

The Roman Catholic Church was morally respected and popular in both countries. It was constrained as a political agent in that theocracies were seen as an outmoded and inappropriate form of government, and by internal constraints on its explicit will to political power. The foundation of a Christian Democratic Party of the post-war German variety was a possibility which the Church in Poland did nothing to bring about. Where the Church in Germany concentrated its attention on social issues, the Church in Poland has concentrated on matters of personal morality, such as abortion and divorce, and has mobilized little of its power in pursuit of issues concerning labour, welfare or social justice.

Solidarity was the only organization which could have acted as a recognized political agent enjoying popular legitimacy and support. The movement stood as a political party in the 1989 elections and won all available seats. At this point the new Solidarity government met the new right consensus, not at the level of cold-war rhetoric in which trade union rights, democratic empowerment and real freedom were the main currency, but on the level of reality in which trade union rights, democratic empowerment and real freedom played no role as policy priorities as defined by the dominant economic, political and military institutions. The message was clear: no union deals, the dismantling of the welfare state, the abolition of workers' councils, a renunciation of freedom of movement in the new Europe and enforced unemployment as a necessary feature of economic recovery. The European Community closed its borders to both Polish labour and Polish goods and no significant aid was forthcoming. At the crucial moment all the dominant institutions which could have facilitated Polish integration in the West were consistent in their response: no integration, no partnership, no help, no aid. Their contribution can be summarized as follows: all we can do is give you a model, which has had no success in any developed industrial nation, but whose adoption is the precondition of any possible recognition as even a subordinate partner in the 'Free Europe' you have struggled for so long to join. Seventy per cent of the Polish national debt was to Western governments, not to commercial institutions. This was widely expected to be cancelled. After a wait of two years, however, it was only halved, thus leaving the new democracies with the added burden of communist profligacy.

Perhaps the supreme achievement of non-abstract Marxism is the renewed plausibility it gave to theories linking nationalism, racism and community which had lost their rational appeal with the defeat of fascism, and the renewed credibility it lent to market utopias which the post-war settlement had discredited. As the unfair consequences of the stabilization plan became apparent, the Polish people were deprived of the language of justice through which they could express their ethical and organizational opposition. Appeals to justice were portrayed as a defence of the *ancien régime*, or as populist, demagogic and utopian. Any alternative to an unregulated market was immediately defined as unfeasible. Communism has victimized social democracy twice over. Having murdered, imprisoned, tortured, banned, reviled and expelled it as revisionism and class treachery, communism now affirms that social democracy is what it has been about all along. Thus the Polish communist party changed its name to the Social Democratic Party of the Republic of Poland just in time to associate the two ideas and to be rejected by the electorate.

If one accepts that agents act with rational purposes on the basis of commitments they consider to be both true and intelligible, an explanation of why reckless, inappropriate and damaging policies were adopted and pursued by an entire consensus, and were not limited to the activities of partisan groups imposing their claims on society, is indispensable. There were two realities. One was failed communism, located in Eastern Europe; the other successful capitalism, located further West. There was, however, no direct access by the Polish people to the realities of Western European capitalism; it remained an abstract category defined by prosperity, the rule of law and democracy. It was an ideal, and it was a model.

The problem with models is that they are by necessity ahistorical. They always assume too much and explain too little. The messy historical truth was that Western Europe, and most particularly West Germany, had inadvertently stumbled upon a distinctive mode of societal organization which has been clumsily labelled welfare, warfare or social capitalism. In this the goal of societal, and not simply market, equilibrium is the regulative ideal. Political and class-based institutions intervene, or rather become entangled in market operations. Democracy and corporate recognition become part of the constitutive rules of economic life. No-one designed post-war Germany; it was the result of the dynamic consensus achieved by the different legitimate agents within the room for manoeuvre given by international constraints (see Glasman, forthcoming, ch. 3). The relationship between the market system, corporate organizations (of both kinds), industrial relations, democratic structures and military constraints led to a 'spontaneous *order*'. There developed stable societal equilibrium characterized by interdependent but autonomous sub-systems composed of the institutionalized representation of different interests. Without stable structures there can only be the self-fulfilling Hobbesian vision of the state of nature with the inevitable consequence of an authoritarian state to clean up the mess. Polanyi's first general rule applied.

The problem for Solidarity was how to conceptualize its constructive, productive and patriotic role. Due to the model of economic reconstruction assumed by the Sachs/Balcerowicz/IMF plan, the only task it could effectively fulfil was to dissolve itself as an economic agent, while acting as a societal pacifier and government apologist. While Solidarity was a necessary force in political reform, it was seen by others and viewed itself as a parasitic and obstructive organization in the economic sphere. The other forces which could have opposed both the stabilization plan and the undemocratic way it was conceived and imposed were either discredited or organizationally weak. The OPZZ kept its head down, fearful of Solidarity revenge. The Communist Party was more concerned with survival and reorientation. The Farmers' Party mistakenly assumed that reforms would be to its benefit. The dominant logic of the government was to impose new economic rules on society, not to work out what the rules were with their representatives (Surdej, 1992). The IMF enjoyed an institutional monopoly of aid and recognition; the EC and the World Bank both handed over their money to it. There was no balance of power within which Poland could gain room for manoeuvre, nor any competing interests within which it could frame its own balance between tradition and revolution.

It is the definition of what it is rational to pursue that has led Solidarity to negate all of its previous policy commitments, and to revise its economic policy on the basis of what it thought was right. It was not betrayal, corruption or weakness that led Solidarity to adopt the policies it did, but inability in 1990 to contest the prevailing orthodox paradigm of economic, political and societal progress institutionalized in the dominant international organizations of political and economic regulation.

Polanyi argued that feasibility was the bench-mark of a morality and that social order was rooted in consensus. The possibility of freedom is given by the possibility of just association under conditions always characterized by dependency and power. Only through stable associative control over societal resources can the preservation of traditional ethical structures of societal reproduction and the new demands of technology and production be reconciled. What is happening in Poland has happened before in Europe, always with calamitous results. The choice before society is understood as one between the state and the market; the possibility of renewing the social order as an industrial democracy is seen either as unfeasible utopianism or as part of the repressive past from which escape is craved. This leaves the institutions of a constitutional democracy without a stable social base and renders both freedom and market reforms vulnerable to overthrow. The West German post-war settlement was never articulated as an ideal or as a model. Its features of market subordination and facilitation through the institutionalization of industrial democracy, subsidiarity and subsidy were unknown in Eastern Europe. There thus seemed no alternative to market Leninism.

FROM 'MANY ARE COLD BUT FEW ARE FROZEN' TO 'FREE TO FREEZE': BOTH GENERAL RULES REALIZED

Marxism presented itself as the defender of community against the ravages inflicted by capitalism but in the end it negated both freedom and solidarity and, consequently throughout Eastern Europe, the removal, not the renewal, of the party was the necessary precondition of societal renewal. This is the central parallel to Speenhamland, but it does not mean that a commitment to the social, the idea of living in a stable society governed by ordered just relations and laws in which work is given respect and protection, is weak. It finds expression in nationalism, Catholic social doctrine, conservative moralism and a residual sympathy for unreformed communist parties masquerading as social democrats. Note the election results from Lithuania where the reformed communists, the Democratic Labour Party, are now dominant, Hungary where a solidaristic Christian Democratic Party is playing a stalling role with respect to market reforms, as well as Serbia, Slovakia and Romania where all kinds of organic irrationality are dominating political and economic decisions. The dilemma facing all these countries is that there is no alternative to the market, but the market is no alternative. *Social*ism is no longer an ideology but a necessity in a market society. It takes many forms but always resists unregulated markets in labour, money and property. In rational choice theory this is understood as either collective irrationality or tribalism. To those with a less Panglossian approach to spontaneous equilibrium, it means not starving, a minimal level of life security, educational opportunity and the means to survival in the modern world generally. The important question is what form associational self-protection takes, and this in turn becomes a question of rational and irrational solidarity.

The market has been embraced because it is seen as a necessary mechanism for improving standards of living, for facilitating integration and communication with citizens and groups in other countries and for breaking the old power elites. It has failed in all these areas. But instead of embedding the market in a web of social relations in which unions, corporate bodies, trade associations and regulations both constrain the market and facilitate social restoration, society has been destroyed yet again in the name of another unrealizable utopian project. The Bolshevik system was unequal and unfair, leading to corruption and waste, thus negating in practice what had been socialism's greatest appeal in theory – the possibility of a fair distribution of society's resources, a recognition of the worth of all who worked and the posibility of equal opportunity irrespective of class, national or ethnic background.

The commodification of labour, land and lodging, the subordination of association to accumulation that must take place in a transition to a market society, becomes a catastrophe in a country such as Poland in which the decommodification of the basic sphere of life through subsidized subsistence was the central feature of the previous regime. Housing, basic foodstuffs, education and health care were all provided either free of charge or with substantial subsidies. There are many ways of conceptualizing the decommodified space that surrounded each citizen of the workers' republic like a coerced bubble of protection, but it had concrete results in improvements in literacy, nutrition, health and shelter. The deal imposed by the party-state on the Polish nation after the war was that the people should surrender their freedom and culture in return for guaranteed subsistence. Life was meaningless, opportunity denied, unfairness institutionalized and reciprocity broken, but at least it was life. Many were cold but few were frozen.

This stagnant paternalism has now been replaced by libertarian atomization in which each naked citizen faces the world in competition with all others without any institutionalized solidarity or protection. Everything is subordinated to the logic of the market. The deregulation of rents and heating have led to home-lessness and hypothermia; people are free to freeze. The rise in the price of basic foodstuffs has led to hunger. The closure of factories has led to sudden unprecedented unemployment and to claims for benefit which the state cannot afford to pay. The educational and health care systems are crumbling, leading to the development of private systems for the old and new rich and the virtual abolition of welfare for the rest of society. The commodification of the basics of life, the destruction of the industrial sector and the vacuum of self-organization left by communist rule leave only one outlet for the people to express their solidarity of despair – the nation-state. Suffering in isolation, they look to collective security and provision. Under these circum-stances the functional rationality of nationalism is not to be dismissed as atavistic tribalism. The disaster is that the one social agent that emerged from Bolshevik rule with an organization and programme capable of renewing the institutions and relations of society during the storm of transition, the workers' movement Solidarity, has also formed the government which implemented the economic reforms. Polanyi's first general rule – atomization is a precondition for collectivism in the form of ethnic nationalism – is already taking effect.

The ways in which the decline of social democratic confidence and New Right hegemony have combined to produce ahistorical and bizarre policy developments is best exposed by asking the original question. Why is it that the most successful programme, combining economic growth, social justice, and fair institutional procedures, has been completely neglected in the discussion of Eastern Europe? Amid all the talk of a new Marshall Plan, fiscal reform, debt rescheduling and privatization, the real precondition of effective reconstruction – the simultaneous reactivation and stabilization of social agents as achieved in West Germany – has been completely ignored. Through co-determination, working-class power was institutionalized and stabilized in German society, knowledge of investment and procedure were guaranteed, and responsible mass movements were legally created, controlled and enabled to grow. Incentives were not only linked to wages but to the co-operative development of industry based on knowledge of the conditions, the sacrifices expected of workers and job security. This was balanced by worker participation in the process of production, not as an advisory force, but as an organized force. By the time that Marshall Aid really got going in 1951, co-determination had already led to the renewal of large-scale German industry within a market framework. Absence of reference to this precedent indicates the power of consensus in framing an agenda; in Poland there was no theoretical alternative offered to the course of action pursued.

The tragedy is that Polanyi's conceptualization of modernist alternatives developed in his final chapter remains fundamentally correct. The degenerative form of organic solidarity is a society without freedom. The form of organic rationality he advocates is the restoration of society through the institutionalization of the greatest possible freedom under conditions of democratic dependence. This he calls socialism. Socialism, however, has been conflated with communism, an equally degenerative form of societyless regulation. The link between socialism and freedom has been severed leaving the people of Poland without a language in which to express their collective yearning for freedom and stability based on justice. Organic irrationality, or aggresive nationalism, is the only basis left for solidarity.

The sooner the utopian and constructivist fantasies of a market utopia are recognized for what they are, and the ideals of political justice and economic democracy that were the unique contribution of Solidarity to political philosophy are reclaimed as the only authentic organic possibility for the recreation of a free Polish nation, the sooner the destination of transition can be changed from autarchy to social democracy. The key practice that can shape a transformation characterized by freedom and solidarity is the self-organization of economic production envisaged by the Solidarity movement. Its historical precursors in Britain, the Owenites and Chartists, the Co-operative Movement and the Labour Party, were all defeated. Even so, they slowed the rate of change, enlarged the sphere of freedom, restored societal institutions and gave hope to those who understood that freedom was based on democratic association. In short, they ameliorated the excesses of market utopianism. This is the burden that Solidarity must assume once more if Poland is to enjoy the freedoms it has struggled for throughout this century of terror.

ACKNOWLEDGEMENTS

There are three primary debts which have to be acknowledged. The first is to Jeff Weintraub who insisted that I study Polanyi's work after reading the first draft of my book on Poland. The second is to Steven Lukes who suggested the title. The third is to Luisa Zanchi who constrained some of the wilder claims concerning economic theory.

NOTES

1 The irony is that sovereignty is a territorial concept and was central to the emergence of the nation-state, but its rise coincided with the dissolution of all patterns of association that linked the land to production through the imposition of a free market in land and its products. Thus the defence of a territory ceased to mean the protection of a way of life and became more a military defence of borders separating countries with homogeneous patterns of regulation.
2 The philosophical roots of organic rationality are analysed in chapter 4 of my forthcoming book, *Unnecessary Suffering*, which concentrates on the German philosophical tradition, its conceptions of society, freedom and reason, and the sources for the peculiar consensus on German post-war reconstruction fashioned by the CDU and the SDP.

REFERENCES

Friedman, M. and Friedman, R. (1980) *Free to Choose*, London: Secker & Warburg.

Glasman, M. (forthcoming) *Unnecessary Suffering*.

Laba, R. (1991) *The Social Roots of Solidarity*, Princeton: Princeton U.P.

Lipton, D. and Sachs, J. (1990) 'Privatisation in Eastern Europe: The Case of Poland', *Brookings Papers on Economic Activity*, no. 2: 293–341.

Polanyi, K. (1944) *The Great Transformation: The Political and Economic Origins of Our Time*, Boston: Beacon Press.

—— (1968) 'The Economy as Instituted Process', in G. Dalton (ed.), *Primitive, Archaic and Modern Economies*, Boston: Beacon Press.

Rawls, J. (1970) *A Theory of Justice*, Oxford: OUP.

—— (1982a) 'The Basic Liberties and their Priority', in *The Tanner Lectures on Human Values*, vol. III, Cambridge: CUP.

—— (1982b) 'Social Unity and Primary Goods', in A. Sen and B. Williams (eds), *Beyond Utilitarianism*, Cambridge: CUP.

Riedel, M. (1984) *Between Tradition and Revolution*, Cambridge: CUP.

Solidarity (1981) 'Programme Adopted by the First National Congress', in P. Raina (ed.), *Poland 1981: Towards Social Renewal*, London: Allen & Unwin.

Surdej, A. (1992) 'Politics and the Stabilisation Plan', Manuscript, Florence: EUI.

Chapter 11

Is there an alternative to market utopianism?
A comment on Glasman

Steven Lukes

In the previous chapter Maurice Glasman asks three related but unfashionable questions and makes extensive reference to an unfashionable author. And indeed the very unfashionableness of his questions and of the author referred to are an inherent part of the argument. For, at the most general level, he is concerned to question the currently prevailing consensus about what forms of socio-economic organization are feasible and viable in the industrial societies of Eastern Europe currently undergoing what is called 'transition'.

First, he asks why the West German post-war settlement, with its distinctive form of welfare state and system of co-determination, successfully combining liberal-democratic institutions and considerable trade-union power, has been so comprehensively ignored in the post-communist transitions in Eastern and Central Europe, among actors, advisers, and observers alike, both within and outside the region.

It is an excellent question, though many will think that there are several answers and that they are rather obvious. They will point to various factors that, they will claim, make the comparison between the two transitions dubiously relevant. There is, first, the enormous change that has intervened in the relationship between the international and the national political economies, above all in respect of the impact of international financial markets on domestic economic policies. There is an ever-diminishing scope for the pursuit of national social and economic policies, in the face of the ever-present threat of capital flight, as the French socialists discovered in the early 1980s. Second, there are the massive changes in the class structure and the division of labour, both nationally and internationally, the fragmentation and feminization of many areas of work, the growth of the service sector, and the secular decline in the manual working class, leading to the declining role of trade unions. Third is the difference in the climate of expectations: post-war Europe was widely held to be ripe for social reconstruction, after the ravages of the Depression and the War, while post-communist Eastern Europe is seen to be in need of social deconstruction and the dismantling of obstructions to economic development. The social interest groups and institutions, if not the personnel, of the Nazi regime perished with its defeat, whereas communism has left behind it a legacy of patterns of interest, dependency and state dependency which at best constitute a constraint and at worst a blocking mechanism upon the privatization and marketization of the economy, and overcoming them becomes a central priority. Fourth is the different international climate: as the cold war set in, the securing of social consensus and stability in West Germany had a high priority for the Western allies, whereas such threats to consensus and stability as exist in various areas of the East, while arguably greater, are endogenous and widely seen as intractable.

At least some of these apparent objections are put into question by Glasman's argument itself, for it does not, as I read it, depend on the claim that the cases are analogous, and that the Poles could now implement a West German-style social market and welfare state. His case is rather that after the war the West Germans and their Western allies created (without designing it) a functioning capitalist order that built upon 'existing institutions and patterns of co-operation' which centred around the the workplace and drew upon indigenous religious and working-class traditions. By contrast, and ironically, the Solidarity government in Poland sought to impose an alien and abstract model, at the behest of international financial institutions and under the influence of advisers with no local knowledge. His case, in short, is that the response of the West to the collapse of communism has been both narrow-minded and short-sighted, echoing and magnifying the reaction within, and failing to take into account the social context or 'embeddedness' of market relations, and thus failing to foresee the likely consequences of allowing it to be damaged further by too headlong a rush towards the implementation of a market utopia.

Here arises Glasman's second question: why has the market utopian 'model' – propagated by Professor Sachs and 'implemented' in the Balcerowicz Plan – seemed so exclusively appealing to all the significant actors in the post-communist states of Eastern Europe, and of Poland in particular. Here he may be exaggerating. Contrary voices – such as that of Jacek Kuroń, Polish Minister of Labour – have certainly been heard, even if they have not prevailed. Nevertheless he is right in broad terms: most of the debate has been over the speed of the proposed reforms, over the dosage of the medicine rather than over the availability of other cures or even an alternative medicine.

Here too many will think that several convincing answers are at hand. They will point to the discrediting of the alternatives – 'real existing socialism' in the East and social democracy in the West. They will probably suggest, as Ralf Dahrendorf has done, that realism was only delayed by long-lasting illusions about the latter (shared, it is often said, by Gorbachev) – a misinformed and inappropriate longing for 'Sweden', as opposed to Sweden. And they will doubtless add that Sweden has in any case run out of steam, in terms of both efficiency and legitimacy. They will point to all the real failures of real socialism – not just the barriers to minimally efficient production and the massive surveillance system, but also the corruption and graft in the provision of welfare and the systematic destruction of self-esteem, trust and initiative. All these interconnected evils seem to call for a radically alternative system based on an alternative principle and indeed an end to the very idea of realizing social solidarity and social justice by design. From this standpoint, the aftermath of 1989 symbolizes the defeat of an indefensible system, not the failure to defend some alternative defensible one. For a long time, in the last years of communist rule, and above all in East Germany in the phoney pre-election period, there was a hankering by many intellectuals for some supposed 'Third Way'. But they could never make clear what this was and came to be seen as timid trimmers whose life-experiences, professional qualifications and interests tied them to the old regime. Moreover, one could indeed argue that the very concept of the 'Third Way' embodied an ideological distortion, suggesting that capitalism was one way (when it in fact is indeterminately many ways) and that real socialism is a second way (when it is no way at all).

Yet here too Glasman's argument puts a question-mark beside these objections. For, following Polanyi, he argues that the trouble with the market utopian model is that it is a utopia and a model – indeed that it is a utopia because it is a model – which abstracts from the historical realities of 'capitalism' as an entire socio-economic formation that can take innumerable forms. In particular it abstracts from the social and moral contexts in which markets can function compatibly with rights guaranteeing basic freedoms, social justice securing fairness for all but especially the weakest, and democracy, including economic democracy. He makes the bold claim that the Solidarity programme of 1981 set out the essentials of a non-utopian conception that defines a historical alternative (capitalist) path that could have been taken but was not. His claim, in short, is that the programme was both feasible and legitimate since it drew upon still living Catholic and working-class traditions.

This leads to the third question which Glasman's chapter raises: was this path indeed feasible? Could one even imagine some future Polish government stumbling back onto it, thereby affording brighter prospects for the Polish transition – suggesting, indeed, that there might *be* a transition, rather than stagnation or disintegration?

Such a question is an invitation to counterfactual history, which is what underlies explanation of actual history. Did the Solidarity government of the early 1990s play a major role in suppressing an historical alternative that Solidarity had itself mapped out nine years earlier? In answering such an intriguing question everything depends on what you take for granted, what you hold to be the parameters of the situation. Here we return to the answers I listed above to Glasman's first question. To what extent did international economic and above all financial constraints set limits to the implementation of the Solidarity programme? To what extent did that programme take account of the changes in the class structure and the division of labour (albeit far less developed in Poland than in Western Europe)? To what extent were the constraints facing the first Polish governments ideological, confining them to a narrower range of options than was objectively available, and inducing them to perpetrate unnecessary social destruction in the name of economic progress? If this last suggestion is right, to what extent are such constraints conjunctural – the product of a particular time and place, and to what extent can they be overcome by developing theoretical and practical alternatives? Such questions are of the greatest theoretical interest and current political relevance.

Index

Poland: agricultural policy 33 (n2), 157; banking reforms 64; civil society 71–2; consensual transformation 184–9; control over army 47–8; culture and values 66–8; debt 174; decartelization 204; decentralization 204; IMF 62–3, 159, 211–12; infrastructure 64; intelligentsia 23–5, 29–31; investment capital 64–5; labour 66–8; lack of economic activity 19; liminality 18; management personnel 65–6; martial law 205; new social contract 188–9; political apathy 28–9; political elites 31–2; post-communism attitudes 81–2; private sector 156–7, 173; privatization 156–61, 177; shock therapy 8, 175–6; trade unions 209; transition goals 192; see also Solidarity

Polanyi, Karl (quoted) 191; first law of transformation 193–6; market utopianism 4–5, 187, 199–202; society concept 6, 196–9

Polish people: capitalism 20–1; political apathy 28–9; privatization 157–8, 177

Polish United Worker's Party (PUWP) 19

pollution 62, 64

Polonia 157

Poor Law Amendment, UK (1834) 5

post-communism, attitudes of people 81–2

poverty 82

power structure, conflicts 129–31

press, parliamentarized 115

price increases 80

privatization: compared in Poland, Czechoslovakia and Hungary 165–8; costs 152; Czechoslovakia 161–8; East Central Europe 147–53; economic 144–7; gradualist approach 147, 154, 167; Hungary 153–6; large-scale

146, 160, 162; by liquidation 183; mass 149, 151, 160, 163–5; methods 147–50; Poland 156–61, 177; shock therapy 147; small-scale 146, 159–60, 162, 167, 178–9; social 145; state assets 40; state enterprise 153, 181, 183–4; trade unions 183–4; see also reprivatization

Privatization Act, Poland 158, 178, 181

property rights, workers 182

Przeworski, A. 3

Public Against Violence, Slovakia 51

purges, elites 111–12

Rabušic, L. 11

racial hatred 91

Ramet, S. 4

Rawls, John 206–8

real socialism i, 2–3, 58–9, 82, 94 (n1)

Reform Bill, UK (1832) 5

religious education 109–10

rendszerváltás 100, 103, 104, 16

Reparation Act 129, 131

reprivatization: Hungary 104–5, 111, 154; property 146; see also restitution

republic, self-governing 206

restitution 151–2, 164, 166–7

restrictions, ownership 152

retroactive legislation 112–13

Révész, T. 64, 70, 153

revolutions 1, 14–15; and culture systems 79; as melancholy moments of history 79; negotiated 104; or system change 100–8; parricidal 14, 16–17, 28; radicalism in Hungary 106–8, 109–16; self-limiting 99–100

Reynolds, P. 63–4

rites of passage 15–17

Roman Catholic Church 55, 72, 209

Round Table Agreement 172, 180

Rzeczpospolita 81